The Work-based Le
Student Handbook

D1459136

Renew by phone or online
0845 0020 777
www.bristol.gov.uk/libraries
Bristol Libraries

PLEASE RETURN BOOK BY LAST DATE STAMPED

18. SEP 10.

04. JAN 11

15. MAR 11.

17. JUN 1

29. OCT 1

26.3.19

Ah

Palgrave Study Skills

Authoring a PhD
Business Degree Success
Career Skills
Critical Thinking Skills
Cite them Right (8th edn)
e-Learning Skills (2nd edn)
Effective Communication for
  Arts and Humanities Students
Effective Communication for
  Science and Technology
The Exam Skills Handbook
The Foundations of Research (2nd edn)
The Good Supervisor
Great Ways to Learn Anatomy and
  Physiology
How to Manage your Arts, Humanities and
  Social Science Degree
How to Manage your Distance and
  Open Learning Course
How to Manage your Postgraduate Course
How to Manage your Science and
  Technology Degree
How to Study Foreign Languages
How to Use your Reading in your Essays
How to Write Better Essays (2nd edn)
How to Write your Undergraduate
  Dissertation
Information Skills
IT Skills for Successful Study
Making Sense of Statistics
The International Student Handbook
The Mature Student's Guide to Writing (2nd edn)
The Mature Student's Handbook
The Palgrave Student Planner
The Personal Tutor's Handbook

The Postgraduate Research Handbook (2nd edn)
Presentation Skills for Students (2nd edn)
The Principles of Writing in Psychology
Professional Writing (2nd edn)
Researching Online
Research Using IT
Skills for Success (2nd edn)
The Study Abroad Handbook
The Student's Guide to Writing (2nd edn)
The Student Life Handbook
The Study Skills Handbook (3rd edn)
Study Skills for Speakers of English as
  a Second Language
Studying Arts and Humanities
Studying the Built Environment
Studying Business at MBA and Masters Level
Studying Economics
Studying History (3rd edn)
Studying Law (2nd edn)
Studying Mathematics and its Applications
Studying Modern Drama (2nd edn)
Studying Physics
Studying Programming
Studying Psychology (2nd edn)
Teaching Study Skills and Supporting Learning
The Undergraduate Research Handbook
The Work-Based Learning Student Handbook
Work Placements – A Survival Guide for Students
Writing for Law
Writing for Nursing and Midwifery Students
Write it Right
Writing for Engineers (3rd edn)

Palgrave Study Skills: Literature

General Editors: John Peck and Martin Coyle

How to Begin Studying English Literature
  (3rd edn)
How to Study a Jane Austen Novel (2nd edn)
How to Study a Charles Dickens Novel
How to Study Chaucer (2nd edn)
How to Study an E. M. Forster Novel
How to Study James Joyce
How to Study Linguistics (2nd edn)

How to Study Modern Poetry
How to Study a Novel (2nd edn)
How to Study a Poet
How to Study a Renaissance Play
How to Study Romantic Poetry (2nd edn)
How to Study a Shakespeare Play (2nd edn)
How to Study Television
Practical Criticism

The Work-based Learning Student Handbook

Ruth Helyer

First published 2010 by
PALGRAVE MACMILLAN

Palgrave Macmillan in the UK is an imprint of Macmillan Publishers Limited, registered in England, company number 785998, of Houndmills, Basingstoke, Hampshire RG21 6XS.

Palgrave Macmillan in the US is a division of St Martin's Press LLC, 175 Fifth Avenue, New York, NY 10010.

Palgrave Macmillan is the global academic imprint of the above companies and has companies and representatives throughout the world.

Palgrave® and Macmillan® are registered trademarks in the United States, the United Kingdom, Europe and other countries

ISBN 978–0–230–22956–3

This book is printed on paper suitable for recycling and made from fully managed and sustained forest sources. Logging, pulping and manufacturing processes are expected to conform to the environmental regulations of the country of origin.

A catalogue record for this book is available from the British Library.

A catalog record for this book is available from the Library of Congress.

10   9   8   7   6   5   4   3   2   1
19 18 17 16 15 14 13 12 11 10

Printed and bound in Great Britain by
CPI Antony Rowe, Chippenham and Eastbourne

I want to dedicate this book to James Marlborough Allen who inspired me so much with his wisdom and gentle intellect

Contents

List of Figures and Tables

● **Figures**

● **Tables**

Acknowledgements

The authors, editor and publishers wish to thank the following for permission to reproduce copyright material:

- David Megginson & Vivien Whitaker and CIPD publishers, for Figure 3.6 'The CPD Cycle' from *Continuing Professional Development* ISBN:0 85292 990 0 London: CIPD, London 2003. Also, from the same publication, Exercise 3.8 'What metaphor would best describe your career and where you are now?'
- Philip Candy for Exercise 3.3, 'Steps to Becoming an Autonomous Learner'. Text adapted from P.C. Candy *Self-direction for Lifelong Learning* (San Francisco: Jossey-Bass Higher and Adult Education Series, 1991).
- Peter Hughes for the list of characteristics (p.75/6), based on his conference paper, 'Autonomous Learning Zones', presented to the 10th European Conference for Research on Learning and Instruction (26–30 August 2003, Padova, Italy).
- Peter Honey for Figure 3.3, 'Honey & Mumford's Learning Cycle', Honey, P. and Mumford, A. (1984) *Using Your Learning Styles* (Maidenhead: Peter Honey Publications), originally devised 1982.
- Ufi for Table 4.1 which is 'based upon the Ufi, **learndirect** Learning Through Work level descriptors © Ufi Limited 2001'.
- Warren Houghton for Figure 4.1, 'Aligning learning outcomes, learning and teaching activities and the assessment'. Warren Houghton (2004) *Engineering Subject Centre Guide: Learning and Teaching Theory for Engineering Academics.* Loughborough: HEA Engineering Subject Centre http://www.engsc.ac.uk/downloads/resources/theory.pdf
- Hodder & Stoughton Ltd. for Figure 5.2, 'Example of a Project Cycle'. This is adapted from a diagram by P. Baguley (1999) from *Project Management* part of the 'Teach Yourself Series', p. 150, fig 11.1.
- Sage Publishers for Table 5.3, 'Knowing Your Position'. This is adapted and referenced from K. Herr & G.L. Anderson 'The action

research Dissertation: A guide for Students and Faculty', ISBN - 0-7619-2991-6 (Sage, 2005, p.31).

- Ian Starkie, Director of Corporate Affairs *fdf* for Figure 8.2, 'How Foundation degrees span sectors'. This chart was plotted using research data collected and analysed by *fdf* and has not been formally published elsewhere but has been presented at conferences.
- Roger Grinyer, Head of Corporate Communications at HEFCE for Figure 8.1, 'Increasing Student Numbers' which illustrates the pattern of growth in Foundation degree enrolments, from the publication *Foundation degrees: key statistics 2001–02 to 2007–08.*
- All of the students whose details appear here anonymously, contextualising the book's content and allowing it to be so much richer because of their interesting examples and experience.

Every effort has been made to trace rights holders, but if any have been inadvertently overlooked the publishers would be pleased to make the necessary arrangements at the first opportunity.

Notes on the Contributors

Adrian Evans is currently the Director of Corporate Programmes at Teesside University Business School. He was recently the Managing Director of 'Mission Antarctica' and has over 20 years' experience of leadership and management development across a diverse range of sectors and learners with current interests in work-based learning, innovation and creativity.

Sue Graham is Work-Related Learning Manager and an Enterprise Fellow at Northumbria University, where she manages a small team which supports the university in meeting employers' higher level skills needs through flexible and responsive provision. Her particular interests lie in lifelong learning policy and practice and, in particular, university level work-based learning.

Dr Ruth Helyer is Head of Workforce Development (Research and Policy) at Teesside University, UK. Her research interests encompass all aspects of academic business-facing activity. Recent publications include, 'Employer Engagement: The New Widening Participation?' in the *Journal of Widening Participation and Lifelong Learning*, Staffordshire University (December 2008). Formerly the Programme Leader of Teesside University's Work-based Studies Programme, she has a particular interest in developing such tailored programmes for employed learners. Ruth has also lectured and published widely in the field of English Studies.

Dr Elaine Hooker is a Workforce Development Consultant at the award winning Teesside University. Located in the Department of Academic Enterprise, Elaine works in partnership with both internal and external clients to manage, coordinate and develop work-based learning initiatives.

Kerstin McClenaghan is a Virtual Learning Co-ordinator at Teesside University Business School where her work includes collaborating with employers and work-based students to design tailored e-learning opportunities. Kerstin's special interest lies in developing innovative ways of supporting students online and she led the e-learning strategy for the programme which won the Times Higher Education Outstanding Employer Engagement Initiative Award for 2009/10.

Dr Jenny Naish is Assistant Dean for Partnerships, Learning and Teaching at Teesside University Business School, the winner of the Times Higher Education Outstanding Employer Engagement Initiative Award for 2009/10. Jenny's special area of expertise is Work-based Learning and she was awarded a National Teaching Fellowship in 2006, the first in the country for WBL.

Alix Pearson is an Associate Director with Foundation Degree Forward (fdf) where her work includes advising employers on higher education for workforce development. She manages the fdf Endorsement Service which awards a quality mark to recognize excellent practice in work-based higher education.

Dr David Perrin is the Manager of the Professional Development Unit at the University of Chester. He manages the university's Work Based and Integrative Studies (WBIS) framework of negotiated work-based learning, currently with around 1000 students. His original background is in politics and applied economics, though in recent years he has developed specialist knowledge of APL and HE credit issues.

Garth Rhodes is Head of Flexible Learning in the School of Health, Community and Education Studies at Northumbria University where he has responsibility for a Negotiated Work-based Learning Programme for over 400 students, the accreditation of employer-based learning and the development of flexible and innovative approaches to employer engagement and workforce development.

Dr Barbara Workman is Director of the Centre for Excellence in Work-based Learning at Middlesex University. Her background is in nursing and health care and she has many years of experience in work-based learning and accreditation of experiential learning. Her current role is to extend and embed WBL across all the university and subject areas.

David Young is Emeritus Professor of Work-based Learning at the University of Derby. He has been engaged in work-based learning at university level since the mid-1990s. He has wide experience in external examination, staff development and consultancy in the field and has published in the UK and internationally. He led the University of Derby team which won the Times Higher Education Award in 2006 for Most Imaginative Use of Distance Learning. He was awarded a National Teaching Fellowship in 2007.

Foreword

Experiential learning is about the acquisition of useful knowledge and the development of a wide range of relevant skills. Learning opportunities present themselves to us every day, at home, work, and even at play but all experiences make us who we are. Gathering and reflecting upon our experiences provides us with our own unique toolkit. It could be said that the real skill of a craftsperson is in selecting the correct tool for a given situation and using it well. Fortunately most of us are not like the artisans of the past where the use of an inappropriate chisel and mallet could lead to the crash of marble and the loss of hours of painstaking effort. But it is true that selecting the wrong tools or attempting to use under-developed tools can be a painful experience. Therefore we are all like the artisans in one respect, whatever our occupation; in that only through the use of highly polished and appropriate tools can a degree of reliability be ensured. The trick is to continuously use and sharpen skills and to apply continuing layers of polish through the acquisition of additional knowledge. There is a salutary lesson to be observed through the use of under-developed knowledge and skills as one is quickly found to be lacking; the painful realities of trial and error are all too swift in arriving. Only through the timely application of knowledge and skills in the real world can we gain a sense of surety in the steps we take.

We are all different and in the text that follows you will find many examples that will help you to understand the benefits that work-based learning can offer and support you through the challenges (opportunities!) that lie ahead. Good luck with your work-based learning journey!

Andy Smyth
Accredited Programmes Manager, TUI UK and Ireland

Introduction

Ruth Helyer

● What is this book about?

If you are new to work-based learning (WBL) then this handbook has been devised specifically with you in mind. Its chapters have been put together by WBL experts from different universities and organizations who have designed their input to guide you through the exciting, but challenging, experience of Higher Education (HE) level study which is based on your workplace and work expertise. Undertaking HE level study is a challenge for everyone but it can seem especially complex if you spend the majority of your time at work, with limited time for study, and little or no recent experience of formal education. There is no one universal model of WBL but this handbook covers the key areas you will need to know about, no matter which WBL route you are taking. For example, you may gain an honours degree via a WBL programme (perhaps called Work-based Studies or similar) or you might be undertaking a much shorter award; the course might be delivered on a university campus, at your own place of work, online, or by some combination of these locations and methods. Whatever the details of your study, this handbook offers you an array of invaluable hints and tips to ensure that you maximize your experience. You can dip in and out of the book, retrieving what you need at any given point in your studies; don't feel that you need to read everything at once, or in a definitive order!

We want to help, support and inspire you, and this is reflected in the text's friendly, relaxed style. However, some of your academic assessments may require a more formal tone, and you may also find this formal tone adopted by other textbooks you use for your studies. We want you to enjoy your learning experience; to feel more confident after reading the book than you did before! Diverse examples of best practice appear throughout; these are clearly boxed and illustrate for you the way in which real people benefit from engaging with HE level work-based learning. The students cited show that it is possible to be employed, juggle personal commitments and flourish in a learning environment despite not attending university at

18, or undertaking 'A' levels. The examples are drawn from real student experiences, but care has been taken not to identify individual students. There are also numerous activities and exercises for you to try, tick-lists for you to use and lists of tips. These are designed to be useful, but fun, activities which will hopefully make some of the learning processes easier for you.

What is work-based learning (WBL)?

The information provided about WBL will help you to place your own experience in context; it will also help you to describe what you are doing to your line manager, colleagues, family and friends. Put simply, work-based learning is what is 'learned' by working – not reading about work, or observing work, but actually undertaking work activities. While reading and research could well be involved, especially if you're aiming for a formal qualification, this is learning from *real* work and *real* life and accepting how inextricably linked those activities are. As the sophistication and level of your job increases, so does the likelihood that you will be undertaking research and studying theory.

Your 'work' may not be full-time paid employment. Perhaps you are learning in a work placement, or as a volunteer. WBL involves many diverse students just like you, but they are all actively *doing* the things they're learning about (and actively learning from this doing!). You learn in your workplace and/or the classroom, further supported by electronic and mobile technologies. Increasingly communication between you, your tutors and your peers will be carried out online and your university or college will offer you introductory support and skills sessions to make sure you get the most out of these new and developing technologies (see Chapter 1 for HE skills and Chapter 7 for online learning).

WBL commonly uses the Accreditation of Prior Learning (APL), a process which acknowledges learning from previous experience and/or qualifications. This reduces the amount of time taken to obtain an award (see Chapter 2). As a WBL student you can gain credit towards your award through APL. This is especially empowering if you initially felt out of place and in a hurry at university. There need be no such thing as 'missing your chance'. You can also include a continuing professional development (CPD) activity which you are carrying out at work already, in your WBL programme (Chapter 3).

As well as the unusual aspects of being a WBL student you will also benefit from the traditional advantages of HE – the development of intellectual, personal, critical and analytical skills, which will support and complement your practical skills and knowledge. You are likely to have much more life experience than an 18-year-old student; furthermore you will probably find that your student peers in your class or study group differ widely in age, background and aspirations (this can even be the case when you are all from the same company!). However, as motivated, employed people prepared to work hard in order to successfully fit studying into already busy lives you will also have much in common. Because Higher Education (HE) level WBL programmes take account of your existing knowledge and expertise they are the best, and certainly most time-effective, HE study route for you.

Let's summarize some of the key benefits of WBL:

- Acknowledges skills and knowledge gained at work.
- Maximizes your time (1) – by offering APL credit and potentially advanced standing (Chapter 2).
- Maximizes your time (2) – by assisting with workplace CPD (Chapter 3), and projects which you would have to do anyway (Chapter 5).
- Combines education and development – for the 'real' world (Chapter 8).
- Offers networking opportunities – your peers will all be employed too.
- Links you into routes to various HE awards (Chapter 8).

And, the key benefits of WBL study routes?

- Use your work role to provide/inform the curriculum.
- Focus on your individual learning plan/contract/agreement (Chapter 3) – some universities re-visit this each year.
- Facilitate cross-disciplinary working, spanning subjects and sectors.
- Actively accredit prior learning, both experiential and certificated (Chapter 2).
- Acknowledge that learning is taking place at diverse locations, not just in Higher Education Institutions (HEIs).
- Offer flexibility re: time, place and style of study for example there may be off campus, out of hours and electronic options.
- Allow longer (and looser) timeframes in which to complete awards.
- Encourage negotiation of title, and content, of award (this differs between institutions).

- Keep compulsory modules and campus attendance to a minimum.
- Offer generic skills modules – invaluable whatever your job.
- Operate beyond the academic calendar – for example, many recruit new starters and/or offer modules more than once a year.
- Support reflective practice and self-analysis (Chapter 1).
- Offer innovative methods of learning, teaching and assessment (Chapter 4).
- Utilize technology, e-learning, distance learning (Chapter 7).

Graduates of these work-based studies programmes frequently state that they could never have undertaken HE level study, without the opportunity such a route has given them:

> I could never have obtained my degree without a scheme like this. I left school with no qualifications and never felt like I could belong at university. The work-based studies programme proved me wrong! It is so flexible, it meant I could attend sessions and tutorials after work. I also completed a lot of the assignments at home, at work and in the library and based all of my major submissions on work tasks which I would have had to complete as part of my job, even if I wasn't studying. (Student A)

They also offer an ideal progression route, if you already hold a Foundation degree (see Chapter 8), a small award; or some kind of professional qualification you can, potentially, accelerate to full honours degree status. The multiple step-on and step-off points characteristic of WBL programmes make this possible. Schemes often use a skeleton structure (see the example below) which can be 'fleshed out' in ways flexible enough to meet your individual requirements.

Example: Programme requirements: undergraduate

Level 4			
Core modules	*Library and IT Skills* 10 credits	*Personal Development and Programme Planning* (Level 4/5/6) 20 credits	Require 120 credits at each level

Level 5			
Core modules	*Research Methods (Level 5/6) 20 credits*	*Personal Development and Programme Planning (Level 4/5/6) 20 credits*	Some modules run at more than one level – to facilitate APL claims

Level 6			
(honours) Core modules	*Continuous Professional Development 20 credits*	*Final work-based project or dissertation 40 credits*	Often modules run more than once a year

The remaining credits needed for your award might come from a combination of:

- APL claims
- taught modules
- skills modules
- WB projects
- open learning
- independent learning.

What does a work-based learning student look like?

Example: student B

Student B is an employed process engineer who already had a Higher National Diploma in Mechanical and Electrical Engineering when she joined the work-based studies programme. She had obtained this within the previous five years. She joined the work-based studies programme at her local university when she found out that her HND could well be counted against a BSc in Engineering Studies. She obtained 120 credits at Level 4 (120 required) and a further 50 credits at Level 5 (120 required) for the precise content of her HND. She then gained further credits at Level 5 for undertaking a core module where she learned about the process of claiming for prior learning (although this module itself carries only 20 credits, through its assessment process – a portfolio of evidence – she was able to claim a further 50 credits at Level 5 for her experiential learning). This completed Levels 4 and 5 (the equivalent of the first and second year of traditional undergraduate full-time study). At Level 6 she studied a taught module about continuing professional development (20 credits, evening attendance), undertook 'Research Methods' (20 credits, evening attendance), an engineering module (20 credits, day release) and two work-based projects, one worth 20 credits and one worth 40. The 40 credit project, equivalent to a dissertation, involved developing a completely new process for her employer. This student was awarded a 2:1 classification for her BSc in just 2 years.

Why would you choose to study this way?

WBL graduates have plenty to say:

Insufficient time to study full-time?

[WBL] is an ideal solution if you can't commit to full-time study but have the right experience. I'd tell anyone to go for it. (IT trainer to primary school teacher)

Thinking of your next career move?

[T]he opportunity to obtain credits for prior learning and professional work-based experience was just the springboard I needed to encourage me to take the first step ... The Business Management degree not only reflected my experience and career path as a professional police officer but will benefit me in being considered for other managerial roles outside policing. (Police Inspector)

Want to accelerate your career in a limited time frame?

I was able to enhance my career prospects in my current position as a teaching assistant. I have always wanted to teach and am pleased that the [Work-based Studies programme] acknowledges my teaching experience and existing qualifications. I've been able to fast track myself. What should technically have been eight years of study has been reduced to three years. I've also been able to personalize my programme to suit my areas of interest, which is Special Educational Needs. (Teaching Assistant to Teacher)

Would you benefit from presenting existing workplace projects in an academic format? (Chapter 5):

> I wanted to do an engineering degree which gave me the opportunity to choose my own relevant modules. The [WBL route] allowed me to do this and, very importantly, claim credit for areas of major experience and learning. I was also able to transfer my previous qualifications into university credits, in effect, reducing my study time. Choosing specific modules to suit my current employment needs has been ideal. I'm a process engineer, responsible for the productivity and optimization of manufacturing equipment. On this degree pathway I can now learn more about managing engineering projects and process improvements, as well as the standard technical modules more normally associated with an engineering degree. (Engineer)

You can see from these quotations how varied the backgrounds and expertise of work-based learners are. The networking opportunities and shared practices you will gain from being part of a HE WBL community will really enrich your learning experience (Chapter 6).

You are probably a 'mature' student, but please don't worry about this; being older than the traditional HE student really is *not* the hindrance new WB learners often presume it will be! You have a head-start on the wisdom and skills front, and experience of practical applications. Now is your chance to monopolize on all of this and connect some of your new educational goals to your professional and personal experience. You might feel that you need to make an extra effort to catch up on the theory and abstraction side of things, but don't give up! This is worth the effort, there is always more to learn but it really enhances your workplace practice. WBL students tend to have a goal-orientated and structured approach (sound familiar?!) – this attitude ensures that you will achieve great things through your engagement with HE, not least because of your professional approach to being assessed (Chapter 4).

What's so good about HE anyway?

HE level learning carries credit. This is what makes it possible to offer you awards and qualifications; there is a system in place to track and quantify what you have learned, and furthermore to compare this learning to other learning which is of a similar level of difficulty and complexity. Credit is used in the HE sector as a portable, international 'currency'. Because HE level learning carries credit, your study pathway is flexible, adaptable, valued, tailor-made and tied into a recognized quality system. The HE credit system recognizes successful completion of modules, courses and programmes.

Why are you engaging with work-based learning? A quick re-cap!

- *Bespoke* – designed around your needs.
- *Relevant* – connects to your real workplace activities.
- *Student focused* – the emphasis is on what you want/need to learn, not what someone else wants to teach you.
- *Credit-bearing* – has a discernible worth attached, recognizable globally.
- *Added value* – encompasses your work and life needs and interests – the qualification can feel like a bonus.
- *Realistic* – in terms of flexible timescales and feasible expectations.
- *Supported* – your employer will see the benefit and may support with mentorship, time off, assistance with fees (ask your line manager).
- *High status* – HE award could bring promotion, pay rise, new job.
- *Ongoing* – ties into progression and your continuous development.
- *Enjoyable* – it really can be! You have such an influence on the content.
- *Cutting edge* – you learn, develop and use innovative, new practice.
- *Different* – this is not run of the mill, it is largely what you make it.

The following chart summarizes where key subjects and activities, of interest to you, are mostly dealt with in the following chapters:

Headline chapter content	Level 4 (1st Year equivalent)	Level 5 (2nd Year equivalent)	Level 6 (3rd Year equivalent)
Accreditation Foundation degrees	Chapter 8	Chapter 8	Chapter 8
APL claims	Chapter 2	Chapter 2	Chapter 2
Assessment	Chapter 4	Chapter 4	Chapter 4
Autonomous learning	Chapters 1, 3 and 6	Chapters 1, 3 and 6	Chapters 1, 3 and 6

Headline chapter content	Level 4 (1st Year equivalent)	Level 5 (2nd Year equivalent)	Level 6 (3rd Year equivalent)
Continuous professional development	–	–	Chapter 3
CV and job description	Chapters 2 and 3	Chapters 2 and 3	Chapters 2 and 3
HE context	Intro and Chapter 1	Intro and Chapter 1	Intro and Chapter 1
HE skills	Chapter 1	–	–
Industry relevance	Chapter 8	Chapter 8	–
Learning contract	Chapter 3 and 6	Chapter 3 and 6	Chapter 6
Learning styles	Chapter 3	Chapter 3	Chapter 3
Level descriptors	Chapters 1, 2 and 4	Chapters 1, 2 and 4	Chapters 1, 2 and 4
Online learning	Chapter 7	Chapter 7	Chapter 7
PDP	Chapter 3	Chapter 3	Chapter 3
Programme planning	Chapters 2 and 3	Chapters 2 and 3	Chapters 2 and 3
Progression	–	Chapter 8	–
Progression Feedback	Chapters 4 and 6	Chapters 4 and 6	Chapters 4 and 6
Reflection	Chapters 1–4 and 6	Chapters 1–4 and 6	Chapters 1–4 and 6
Research methods	–	Chapter 5	Chapter 5
Support networks	Chapters 6–8	Chapters 6–8	Chapters 6–8
WB projects	–	Chapter 5 and 6	Chapter 5 and 6
Work placements and live briefs	Chapter 8	Chapter 8	–

1 Adapting to Higher Education: Academic Skills

Ruth Helyer

In this chapter you will learn:

- ▶ how far you have already come in your learning journey;
- ▶ what higher education (HE) is and how it works;
- ▶ how to make the most of reflecting on your activities;
- ▶ about different styles of academic writing;
- ▶ what the different levels of study are;
- ▶ how to manage your time better.

Where am I now?

The fact that you are now looking through this handbook suggests that you have made a decision to study for a higher education (HE) level work-based learning (WBL) qualification, perhaps to enhance your professional profile and advance your career. This journey, from where you are now to where you want to be, will also offer you a good deal in the way of personal enjoyment and satisfaction. Most university programmes which include WBL start with questions about 'where you are now', and a combination of exercises, discussion and self-audit procedures designed to help you to form a clear picture of what you have achieved and learned already at HE level and how to progress with this.

Personal development plans (PDPs), or personal plans of action, will help you with this (see Chapter 3). Exercise 1.1 will help to begin to organize your thoughts before you write your PDP. The bullet points are suggestions; populate the lists with what is important to you personally.

Exercise 1.1: Achievements and ambitions

What have I achieved already?	What do I want from my job?
● Specific	● Power?
● Personal	● Status?
● Work-related (or not)	● People/relationships?
	● Creativity
	● Challenge?
	● Structure?

What skills and qualities enabled these achievements?	What would facilitate (F) and prevent (P) me getting what I want?
● Your abilities? ● Aware of them?	● Required qualification (F) ● Lack of above! (P) And so on.

Because work-based programmes usually allow what you have learned already to count towards your new award, it is very important to give this introspective part of your study as much time and effort as you can. By claiming for credit via the APL process (mentioned in the introduction and fully explained in Chapter 2) you locate the starting point for your new programme of learning. Most WBL students comment on the empowerment this part of the programme gives them; gathering strategic evidence about your prior learning requires you to focus on your key strengths, which perhaps you take for granted. Measuring what you know already against your Higher Education Institution's (HEI's) level descriptors (see later in this chapter and Chapter 4 for more information on these) proves to you that you are operating in the workplace at a level comparable with HE study. This will improve your confidence and feelings of belonging as you embark upon your HE adventure. Although all students differ greatly from one another, and WBL students like you come from a wide variety of occupations, there are certain character traits which frequently reoccur. You may find these coming to the fore as you begin to ask questions of yourself (they are shared by all WBL students so don't worry!):

- *New to HE?* Have not been in any educational setting for some years? You will require generic and academic skills alongside subject-specific skills – don't worry!
- You bring *professional knowledge* – perhaps working at levels far higher than your formal qualifications suggest. Your incidental and opportunistic learning applied in an academic setting creates an empowering synergy (see Chapter 5, 'Work-based Projects').
- WBL programmes attract, and welcome, learners from *all sectors* and backgrounds (Chapter 8).
- You are probably *older than traditional students* at the same level. WBL courses encourage claiming credit, which offers advanced standing; it is almost a prerequisite, and certainly a benefit, that you are old enough to have gained learning through experience (Chapter 2).

- You have certain *motivations* for entering HE. These could be: to expand your qualifications; improve your career prospects; justify your job position; fulfil a long-held personal wish; respond to a turning point in your life – these are all normal.

- You are a *part-time student* but you are also *employed*. This may be part or full-time work, paid or unpaid (for example voluntary or family business), self-employment and/or business owner, seasonal or contract work – again, all normal.

- You can only attend the campus *outside of 'office hours'* (your employer might give you 'day release' to attend certain 'daytime only' modules). However, due to the flexibility of these awards and the APL process it is possible to complete awards in a relatively short period of time.

- You will be *paying your own fees*, self-supported and financially independent. If you have your fees paid by your employer they may expect some input into your choices.

- You will have a *complex* life, and commitments (family, work, community). But, coping with this complexity proves you are capable, motivated and prepared to juggle the demands on your time, finances, energy, intellect and emotions.

- Along with this personal complexity the *study route* is non-regular, first because it is individualized but also because of the varying methods of attendance and assessment. You will need to be a flexible, adaptable individual to survive.

- As well as intellectual challenges there are *logistical* ones, such as the impact of evening attendance on tutor and facility availability – cafes, car parks and so on.

- You will rely on *virtual learning environments* for some sessions and for pastoral support (you will need access to a computer for this) (Chapter 7).

- You will be relying on family, friends and work colleagues for *support* and understanding. Line Managers might need to give permission to access work-related information needed for assignments and so on (Chapter 6).

- You will need to develop the ability to negotiate and manipulate the *HE credit system* – that is, understand how many credits at each level you will require to obtain your award (see Appendix 1 for a table of these, and Chapter 2).

These traits are widespread and reoccurring; they should help you to feel part of a group of learners who have a lot in common. The questions you are asking about 'where am I now?' are shared by your peers; you will all relate to at least one of the categories below, in feeling:

- *At a crossroads* – there are several options open to you. You feel that work-related study will focus your mind as well as giving you extra HE qualifications.
- *At a dead end* – you have gone as far as your current job role will allow and you need a new, higher level, qualification to move on.
- *On a plateau* – you are unable to progress any further in your career/sector without a degree.
- *Confused* – the discipline of study will help you to sort your profile/thoughts/aims into a format for progression and development.
- *Bored* – it is time to do something new with your working life.
- *Frustrated* – you are being passed over for promotion by younger, less-experienced colleagues who all have HE level qualifications.
- *Like you have time on your hands* – maybe your responsibilities towards dependants have altered.
- *Slightly envious* – partner/friends may have recently experienced academic success.
- *Inspired* – your own offspring are doing well at university or college.
- *Underpaid* – there is increasing pressure on you at work to take on extra responsibility, yet rewards for this, in your company, are tied to level of qualification.

There are numerous reasons for taking stock of your own learning and development, but embracing WBL is far more demanding than just signing up for night classes, or attending a training course provided by your employer. WBL is an all-encompassing life change and the results of your engagement with it will, like all worthwhile activities, be directly related to what you put into the experience. The initial exercises and activities of WBL programmes usually include compiling a CV and a job description – not exactly like the ones you periodically use for job applications but a version specifically designed to get to the heart of what it is you actually do (and have done) and how much you have learned from that 'doing'. These activities act like a self-audit and encompass looking back to gather evidence which exemplifies your skills, expertise and learning. This body of evidence helps to truly ascertain where you are 'now', as well as being the catalyst for where you are going next. There is much more detail about these activities, which are sometimes part of a module with a name like 'Make Your Learning

Count' or 'Recognition of Prior Learning' in Chapter 2, where you are guided on a step-by-step journey of unpicking, evidencing and claiming what you have previously learned.

You have probably already decided that you want to study in relation to your occupation (Chapter 8). If part of your desire to engage with HE level learning comes from a long-cherished dream to study a particular subject, and this subject does not relate in any way to your employment, then a WBL route is probably not the best choice for you. A course of study which includes a large percentage of new (to you) theoretical input will probably be best approached via the more traditional undergraduate route. If you have decided that you would like to obtain an HE level award and that the WBL route is the best way for you then the next question you probably need to ask yourself is how much involvement will your employer have? For example, do you need to ask if it is OK for you to enrol on a course? As WBL courses are often held outside of office hours you might not need your employer's permission. However, your university assignments (Chapter 4) will almost certainly need information and real-life activity from your workplace and this will be enhanced by your employer's involvement; indeed, you may not be allowed to quote details about the company without this involvement.

They could also offer to pay your fees and/or perhaps let you negotiate some time away from the workplace within office hours. The more positive the impact of your studies on the organization the better it is, as this will make your employer feel more inclined to offer you support (Chapter 6). Perhaps you wish to keep your university attendance from your employer because you are planning to change your career and/or job? This closes down options for certain means of study and development, but is sometimes unavoidable. Alternatively, your employer might be the driving force behind your university attendance. If this is the case, are you part of a group of students all from the same company? This changes the focus of your studying by placing a stronger emphasis upon your employer's expectations. Or you may be part of a mixed group or class, made up from students from across the same sector but from diverse companies? Or even, differing sectors, if your chosen course of study is suitable for many sectors (for example, Leadership and Management).

To get the most out of your learning experience you need to think about how you learn best (Chapter 3). Be honest about how much of an independent learner you can be; if you need the constant input of a tutor or teacher then WBL is probably not going to work for you. Instead you need to be capable of self-direction (even if this doesn't come naturally to you!). You will not be left totally alone and told to 'get on with it', especially not at first, but you will be expected to be a motivated, self-starter who is capable of using their initiative, and probably somebody who is intellectually curious. If you do not find the subject matter engaging then you probably won't feel motivated to do as much independent work as will be expected of you. This means taking responsibility for your own learning and your own time management (see the section 'Time management' below), nobody is going to hand you the answers or write the syllabus on the black/white board. Your study will be about *your* work and how *you* learn and therefore is far too personalized for a didactic style of teaching to be useful. WBL programmes are usually negotiated programmes driven by a personal learning contract (Chapter 3); this increases individuality and appropriateness but reduces commonality. It can also reduce interaction with your peers; you might find yourself, on the odd occasions when classroom attendance is necessary, among other students with whom you feel you have little in common. However, although these other students come from different work disciplines they are embarking on a similar journey to yourself – one that involves time and effort on top of holding down employment – and this similarity is enough to spark friendships over coffee. Traditional undergraduates on the campus for three years full-time doing the same course cannot escape each other – for you and your peers interaction may require a bit more conscious effort! Your individually planned programme will differ in content and pace from other students but hopefully you might spend enough time with other learners, in generic core modules for example, to form supportive relationships and networks with them.

TIP Challenges for (WBL) students (in particular!)

- Academic expectations, policies and procedures.
- Academic skills (writing, presentation, note-taking, literature reviews and so on).
- How does the HE credit system operate?
- Learning Agreements or Contracts – planning your own study route.
- Being part of a group of diverse students.
- Unfamiliar HE setting.

You could well need extra support and feedback, and your tutors will provide this (Chapter 6). *But* your increased professional profile, when compared to the average 18-year-old student, means that you are far more likely to have the confidence and experience to ask for help and guidance – please do.

What is HE?

In the UK we have standard secondary education (11 to 16-year-olds) followed by sixth form (post-16) colleges and further education colleges (FECs). Then there is higher education (HE), offered through universities and some FECs and specialist institutions (often banded together as HEIs). Originally HE was aimed at 18-year-olds, but increasingly its culture of developing the whole person, something very attractive to employed students, means that it is attracting students of all ages and backgrounds wishing to undertake an HE level qualification (for example FdA, BA, BA Hons, MA, PhD and so on, see Appendix 1). HE awards are widely recognizable, carrying an impressive reputation and a high profile. In order to justify this they are rigorously quality assured by the Quality Assurance Agency (QAA), see: http://www.qaa.ac.uk/aboutus/default.asp. WBL HE level qualifications undergo exactly the same processes and are of an equally high standard to the more traditional qualifications; they also use the same terminology – if you study for a BA it will still be called that. HE quality processes are externally monitored and strictly adhered to in order to keep the qualifications which UK HEIs award at a recognized level. The variety of HE courses available is constantly increasing (Chapter 8). WBL programmes have differing kinds of demands but utilize the same levels of academic rigour as comparable taught courses. It is not an easier or lesser way of obtaining a qualification, indeed it could be argued that this is a more demanding route as you have to be self-motivated and largely unsupervised.

Exercise 1.2: Different courses

Draw up a personal list of what you perceive to be the *similarities* and *differences* between a traditional university course and a WBL programme in higher education; you probably haven't attended an HEI yet, but you will have ideas about what happens there.

Traditional university course	University level WBL programme
Similarities	**Similarities**
Challenging high level learning – demands critical thinking	Challenging high level learning – demands critical thinking
Leads to university qualification	Leads to university qualification
....	....
....	....

Traditional university course	University level WBL programme
Differences	**Differences**
Focus on one or two subject areas	Focus on my work and work activities – applied learning
Taught in lectures on campus	Tutorial and other support at a distance
....	....
....	....

You gain some significant advantages by undertaking some/most of your university level learning off campus. Perhaps the main one of these is flexibility – the ability to fit learning around the demands of your work or family and to study at your own pace and at times and in locations that suit you, rather than following a totally pre-set timetable is a massive bonus. There is also the opportunity to design your programme around the interests and concerns of your workplace and professional practice, therefore combining academic and theoretical knowledge with work-based skills.

Historically universities have been viewed as seats of knowledge where specialist lecturers transmit information to pupils through timetabled tutorials and lectures, using set texts from a pre-decided syllabus. This content-heavy position has shifted considerably in recent years and you will find that interaction between you and your tutors is far more negotiated and personalized. Rather than the curriculum being carved in stone and designed around material that must be covered (and all of the suggestions of 'correct' answers and 'cramming' which go with that), you should view it as a personal vehicle that you can use to get you to where you want to be. This new kind of learning/teaching relationship hones and alters learning opportunities, while retaining the established strengths of HE.

TIP **How to tell it's HE**

- Awards credit which values, describes, measures and recognizes all learning (at level).
- Develops intellectual and personal skills together with specific knowledge in key areas.
- Improves the many facets of every individual student with holistic programmes, courses and modules.
- Acknowledges and validates skills, knowledge, experience, work-practice.

- Facilitates learning which transforms and improves lives.
- It is innovative – which inevitably includes rethinking, changing and some disruption!
- It offers all of this to everyone who stands to benefit from it.

The changing culture of HE

So while you may feel that your WBL journey is unusual you need to set this within the context of the culture of HE itself changing considerably in the last ten years, and continuing to change and evolve. The largest component of this changing landscape is the growing number of non-traditional students. This shifting HE population can be attributed to many factors, but they include: equalization of opportunity; an ageing population; changes in the economic and employment markets; rapidly developing technologies and so on. The increasing number of work-based students, like you, means that HEIs have had to be innovative about how they acknowledge non-traditional educational experience. This innovation has led to a marked increase in the use of articulation of achievement and accreditation of company in-house training, both practices with the potential to offer you advanced standing, which obviously affects HEI's admissions processes. Building relationships with different kinds of students, like you, and increasingly also with your employer, means that HEIs are behaving more commercially and taking more risks. This is bound to challenge a culture more accustomed to behaving in established, and somewhat risk-averse, ways, but it assists with the continuous development of HE as a stretching environment. Working with you and your employer makes HE more responsive and more likely to develop and deliver learning opportunities which are relevant in the twenty-first century; programmes of a bespoke, negotiated, adaptable and often multi-disciplinary nature.

HE qualifications hold a parity of esteem across the learning sector and beyond. Some career pathways demand graduate status, but this is not the same as having a professional licence to practice. Your WBL qualification will not enable you to become a police officer, nurse, teacher and so on; you will still need to undertake the requisite training for these careers in order to also obtain the professional qualifications, usually strictly overseen by the appropriate professional body. Your HE level WBL study adds a further dimension to your very job-specific qualification and it includes the rounded qualities which the majority of employers state they are looking for, a mix of cognitive and non-cognitive skills and achievements which help you to become a fully developed person – useful at work, at home and in your community.

Employability is clearly a complex mixture of elements; elements which differ from job to job but with the same basic outcome – they make you a desirable employee. In a rapidly changing society it is clear that you need to be adaptable and multi-faceted. It is unlikely that as a twenty-first-century worker you will hold one position, or even one occupation, for your entire working life. You will work for longer than previous generations and perhaps in changing circumstances; this need for reinvention requires a receptive and self-aware person and your employability skills need to be honed and enhanced (Helyer, 2007). These skills include those of analysis and critical debate, being able to make connections and read widely; they also include broader multi-faceted skills including creativity, imagination and entrepreneurship.

You will find that in common with the majority of HE award routes, on work-based programmes you must undertake a large project or dissertation to achieve an honours degree. This usually represents 40 or 60 credits at Level 6 (the equivalent of the third year for full-timers). Your project will investigate a work-based issue and, like all learning, will result in changes. The impact this could have on your workplace will very much depend on your individual role and the size and scope of your employer; however, there is the potential here for you to make a real difference to the workplace practices of you and your colleagues. There are many excellent examples of WBL students greatly increasing the profitability of their workplace by applying the discoveries of their work-based projects and this has ensured that WBL has become positively associated with not just personal change but also organizational change (Chapter 5).

One key difference between most work-based programmes and the traditional degree programme, and a real plus for you, is that as well as this large summative piece, you can often also undertake almost as many extra projects as you wish to, taking into account level, subject and requisite core modules. If it is in keeping with your profile and areas of expertise then it is permitted and indeed valid for you to largely populate your programme with work-based projects (Chapter 5). Work-based projects will help you to manage your time and effort, both of which are at a premium when you are attempting to combine work and study. You and your employer stand to gain from combining a piece of work activity (which needs to be carried out anyway) with an academic assignment (Chapter 4). For you, a busy employed student, this reduces campus attendance; for your employer it offers unrivalled research resources and a superior piece of written work, usually exceeding the report expected in terms of research skills, depth and academic rigour.

Much of your learning will be taking place at work; reading and writing about WBL needs to be fitted into your own time and you will have to develop timetabling skills to deal with this. Your studies might demand extensive use of the internet and other web-facilitated technologies: searching the web; communicating with fellow students and tutors; using your university's virtual learning environment (VLE). Increasingly, all university courses utilize these technologies as much as is possible and appropriate but it is even more important for you because WBL students are almost always employed, perhaps spending periods of time away from their homes and their office/work-base, at distant branches of their company, potentially across the world. Online technologies mean that so long as you have access to a computer and the internet you can progress your studies wherever you are. Some WBL programmes are totally online and to get the best from these you must develop your IT skills to your fullest capacity (Chapter 7).

You are probably starting to see just how much WBL is pushing boundaries on many levels: by acknowledging previous learning and encouraging you to evidence and build upon your knowledge and expertise; by utilizing different ways of learning – such as extensive use of mobile technologies; and by encouraging change and growth in the HE sector itself as WBL can often exceed what the academy knows already.

Exercise 1.3: The good and the bad

With some of this in mind draw up your personal list of the advantages and disadvantages of undertaking a WBL programme in higher education. For example: time needed to study; balancing other commitments; cost implications; travel; self-confidence and so on.

Advantages	Disadvantages

You (and your employer) bring expertise and a new kind of knowledge into the university, adding to and enhancing what is already going on there; this makes you more like a partner than a student and has the potential to facilitate truly cutting edge work, vastly different to the old model of an HEI where subject-based knowledge trickles downwards towards an empty recipient (you!), usually in a classroom setting, on a full-time basis, over a set period of weeks and years. This 'learning' would be then typically assessed by you being required to write essays and sit examinations. Contemporary and future methods of learning, teaching and assessment need to go way beyond this if they are to fulfil your needs, as part of a new, varied body of learners, and do justice to the type of learning which is entwined with workplace and life activity (Chapter 4).

Within traditional subject disciplines, such as history or philosophy, the way in which you actually study the subject is part of the subject's formation and integrity; there are well-established expectations around what the curriculum contains and how it is accessed. However, as Gibbons et al. suggest, 'The bounds of the intellectual world and its environment have become blurred' (Gibbons et al., 1994: 37). With new knowledge, that which is produced outside of the university, a more active style of learning is involved and it is impossible to separate the learning from the activity. You are not learning something then applying it, you are learning while you personally work (Gibbons et al., 1994 describe these distinctly different styles as Mode 1 and Mode 2 knowledge). Similarly Biggs (constructivist debate 2003) claims that you construct something personal from your activity which makes you learn, and that *what* you construct depends upon your motives, your intentions, your previous learning, your previous knowledge and probably also other factors.

So while formerly HEIs' strengths have been summed up as focusing on research and theory there is much evidence now to suggest that learning and doing cannot be separated and therefore to use knowledge to its fullest potential it must be implemented, performed and enhanced as part of a synergy. Ideally, as a learner, you will not only 'do', you will focus on *why* you are doing what you are doing, *how* you are doing it and the theory behind it. It is well worth you doing some research for yourself into the interesting debates around the nature of knowledge. Postmodern theory, for example, has considerably weakened the position of strength HEIs may have thought they held over deciding what could be legitimately classed as knowledge (see, for example, the work of Jean-François Lyotard).

Reflective practice

Elda Nikolou-Walker describes this learning revolution as, ' "marrying" academic skills within "real life" circumstances', a process which 'brings theory out of the classroom, right onto the desk in the office, onto the shop floor, or wherever individuals seek to *build* and *use* knowledge' (Nikolou-Walker, 2007: 539, italics in original). One of the key skills you must develop to get the most from your studies is actively reflecting on your work activities, as part of continuously evaluating, reviewing and improving performance, satisfaction and results. Combined with your new academic skills this reflection will encourage you to change your practices within the workplace, hence enhancing your personal performance, but also the overall performance of your organization. You will almost certainly already be utilizing critical reflection even if this has been subliminal up until this point!

David Gray cites reflecting actively and usefully as a process which generates the development of 'a dynamic synergy and dialectic between academic learning and work-based practice' (Gray, 2001: 24).

TIP   **Reflect to gain maximum credit**

- Reflect strategically on your learning through past experiences.
- Remember, the activity and the learning process are entwined – not separate entities.
- Reflect not just on your programme of study but also more generally along your life path.
- Make the most of your programme's guided self-audit (Chapter 2).
- Establish where exactly you are – in terms of career, personal development and learning.
- Acknowledge what you can already do – for example 'write reports' – this feeds into academic writing, an area you might be convincing yourself you know little about.
- Reflection makes you realize that you already have a good base on which to build your next stage of development.
- Don't worry, reflective skills can be 'taught' and measured.
- Become a reflective practitioner – strive to continually improve your practice – active reflection is key to this.

Humans automatically reflect on their actions, to a certain extent, but focusing this activity into a structured response maximizes its usefulness and encourages you to become a reflective and self-aware person. This means that you will be looking both backwards and forwards (and sometimes sideways!) to make connections with what you are currently undertaking. This kind of evaluation can feel fragmented and disjointed – don't worry, that is normal – it utilizes the knowledge which lies deep within you (tacit knowledge) – so deep you probably take it for granted and don't explicitly acknowledge it, but it is the data you use to make instinctive decisions based upon your accumulated knowledge from past actions and experience. Michael Eraut (1994) discusses the subtle nuances between the tacit, that which is implicitly acknowledged and referred to, rather than that which is explicitly pointed out. You might choose to use formalized reflection as a method for offering feedback to your employer; it is a good way to share outcomes. Because reflection is a vital part of personal development work-based learning programmes encourage you to become actively reflective.

Exercise 1.4 will help you with the thought processes.

Exercise 1.4: Reflect and plan

Describe a significant work-related incident (*describe and interpret*)

Information

Context

Perspective

Others involved

Actively reflect on this incident (*analyse your actions*)

Results?

Consequences? (for self and others)

Feelings?

Influences?

Alternatives?

The Learning Process (*explain*)

Feelings now?

New/different ideas?

Learned anything?

Progress?

Future practice?

By trying this activity you are required to 'look back' and analyse past events and experiences. This enables those experiences to be then placed within the context of what is happening in the present and what may happen in the future. Within your WBL study you will encounter sessions which include learning theories and styles, meta-cognition, self-analysis of strengths and weaknesses and personal statements (Chapters 2 and 3) and you will be encouraged to think about what has worked well for you in the past when you have undertaken tasks and tackled situations in certain ways. This kind of reflection will also be usefully formalized into reports, essays, journals, logs or diaries. Your reflective writing can take a more personal style than that which you might have at first expected to be producing for university assignments, but it still needs to be structured and purposeful. Writing about your active reflection embeds within you good practice for your future continuous professional and personal development activities. Developing an ongoing ethos of reflection means you challenge and question *why* tasks were undertaken in a certain way rather than *how* they were carried out, and furthermore become accomplished at recognizing that you are learning continuously; it is not a standalone process. Tutor interaction will be built into this process with debriefing and support and the possibility of observational visits to your workplace. Your employer has much to gain from encouraging you to actively reflect on your work practices. As Cox claims, '"learning through work" is integral to the whole reflective practice process and can provide valuable opportunities for individual action research in the work context' (Cox, 2005: 471). It is crucial to remember that you are not separate to that context, but an intrinsic part of it. Reflective practice has the potential to impact positively upon you and your workplace/job-role; feedback from former WBL students refers to its transformative effect.

Active reflection is usually included in the core modules of a WBL programme. You may find that you are collecting a series of short narrative statements (500–1000 words) in which you actively reflect upon your learning

Figure 1.1 Review, research, reflect and learn

processes during different modules, these statements are often transformed into a 'Portfolio of Active Reflection', which includes your experience of various modules, your current and past activities and your future plans – all situated within a framework of personal and professional development. By embedding the value of reflecting and learning from experience your university hopes to create 'reflective practitioners' (Schon, 1983 and 1987); the ideal scenario being that as a reflective practitioner you share your ability to critically reflect and analyse and your higher level ideas with your company colleagues. You will become a practitioner for whom it is the 'norm' to continuously reflect, plan and develop; routinely revisiting the manner in which activities are conducted, rather than assuming that the 'old way is the best'. This is often illustrated in a circular format (see Figure 1.1) which can be slightly misleading as the process of reflection is more iterative and messy than a neat circle suggests. There *is* a certain circularity to moving through the stages of Review, Research and Reflect but it is a forward moving loop of enquiry – rather than a 'closed off' or 'fenced in' circle. To prevent an emphasis on looking back (despite this being needed) some prefer the term 'reflecting forwards', which foregrounds the developmental nature of the process.

In work-based degree programmes the acknowledging of what *has* been, *is* being and *will be* learned is at the core of your interaction with your tutors and your peers. This questions the 'correct' order of things, as you repeatedly look back, forth and across through your experience. This postmodern approach to learning can be seen as simultaneously liberating, because of the opportunities it offers, and frightening, as it removes boundaries and the purported 'safety', they bring (Helyer, 2007). WBL programmes inevitably involve a personal and professional 'stock-take' (Chapter 2). An important element of this is 'looking back' to analyse your past learning experiences. This might feel uncomfortable. Invariably as a WBL student you will be a mature student feeling the need to 'catch up'; you want or need that qualification (perhaps others in your workplace are graduates, or your career has changed into a graduate profession since you joined it) and you feel aware that you are not 18 and do not have A levels. I am positive that you did not enrol with a university in order to look back; you want to move forwards towards a qualification, like every other student. Being genuinely reflective takes time, it can be painful and is invariably more difficult than you anticipate; some facets of your practice may need to be 'un-learned' or at least amended. As Elaine Cox (2005) states, 'encouraging reflective practice at all levels is beneficial for students undertaking any kind of work-based activity, even though ... there is often resistance to the process and difficulty in initial development of the reflective and analytical skills required' (Cox, 2005: 461). You will be guided through the process; an issue in itself as you must learn to trust your tutor (who will be adept at reflective processes) in order to be open and honest with them: 'To engage in reflective practice, people need a sense of security' (Osterman and Kottkamp, 2004: 68).

Writing for academic purposes

One of your major worries may be that you will be expected to write, read and respond like a student, and that this will be judged against others who have more recent experience of studying than yourself. This is not the case; you will be offered help and advice about academic practices, including modules that have been specifically devised to bring you 'up to speed' with academic writing conventions, (including presentation and format) in a limited timeframe. Due to the negotiated and personalized nature of your programme and your working environment (requirements of your sector and so on) it may be that your assessments will not involve writing essays or sitting exams – not all university assignments do (Chapter 4). What you will find is that it is now far more commonplace to undertake an assessment tailored to your work activities; for example, some of your tutors may observe you giving a presentation to your managers about a workplace initiative and then mark a copy of the subsequent report you produce.

Your tutors will fully appreciate that although you have been offered a fantastic opportunity by enrolling on a work-based route (there was probably no other suitable route to HE for you) and, furthermore, you stand to gain advanced standing, that there is a downside to this. This downside is not insurmountable but it means that the very advanced standing which is claiming to help you also disadvantages you with its speediness, for example you may undertake an introductory module in which you claim APL and find that you are propelled into the equivalent, for example, of the second or even third year of undergraduate study (or the corresponding stage of your post-graduate route). Obviously this is a deserved recognition of the amount of previous learning you have undertaken and the level of the experiences, skills and responsibilities of your job. What you do not get is the time and space of multiple years' full-time study and campus attendance in which to gradually become familiar with academic conventions and to learn how to read, write, take notes, research effectively, understand marking systems and so on, which your fellow students who opted for more traditional routes get. You have to learn fast! But also, realistically, some of what a typical full-time student is learning is not appropriate for you, and many of your skills are far in excess of theirs. They are being taught about learning; your job has already taught you how to learn. What you need now are some methods of translating that learning into formats that can be ratified by HE. Make the most of the self-audits and exercises your university utilizes to highlight your areas in need of development and try your best to address these areas. Most universities, as well as having specific modules to polish up these skills also have web pages and drop-in centres, typically in the library. There are also excellent study skills books available on the market (see suggested further reading, at the end of the chapter). You will also find that your university provides handbooks for each module and programme and these are always an excellent resource for getting up to speed with the skills that particular module needs. Many universities also have websites designed to help you with study skills – for example, see http://dissc.tees.ac.uk/ – sites like this have pages dedicated to improving your writing and so on and give you invaluable, down-to-earth tips to help you sharpen your skills.

Level descriptors

One of the ways in which you can be sure you are attaining HE level academic standards is to familiarize yourself with your institution's level descriptors, these are published standards which state the institution's expectations of student achievement at each level of their study. In this context 'level' refers to the difficulty of study – that is, year one for a full-time undergraduate is the equivalent of Level 4. It is not about the level of your mark or grade, but the level your *course* is at. Just as National Vocational Qualifications (NVQs) expect you to demonstrate certain things – they usually use defined competencies against occupational standards – your HE work-based learning will be measured against your institution's level descriptors. These differ from one university or college to another but all are predicated around those set out as suggestive by the QAA – see: http://www.qca.org.uk/libraryAssets/media/qca_05_2242_level_descriptors.pdf.

TIP **Typical words you will find in descriptors**

Level 4
- *Demonstrate* you can use a systematic approach in *acquiring knowledge* and the *underpinning concepts* and *principles* associated with this *knowledge*.
- *Use* a range of *subject-specific, cognitive* and *transferable skills.*
- *Evaluate* the appropriateness of *differing approaches* to *solving problems.*
- *Communicate* outcomes in a *structured* and *clear* manner.
- *Discuss* your findings from texts, journals and other data.

Level 5 – Level 5 is the equivalent of a second year undergraduate – expectations increase
- *Demonstrate* your ability.
- *Apply* and *evaluate* key *concepts* and *theories.*
- *Select* and *use* a range of *cognitive and transferable skills* and *problem solving strategies.*
- Effectively *communicate information* and *debates.*
- *Accept responsibility* for personal outcomes.
- *Reflect* on, for example, workplace experience.

Level 6 – The level of difficulty and sophistication increases for honours level students in their final year
- *Demonstrate* that you have certain abilities.
- *Critically review*, consolidate and extend a body of knowledge.
- *Critically evaluate* ideas and material from a range of sources.
- *Transfer* and *apply* subject-specific, cognitive and transferable skills to complex situations.
- Your skills *of* communication and argument should be considerably honed by this stage.

- *Demonstrate your acceptance* of your accountability for determining and *achieving* both your own outcomes but also team outcomes.
- *Evidence* your *critical* and *analytical reflection.*
- You will be expected to give *evidence* in a variety of formats.

These lists are not definitive but they give a flavour of the expectations of those assessing your work and begin to show the stages in your journey from novice through competence and proficiency to expert. As stated above, you should also refer to the particular level descriptors used by your own institution. If you are undertaking postgraduate study there will be separate descriptors for this. Whichever descriptors you are using make sure that you interpret them through your own sector's legal requirements and governing bodies. Do not view them as something devised to test you or catch you out, but as helpful guidelines for you to aim at. Having something clearly defined is far preferable to nobody bothering to point out what success might actually look like.

Time management

WBL students are without exception busy working people; to make a success of your HE study you will need to be accomplished in time management. There are many things that occur during the day that waste your time: the telephone interrupts you; visitors surprise you; feelings of stress and tiredness, even illness, catch up with you. Sometimes you find yourself avoiding what you need to do for no very good reason – even allowing yourself to be distracted by something less important and often less interesting. Why does this happen? Procrastination is not necessarily a sign of laziness; maybe you are avoiding facing up to what you should be doing because it is difficult to work effectively without all of the necessary information. Or because your line manager hasn't really made it at all clear what is expected of you. Having all of the necessary information and planning your time appropriately, and realistically, makes it easier to carry out your tasks in an organized, efficient manner. Trying to work in an unplanned (even shambolic!) way may initially feel like 'getting straight on' with something, but in the long run unplanned activity is a proven time waster. This is not to suggest that there is no place for spontaneity in the workplace – there is – but when trying to achieve certain outcomes, within a set timescale, a plan is necessary. If you think about what kind of events or issues regularly disturb your working environment you will be well on the way to developing a plan which will improve your effectiveness.

Exercise 1.5: 'What disrupts you?' (and what you can do about it)

Interruptions?	Poor planning?	Things out of your control? (or seem to be?)			
Meetings	Working without necessary tools and/or information	Tiredness			
Phone calls		Illness			
Emails	Lack of/poor communication	Procrastination			
Uninvited visitors (even invited ones sometimes!)	Unclear objectives	Personal responsibilities			

What else have you added to the list? Disruptions are sometimes out of your hands, but at other times they are self-inflicted, with some disruptions falling into both of these categories! They are out of your hands – yet your response is making the situation worse not better! You may not have been given the necessary information, but perhaps you have not sought it out either? Or perhaps chosen to ignore it thinking you know better? Some disruptions are the knock-on results of an earlier disruption, in a vicious circle of insufficient time – for example, the stress you are feeling which is significantly compromising your performance may well be a direct result of you attempting to achieve something which was *never* possible. Unclear, or wildly ambitious objectives can often create this situation especially when these objectives are linked to an overall lack of good communication. Modern life is undoubtedly complex, hopefully these ideas will help a little.

TIP   **Good time management skills**

- Be *realistic* – don't set yourself up to fail.
- *Record* your activities, and how long they take on a *log* – you might be surprised.
- Set *boundaries, clear goals* and *time limits.*
- Use a *calendar* – something like *Outlook diary* on your PC can send you reminders and really help you to plan your time – as well as letting (chosen) others see when you are busy and when you are free.
- *Contacts* – keep well-ordered records – saves time looking them up – use your mobile phone or PDA to the best of its ability.
- *Delegate* – pass things on – nobody can do things just like you – but it doesn't matter.
- Similarly *accept help* – welcome the involvement of appropriate others.
- *Minimize distractions* and deflections – create a working environment for yourself which suits you.
- *Overall schedule* – keep perspective of the bigger picture.
- *Plan/prioritize/balance* – what is really important? (urgent isn't the same thing).
- Say *'no', 'not now'* and *'later'*!
- Use a clear *task list* and subsidiary *'to do lists'* – breaking tasks down helps.

Try to utilize a number of key suggestions from the Tip above, and monitor and adapt your use of them; this will result in you keeping track of your activities via an approach which produces the best results for you. It is important that you focus in this way on what works for you because WBL does not rely on a pre-set curriculum, but encourages and facilitates a negotiation of the programme content, pace, location and so on between you and your tutor(s). There is minimal pre-decided content – instead you bring the content with you – of course this requires enhanced levels of responsibility from you as learner. You have freedom – which is great – but you are also largely responsible for using your time wisely and not abusing this freedom. Your flexible programme will be bespoke to you, but you will have many interested stakeholders. It is your responsibility to ensure that you do your best to satisfy them all: your employer, colleagues, fellow learners, tutors, mentors, customers, partners, family, friends and of course, yourself. This demands a high level of commitment to your course of study as while tailoring your programme brings relative freedom and self-direction it also requires that you take ownership of your own learning. But don't be daunted, remember you are already operating as a professional, as Burns and Costley suggest: 'These learners already have intellectual capital, what they seek from HEIs is not so much factual knowledge as ways to research and develop knowledge, reflect and evaluate situations and think autonomously' (Burns and Costley, 2003: 45).

Summary

1   WBL is facilitated learning; not a teacher writing on the board, but heavily relying on you.

2   You are required to behave differently to how you might expect a 'typical student' to behave.

3   You personalize your study and focus on what is of interest to you and appropriate to your job.

4   You must be prepared to be pushed beyond your comfort zone.

5   The speed and route of learning is under your control; a bit unnerving at first.

6   You will get to know and understand your own learning styles, strengths and weaknesses – leading to greater autonomy as a learner.

> **7** You will develop a critical distance and ability to reflect which will allow you to monitor your own progress – the following chapters will assist you with this.

References

Biggs, J. (2003) *Teaching for Quality Learning at University: What the Student Does,* 2nd edn (Maidenhead: Society for Research into Higher Education and Open University Press).

Burns, G. and Costley, C. (2003) Non-Traditional Students and 21st Century Higher Education. In: *Knowledge, Work and Learning: Conference Proceedings of the Work-Based Learning Network of the Universities Association for Lifelong Learning,* compiled by D. Hollifield and issued on CD.

Cox, E. (2005) 'Adult Learners Learning from Experience: Using a Reflective Practice Model to Support Work-based Learning'. *Reflective Practice,* 6 (4), 459–72.

Eraut, M. (1994) *Developing Professional Knowledge and Competence* (London: Falmer).

Gibbons, M., Limoges, C., Nowotny, H., Schwartzman, S., Scott, P. and Trow, M. (1994) *The New Production of Knowledge: The Dynamics of Science and Research in Contemporary Societies* (London: Sage).

Gray, D. (2001) 'A Briefing on Work-based Learning', *LTSN Generic Centre Assessment Series No 11* (York: Learning and Teaching Support Network).

Helyer, R. (2007) 'What is Employability?: Reflecting on the Postmodern Challenges of Work-based Learning'. *Journal of Employability and the Humanities,* (University of Central Lancashire), 1.

Nikolou-Walker, E. (2007) 'Critical Reflections on an Evaluative Comparative Analysis of Work-based Learning through Organizational Change Mechanisms'. *Reflective Practice,* 8 (4), 525–43.

Osterman, K. and Kottkamp, B. (2004) *Reflective Practice for Educators: Professional Development to Improve Student Learning,* 2nd edn (Thousand Oaks, CA: Corwin Press).

Quality Assurance Agency, *About Us* (online). Available at http://www.qaa.ac.uk/aboutus/default.asp (accessed 28 November 2009).

Schon, D. (1983) *The Reflective Practitioner: How Professionals Think in Action* (London: Temple Smith).

Schon, D. (1987), *Educating the Reflective Practitioner: Toward a New Design for Teaching and Learning* (San Francisco: Jossey-Bass).

Suggested further reading

Billett, S. (2001) *Learning in the Workplace: Strategies for Effective Practice* (London: Allen & Unwin).

Boud, D., Keoghr, R. and Walker D. (eds) (1985) *Reflection: Turning Experience into Learning* (London: Kogan Page).

Burns, T. and Sinfield, S. (2008) *Essential Study Skills: The Complete Guide to Success at University,* 2nd edn (London: Sage Study Skills Series).

Cottrell, S. (2005) *Critical Thinking Skills* (Basingstoke: Palgrave Macmillan).

Cottrell, S. (2008) *The Study Skills Handbook* (Basingstoke: Palgrave Macmillan).

Cunningham, I., Dawes, G. and Bennett, B. (2004) *The Handbook of Work Based Learning* (Aldershot: Gower Publishing).

Dawson, C. (2006) *The Mature Student's Study Guide: Essential Skills for Those Returning to Education or Distance Learning,* 2nd edn (London: How To Books).

Durant, A., Rhodes, G. and Young, D. (eds) (2009) *Getting started with University-Level Work Based Learning* (Middlesex: Middlesex University Press).

Grix, J. (2010) *Information Skills* (Basingstoke: Palgrave Macmillan).

Groucutt, J. (2008) *Business Degree Success* (Basingstoke: Palgrave Macmillan).

Hobbs, V. (2007) 'Faking it or hating it: can reflective practice be forced?' *Reflective Practice,* 8 (3), 405–17.

Hoult, L. (2006) *Learning Support for Mature Students* (London: Sage Study Skills Series).

Moon, J. (2000) *Reflection in Learning and Professional Development: Theory and Practice* (London: Kogan Page).

Moon, J. (2004) *A Handbook of Reflective and Experiential Learning: Theory and Practice* (London: Routledge).

Moon, J. (2007) *Critical Thinking: An Exploration of Theory and Practice* (London: Routledge).

Nikolou-Walker, E. and Garnett, J. (2004) 'Work-based Learning. A New Imperative: Developing Reflective Practice in Professional Life'. *Reflective Practice,* 5 (3), 297–312.

Pears, R. and Shields, G. (2010) *Cite Them Right: The Essential Referencing Guide,* 8th edn (Basingstoke: Palgrave Macmillan).

Peck, J. and Coyle, M. (2005) *The Student's Guide to Writing: Grammar, Punctuation and Spelling,* 7th edn (Basingstoke: Palgrave Macmillan).

Raelin, J. A. (2008) *Work-Based Learning: Bridging Knowledge and Action in the Workplace,* revised edition (San Francisco: Jossey-Bass).

Rose, J. (2007) *The Mature Students Guide to Writing,* 2nd edn (Basingstoke: Palgrave Macmillan).

Russell, T. (2005) 'Can Reflective Practice be Taught?'. *Reflective Practice,* 6 (2), 199–204.

Williams, K. and Carroll, J. (2009) *Referencing and Understanding Plagiarism* (Basingstoke: Palgrave Macmillan).

2 Make Your Learning Count: How APL Can Enhance your Profile

Adrian Evans, David Perrin, Ruth Helyer and Elaine Hooker

In this chapter you will learn:

▶ what the Accreditation of Prior Learning (APL) is;
▶ how it works;
▶ how to use certificated learning as part of an APL claim;
▶ how to scope out your strengths and expertise as 'areas of learning';
▶ how to make and submit an APL claim;
▶ what you can use as good evidence to prove your APL claim.

● **Accreditation of Prior Learning: context and background – the 'what'**

The Accreditation of Prior Learning (APL) process is used widely across the HE sector in the UK and abroad. Many work-based learning (WBL) students state that without it, they would never have gained their HE qualification. APL is a process which means that credit can be granted for learning that has already taken place; therefore, to you as a work-based learner it offers a time-saving, empowering device: time-saving because if you have already learned something in the workplace (and can evidence that learning) you will not be asked to do it again as part of your HE course, and empowering because it is a method which helps you to see just how complex and challenging your work role actually is. By attaching HE level credits to learning you have gained elsewhere the university acknowledges your expertise, skills and rich hands-on experience. For whatever reason, you have not had the opportunity to attend a university in the past but the APL process can help to show you that you have amassed important knowledge from other sources. There is a lot to be said for lifelong learning and the 'University of Life' but APL can actually transform your experience of learning into academic credit.

A fairly modern concept and process, the Council for National Academic Awards (CNAA) agreed in 1986 that: 'appropriate learning at higher education level, *wherever it occurs,* provided it can be assessed, can be given credit towards an academic award' (cited in Garnett et al., 2004: 6, italics added).

Since then, more and more institutions have realized the real benefit of APL, resulting in its widespread use throughout the HE sector. What has really helped to embed the process is the simultaneous spread of the Credit Accumulation and Transfer Scheme (CATS). CATS is:

> Arrangements within institutions which determine student progression towards defined learning outcomes, including formal qualifications, and recognition of these arrangements between institutions to facilitate the transfer of students. (http://www.qaa.ac.uk/aboutus/acronyms.asp)

CATS is based upon contemporary academic levels and includes an accepted tariff for recognizing volumes of learning (ten hours of notional learning time = one HE credit). The framework of academic levels currently in use is illustrated in Figure 2.1. HE levels of study begin at Level 4 in the National Qualifications Framework (the equivalent to undergraduate level, or year 1, in some universities).

The development of APL has been closely linked to the growth of credit and modularization in HE because only credit-based systems, with defined units of learning (like modules), fully allow the kind of flexibility and transferability that is needed for APL opportunities and practices. For example, you may well have already signed up for modules which state they carry 20 or 30 credits. These will have agreed levels of study explaining what stage you are at with your learning; as Figure 2.1 shows. Without this sector-wide accepted framework, one university could not be sure that particular learning acquired in another university was appropriate and comparable to its own awards at that particular level. It is not necessarily about being exactly the same – difference is fine, it is equivalence and comparability that the framework upholds. For further information see the Quality Assurance Agency's website: http://www.qaa.ac.uk/england/credit/creditframework.asp.

The credit framework gives you some idea of what academic levels mean; they relate to the degree of *complexity*, *depth* and *sophistication* of both thought and practice with which you engage in your study, together with the level of *autonomy* expected from you. The credits you receive through your APL claims relate to *volume* of learning.

APL takes one of two forms – and you might find that both of these forms are applied to your claim for credit. The two different methods are:

- Accreditation of Prior Certificated Learning (APCL);
- Accreditation of Prior Experiential Learning (APEL).

National Qualifications Framework (NQF)		Framework for Higher Education Qualifications (FHEQ)
Previous levels	*Current levels*	*Levels*
Level 5 Level 5 NVQ in Construction Level 5 Diploma in Translation	**Level 8** Specialist awards	**D (Doctoral)** Doctorates
	Level 7 Level 7 Diploma in Translation	**M (Masters)** Masters degrees, postgraduate certificates and diplomas
Level 4 Level 4 NVQ in Management Level 4 BTEC Higher National Diploma in 3D Design Level 4 Certificate in Early Years Practice	**Level 6** Level 6 National Diploma in Professional Production Skills	**H (Honours – undergraduate Level 3)** Bachelors degrees, graduate certificates and diplomas
	Level 5 Level 5 BTEC Higher National Diploma in 3D Design	**I (Intermediate – undergraduate Level 2)** Diplomas of higher education and further education, foundation degrees and higher national diplomas
	Level 4 Level 4 Certificate in Early Years Practice	**C (Certificate – undergraduate Level 1)** Certificates of higher education, higher national certificates
Level 3 Level 3 Certificate in Small Animal Care Level 3 NVQ in Aeronautical Engineering A levels		
Level 2 Level 2 Diploma for Beauty Specialists Level 2 NVQ in Agricultural Crop Production GCSEs Grades A*–C		
Level 1 Level 1 Certificate in Motor Vehicle Studies Level 1 NVQ in Bakery GCSEs Grades D–G		
Entry level Entry Level Certificate in Adult Literacy		

Figure 2.1 Comparing levels

Source: Adapted from the Qualifications and Curriculum Development Agency (2006).

Accreditation of Prior Certificated Learning (APCL)

Previous learning which has led to the award of a formal qualification, and probably a certificate, is called 'certificated learning' (the 'C' in the APCL) and when this previously rewarded learning is used in a new programme of study it is called Accreditation of Prior Certificated Learning (APCL). This is usually allowed for learning that has contemporary relevance; there is an obvious coherence between your past certificated learning and what you are proposing to study now – it is not a completely different subject. It should also still have academic currency – this usually means that it has to have been gained within the last 5 years. However, don't worry too much if this is not the case as most HEIs will still allow you to make a claim for appropriate certificated learning, whatever its age, if you can submit a narrative commentary which proves that you have built on the learning in question and that it has informed your professional practice (and continues to). 'Credit transfer' is the name of the formal process by which credit which has been awarded for the learning achieved on one programme (the certificate you hold already) can be recognized and accepted as part of the overall credit requirements on another programme (your new WBL study route).

Accreditation of Prior Experiential Learning (APEL)

Prior learning also includes your learning *for which no award has previously been conferred at all* ('uncertificated learning'). This type of learning has often been acquired in your workplace and has not involved conventional forms of HE study or assessment. Instead it typically takes the form of what is called 'experiential learning' – that is, learning while doing your job, so through experience. When this learning has credit attached to it via HE processes it is called the Accreditation of Prior Experiential Learning (APEL). Work-based learners like yourself are then given a really useful opportunity to gain academic reward by describing and evidencing what you have learned from your workplace learning experiences and development activities.

These types of APL can be used in one of two ways: either for the purposes of admission into a HE programme, for example instead of the more standard entry requirements, such as 'A' levels; or for the purposes of gaining academic credit towards a named award, which in effect gives you advanced standing. APL is usually dealt with at your point of admission to an educational institution, whichever of the two outcomes above you are aiming for. On negotiated programmes of WBL, however, APL is often engaged with after your initial admission, and during the negotiation of your learning pathway or learning contract in your institution's version of a 'diagnostic' or negotiation of learning module – these do differ between universities. One of the many advantages of negotiated WBL programmes for adult learners is the way in which APL (especially APEL) is addressed systematically as an intrinsic part of the negotiation of the learning pathway. In this way you are made aware of its existence and its possibilities and therefore do not miss out on the opportunities it offers. Many students do not even know that the APL process exists, which is a pity and also a missed opportunity. So please don't be put off by how complex it might be sounding at the moment!

Exercise 2.1: Consider APL

Think about any areas of your learning – both certificated and experiential – which could be awarded credit through APL. Start to make a list!

Because WBL programmes are designed to be flexible – and are often individually negotiated – they are ideal vehicles to make the best use of APL, particularly APEL. As previously mentioned, this differs from one university to another; some have a specialist APL adviser who deals with all claims, and others have wider numbers of staff who are able to engage with the APL process as part of the facilitation of a negotiated learning pathway. Most HEIs with negotiated WBL frameworks fall into the second category.

We can't leave this section without first clarifying the difference between specific and general credit:

- *General credit* refers to the credit value attached to successful completion of a block of learning or a programme, which will all map comfortably onto an award.
- *Specific credit* refers to credit awarded towards a specific route or award. It is 'specific' because it relates directly to the content of the course you are following. In this sense, what you possess as general credit might not be applicable or allowable for your programme of study, or may be only partly allowable (for instance, if you hold a professional qualification rated as 60 points at Master's Level you might not be able to bring all those points into a prescriptive course like an MBA as there might not be a sufficient 'match').

This is an area of WBL that continues to be debated and still lacks clarity in terms of application from university to university. You will need to look carefully at the learning outcomes of the award you are making a credit claim against and discuss with your tutor prior to submitting your claim. There is more detail about specific and general credit later in this chapter.

How is APL facilitated practically? – the 'how'

Understanding how universities go about facilitating APL in a practical sense reveals there is a variety of practice across the sector, and you really need to be aware of this when putting together your claim. Be sure you take your tutor's advice; whichever process is used, you should always be clear who it is you should speak to and consult about APL – typically an academic member of university staff often called an 'APL adviser' or similar.

Exercise 2.2: Find your own APL expert

Who is it in your institution? Find out their details and go and talk to them.

This designated person will certainly guide you through the process. There are various ways in which the procedures differ; for example, some programmes allow you to submit just one APL claim, whereas others will allow multiple claims (especially for APEL). Alternatively, some WBL programmes encourage you to think about APL claims in an initial 'diagnostic' or programme planning module; where other programmes facilitate APL through the means of a credit-rated and assessed module in its own right, usually with a title such as 'Recognizing Your Learning'. In this type of module you get credit for the processes of identifying and planning your APL claim, as well as credit for the claim itself, the module might carry 20 credits but the APL claim you put together in that module will bring you extra credits, if successful.

The diversity of students' learning experience means that there can be a whole range of credit awarded. The following example, taken from a cohort of WBL students undertaking a negotiated learning, undergraduate degree programme, clearly shows the varying amount of credit that can be achieved through APL. From a cohort of 18 students, the credit awarded ranged from 10 credits, through to 100 and 120 credits, with one student reaching 260 credits; plus credits for undertaking the modules. Broken down, the student profiles are shown in Table 2.1.

Students	Level 4 credits	Level 5 credits	Level 6 credits
a to d	10 (exp)		
e and f	20 (exp)		
g and i	30 (exp)		
j to m	60 (20 cert)		
	40 (exp)		
n and o	70 (exp)		
p	60 (cert)	20 (exp)	
	20 (exp)		
q	100 (cert)	20 (exp)	
r	100 (cert)	80 (exp)	40 (exp)
s	120 (cert)	100 (cert)	20 (exp)
t	120 (cert)	100 (cert)	40 (exp)

exp = experiential AP(E)L, cert = certificated AP(C)L.

Table 2.1   What can be achieved

Universities look at APL in differing ways – but the processes will always be similar:

- You will focus on current and recent working arrangements, skills and practices. For example, how you have been involved during your career or job role with: company staff development issues; disciplinary matters; HR policies and practices; managing projects, such as setting up a 'breakfast club' for schoolchildren; and numerous other topics depending on your job and sector.
- You will think precisely about how your knowledge and talent has been built up over the years. This might be called a 'skills audit' and be a formal part of your course.
- Adult learners tend to undervalue their talents – you will be discouraged from using phrases such as 'I am only a nurse' or 'I am only a gardener'.
- You will be encouraged to develop an awareness of the skills you possess, and to avoid being modest or taking your skills for granted.
- Your progression over the years represents considerable learning – much of which is probably *experiential* learning – 'hands-on' in the workplace; this will be teased out.
- The APL guidance you receive will show you how to differentiate between this *experiential* learning and any *certificated* learning

(courses you have already passed which carried credit and perhaps a qualification).

- You will be able to claim for either – or both – depending on your profile.
- Areas of Learning (see section later in chapter) are a commonly used way of claiming for experiential learning – they are like short essays backed up with evidence.
- You can only claim for HE Level 4 and above (your tutor will guide you).

Using certificated learning – the past

Exercise 2.3: Consider APCL

Remember the list you started that made you think about initial areas of learning? Return to that list and think about certificated learning. What learning have you previously done that has led to a certificated award? Refine your list in order to separate APCL from APEL.

TIP **It's good to talk**

You must speak to your APL adviser about any certificated learning you may have. There are a number of key considerations when APCL is being discussed; the most important are described in the steps below.

Step 1: Size – establish the academic learning level and credit value

Much certificated learning is useful and represents significant learning – but it may not necessarily be credit-rated in HE terms (because it is not at HE level or simply does not have a credit/level). For example, City & Guilds qualifications are almost invariably pre-HE in nature and cannot, of themselves, be directly used towards HE awards. National Vocational Qualifications (NVQs) exist at a variety of levels – some do map across to HE level awards, but this is not always straightforward. NVQ portfolios are more normally used as the basis for APEL claims, rather than APCL, as a result. It is usually up to you, as the student, to establish the level and credit-rating, if any, of your certificated learning (internet searches are useful, but nothing beats contacting the awarding body directly to establish level and CATS points rating).

Step 2: Time – when did the learning happen?

This is important as most universities have rules concerning 'academic currency', meaning whether an academic award can be considered to be usefully still in date. Typically, this is five years, meaning that you should consult your APL adviser about any credits you have that are over five years old. If credit is deemed to be 'out of date' in this way all is not lost – many universities (including most operating flexible WBL frameworks) will allow you to demonstrate currency with a reflective review and/or presentation of evidence concerning how the learning has been applied and updated since, usually through engagement in the workplace. A typical example would be a manager with a HND in Business awarded seven or eight years ago who is encouraged to put together a reflective commentary with evidence about how the key areas of learning in their HND has been applied and extended in the years since (a general outline of the curriculum is often helpful for this process).

Step 3: Relevance – what was the learning for?

For instance, if you are now on a WBL programme, working as an office manager, but flunked a geography degree several years ago, you may struggle to demonstrate the relevance of the credits you got. Even if the credits, level and academic currency are clear, the relevance to a WBL programme in the field of current practice might not be! Here the notion of specific (rather than generic) credit comes into its own. On a negotiated WBL programmes it is possible to use credit creatively, much more so than on a traditional or prescriptive programme, where credit is required to very closely match modules in the programme concerned. This is because negotiated WBL allows you to work towards creating your own curriculum, within certain parameters. This very design determines what is relevant and what is not. Many universities will only accept generic credit at certain levels of study too, sometimes only Level 4 (undergraduate first year equivalent).

Step 4: Evidence – what is appropriate evidence?

This usually takes the form of photocopies of certificates and any accompanying documentation referring to modules, credits and levels (such as a transcript from a university Registry department).

'Scoping' areas of learning for APEL – the potential

You have a large role to play in the design of the curriculum for your WBL pathway; this is one of the key advantages of WBL and APEL plays a large part in this. WBL is predicated on the notion that the workplace is an important site of knowledge generation and experiential learning (Armsby et al., 2006). Much of your learning will already have taken place before you enrol at university and will have undoubtedly informed your current workplace practice.

The process of 'claiming' APEL should be considered to be just that – 'making a claim'. You are proactively claiming that learning you have previously acquired legitimately, but which has gone unrecognized at university level, is usable and useful. It is therefore helpful to not see APEL as a process of 'opting out' of learning but of 'opting in' – it is the (albeit retrospective) granting of credits for learning that is just as genuine and powerful as that acquired through a traditional university course. Indeed, the very process of identifying APEL opportunities, assembling a claim and reflecting on practice with a view to future enhancement is a valuable learning process in itself; so valuable in fact, many universities dedicate a module to the process.

Whatever method your institution uses for acknowledging APL claims, their aim will be the same – to assist you in outlining your main areas of learning so that a claim can realistically be made for credit – this is the 'scoping' referred to in the title of this section. The scoping process will either take place in your initial programme planning module, or in a special module (as previously mentioned called something like 'Recognizing Your Learning'), which also gives credit for the module itself. Whichever style of module is used, the relationship between you and your APL adviser or tutor is crucial at this stage. In order for your APL adviser to ensure that you are able to identify appropriate, relevant areas of prior experiential learning to claim for (for which you can also provide evidence), you will need to engage fully with the process. APL considerations also have to sit alongside wider considerations about your pathway of learning as a whole; it is important that any negotiated pathway has coherence and is assembled in a way that will provide a meaningful and holistic learning experience.

Provisional areas of learning

Exercise 2.4: Consider APEL

Return to your APL/APCL list from the beginning of the chapter, take it a step further by considering your experiential learning; start by compiling a list of provisional areas of learning.

To complete Exercise 2.4 you will need to:

- look closely at your past and current achievements;
- from all this experience, select themes or areas in which you feel you have significant learning;
- focus on what can you provide evidence for – evidence of learning is very important to your claim so if you don't have any evidence then you will not be able to make a claim;
- decide what has the most relevance to your new award's other proposed content and title;
- determine what you have done that you would like to progress or build on.

When scoping out potential APEL claims, your curriculum vitae and your job description (possibly previous job descriptions too) can be especially helpful. These documents structure experience in terms of roles and activities – they are about what you do and have done. Underlying and informing these duties are skills, abilities and knowledge that you have learned – some generic and transferable to other occupations, like project management skills; some specific to particular work roles such as skills needed to teach – for example, being able to construct a viable lesson plan. In this way, areas of expertise can be categorized into themes or topics, which are often called 'areas of learning'.

Exercise 2.5: Areas of learning – compiling a provisional list

Job title	Main areas of responsibilities	Potential area(s) of learning?
Classroom assistant	Supporting teaching, research, health and safety etc.	1. Teaching on unqualified status 2. Truancy 3. Early years development
Marketing manager	Key client account management, research, planning etc.	1. Customer relationship management 2. Branding 3. Market research
Technician	Repair, maintenance and technical support etc.	1. Digital Media 2. Project planning 3. Human machine interface

Look at the above examples and start to make a list of your own:

Your current job title	Areas of responsibilities (see job description)	1._____
		2._____
		3._____

Developing a learning CV

When you are working on your CV you probably think about your work-based and other experience in a chronological way. When you are developing your list of possible areas of learning for an APEL claim, it is more helpful to think thematically about experiences, rather than chronologically and instead pick out recurring and/or significant themes of learning which you can group together into areas (Chapter 3). For example, if you identify 'Teaching young adults' as a possible area of learning for your claim, you have probably developed this area of learning through a number of activities; they might be:

- teaching maths in a secondary school;
- running a youth club;
- teaching a son or daughter how to play a musical instrument.

Each of these activities may have enhanced and developed your teaching abilities over time. It is these key areas of knowledge and skill that are identified in the areas of learning, that are then turned into an APEL claim and assessed for credit, rather than the work activities listed in your usual CV or job description. Many work-based study routes ask you to create a further CV and job description which focus more clearly on your areas of expertise, what you do at work and what you have learned from that activity, and so on (see Appendix 4 and 5). Formulating a coherent list of your possible areas of learning usually involves looking back over experiences to date across your entire career pathway. You are likely to have developed a great deal of skill, ability and knowledge over the years that has accumulated and informed your current practice – so how do you decide what to use as areas of learning for your APEL claim(s)?

Narrowing down your list of provisional titles

There is no single straightforward answer; you need to negotiate with your university APL adviser; ideally, and as a general guide, chosen areas of learning for APEL should be:

- **C**apable of being clearly evidenced in terms of supporting workplace artefacts.
- **R**elevant to the chosen pathway of learning and award you have negotiated.
- **I**ndicative of the type of skills and knowledge that are commensurate with the level of HE study currently being pursued.
- **S**ubstantial enough to have had a significant effect on your development, professionally and/or personally.

Used as a memory guide, the acronym **CRIS** might help you to remember these important points.

It is vital that you get feedback on initial ideas before they are developed further. APL advisers have experience of seeing a variety of APEL claims from a range of students and occupation types over time and will be able to tell you whether or not your ideas, at this stage, are likely to result in areas of learning of appropriate size, content and academic level.

Exercise 2.6: Scoping APEL

To help you scope areas of learning for APEL in relation to your present job, try the following:

- List all the types of education and training necessary/ currently provided for the type of job you do, that you can think of.
- Now list how *you* have attained knowledge and competence in the fields covered (perhaps not by traditionally studying – but how?).
- Identify the aspects of this learning you have never received formal academic recognition for (or which you have developed/added to significantly since gaining relevant qualifications).
- Think about whether there is knowledge and a body of skills that you possess that others typically entering into your type of role don't have.

> **TIP** **This is a gradual process**
>
> It is important to remember:
>
> ● This is a step-by-step process that can help you identify some viable areas of learning for APEL purposes.
> ● The approach can also be adopted in relation to other jobs you have had in the past.

Mapping against existing modules

At this 'scoping' stage you also need to decide whether APEL is going to be claimed:

● against existing modules (so specifically matched against their outcomes);
● as a 'block' of generic credit that is relevant to the pathway, and perhaps split into named sections, which all map comfortably onto the award you and your advisers have planned out;
● as a combination of the two.

This was mentioned earlier in the section 'Accreditation of Prior Learning: context and background – the "what"' when discussing general and specific credit. If you were undertaking a traditional degree you would be more typically guided towards claiming for existing, specific modules. This is because most HE programmes are largely prescriptive with a set modular pathway and limited choice. However, the experiential learning acquired by you in the workplace is rarely an exact match for the learning identified in existing university modules, which is precisely why increasing numbers of universities are now offering work-based study routes – in acknowledgement of the need to be more flexible and to recognize how much is being learned in the workplace – at HE level.

WBL frameworks possess built-in advantages for experienced adult learners like you. They allow you to claim APEL for specific taught modules as an option, but the real flexibility, when assembling your claim, comes through allowing you to identify areas of learning, which you can claim for, and which are consistent with your pathway and award. To verify the value of these blocks of credit they are matched against your university's level descriptors (Chapters 1 and 4). Work-based projects (Chapter 5), 'independent learning' or 'experiential learning' template modules also exist. These 'empty', or 'shell-like' modules allow you to design your own content – this content revolves around experiential learning activities upon which you will be assessed. The APEL process can be used to facilitate a claim being presented retrospectively for these modules – this aspect of the process is also useful for applying credits to a work-based project that has already been completed (Lester, 2007). These types of module provide handy 'containers' for APEL and will help you to identify clear learning areas, which can be claimed for separately or in a linked APEL portfolio.

Amount of APEL claimed (volume)

Deciding on the level of credit is fairly straightforward as universities have their own established *level descriptors* (Chapters 1 and 4), which elaborate on the discernible characteristics of each level of study, complete with many examples of how these levels might be attained and what kind of evidence will prove this attainment.

Exercise 2.7: Find your own level descriptors

- Do some research and find a copy of your learning institution's level descriptors – they will really help you to map your experiential learning against academic credit.
- Sometimes they are reproduced in your course handbooks.
- Often they are online.
- Ask your tutor!

However, deciding on the *volume* of credit to be legitimately claimed is more complex (Workman, 2008). Generally in HE it is accepted that each credit represents ten hours of notional learning, though, as very often with taught modules, an emphasis on the word 'notional' is required because exact measurements are usually near impossible. Quantifying learning time on a discrete project at work may be easier than when an APEL claim is based on learning in a subject or skill area (say, for instance, presentation skills) which may cross-cut a variety of workplace activities and represent learning accrued over an uneven period of time. Evidence is important too – a significant report written for the workplace is likely to underpin a far greater volume of APEL credit than sketchier or less substantial evidence like minutes of meetings. It is worth noting that because of the complexity involved in determining appropriate volumes of credit for APEL some universities have broad indicative word count guidelines for APEL as well as for conventional modules, this is explained in more detail later in this section. This has the advantage of clarity for you, though some have argued that it is an approach which places an undue emphasis on outputs rather than inputs (Prince, 2004). Some universities, yours may be one, try to equate areas of learning to essay sizes which may be used for other, more traditional modules. For example, if a module carrying 20 credits assesses its students with an essay of a certain word-count, could some comparison be drawn between this and your 20 credit claim? This is not to say that you should also produce the same amount of words, but it provides something for your area of learning, plus its accompanying evidence, to be compared to, though very different. You also need to be aware that some universities rely almost solely on their assessors to determine APEL credit volume *after* submission (Workman, 2008) although this practice seems to be less common in HE than it was.

Case Study: APEL in practice

Below is a practical, recent example of a student from the University of Chester who entered the negotiated work-based learning framework at undergraduate Level 1 (NQF 4) on the initial programme planning module, 'Self Review and Negotiation of Learning'. As part of her programme planning process she identified a number of likely areas of learning for APEL claims.

Davina is a health service manager in an NHS Trust who has risen 'through the ranks'. She has negotiated to work towards a work-based honours degree in Health Service Management. She doesn't have any certificated learning that is relevant to gaining credits for her degree but she *does* have a lot of experiential learning built up over recent years managing a unit in the local hospital. In consultation with her tutor she was able to identify the following significant areas of learning:

- She had set up a new committee, which she still chairs, into an important new area of working in the Trust related to clinical audit.
- She wrote a comprehensive set of patient admission procedures that are still in operation in the unit she manages.
- She investigated the impact of a new piece of government legislation and disseminated her findings on its implications for hospital workers, giving presentations to staff at all levels and in all departments.

There were lots of other, smaller areas of learning too, but these were the main ones she was confident of making a claim for. Treating these areas of experiential learning as work-based projects (Chapter 5) she had already completed, she wrote claims (with supporting evidence) for each of these projects to show that she had met the learning outcomes of the undergraduate Level 4 Negotiated Experiential

Learning Module. And in consultation with her tutor regarding the amount of work and effort she'd put into these projects, she decided to claim:

- *20 credits* for setting up and chairing the committee;
- *40 credits* for the new procedures, as this was a major piece of work that had probably taken as much as 400 hours of her time in learning the things she needed to, with copious evidence of how the procedures had been drafted and developed;
- *40 credits* for the dissemination project to other staff, another significant piece of work that she estimated was the equivalent of around 400 hours learning, with a variety of written evidence plus a video presentation.

When she submitted her prior learning claim with her Self Review module (20 credits) she hoped to gain 100 credits worth of APEL (20 + 40 + 40) at undergraduate Level 4, which would have given her enough to complete that level of her degree programme (120 credits in total).

Her next module would then start her off at the beginning of undergraduate Level 5, after she had achieved almost an entire level's worth of accreditation for her prior experiential learning.

Case Study: APEL in practice

Nick is a police sergeant in his local police force. He had career aspirations of moving through the police ranks but felt that he needed a degree to improve his prospects within the force. He chose Teesside University because of its reputation and commitment to work-based learning. He enrolled on the Work-based Studies degree in Business Management, as this programme offered flexible learning which fitted in with his personal and professional commitments. Through the 'Make Your Learning Count' module Nick identified that, having been in the police force for 20 years, he had a large amount of experiential learning as well as a strong claim for certificated learning. He submitted his portfolio and was awarded the following:

Level 4: 120 credits for:

- Certificate in Management

Level 5: 120 credits for:

- UCPD in Domestic Violence (30 credits)
- UCPD Ethics and Policing (30 credits)
- Intermediate CID course (20 credits)
- Senior Investigating Officer's Appreciation Course (40 credits)

Level 6: 40 credits for:

- Firearms Incident Commanders Course (10 credits)
- Serious Crime Investigation Review Training (10 credits)
- Certificate in Professional Policing (20 credits)

Nick then achieved his degree by completing Level 6 (equivalent of the third year) through studying core modules:

- Research Methods (20 credits)
- Dissertation (40 credits)
- Managing Own Learning (20 credits)

Nick graduated with First Class Honours in Business Management and has been able to relate the knowledge he gained from his learning to his role in the force.

Timing issues

Timing is crucial for your APEL claim both in terms of workload and in maintaining momentum. Many universities prefer the presentation of an APEL portfolio that contains all the prior experiential learning being claimed for, so that APEL is assessed and dealt with all at once. This allows you to move on beyond the APEL process to the next stage of your pathway in the knowledge your APEL credits have (hopefully) all been granted and that this part of your learning pathway is complete. However, it can also mean you working on very significant and often time-consuming claims before receiving credit for any of them, and, in such circumstances, it is not uncommon for you to become slightly nervous while awaiting the outcome of your submission and even to find it difficult to carry on with other study until you know how much you have been awarded.

Other universities allow you to submit a number of APEL claims over time, especially those universities that invite learners to package their APEL into a series of retrospective work-based projects or similar. This is a more piece-meal approach but has the advantage that you can concentrate on one claim at a time and progress in an incremental fashion, in keeping with the spirit of modular programmes more generally and, indeed, with how you will most likely complete the rest of your study, if your pathway is negotiated. You may even take other modules (taught modules or current work-based projects) alongside working on your APEL claims.

● Compiling APEL claims – the process

Once you have scoped out the APEL areas of learning and agreed some timescales, the second stage of APEL begins – the writing and compiling of your claim(s). This is the really substantial (and exciting) part of any APEL submission and comprises the specific identification of the prior experiential learning you are claiming, usually in written form (though presentations and dialogue assessments are also usefully deployed by some universities). It must also include your appropriate supporting evidence, drawn usually from workplace artefacts which you have generated. So the majority of APEL claims will include these two key elements as standard:

- a *written claim* about the learning;
- complemented by an *appendix of supporting evidence.*

TIP   It's about breadth and depth

Remember that the number of Areas of Learning you submit and the overall size of your claim for credit will depend upon how extensive your experiential learning actually is and how much of it you wish to claim for (with supporting evidence).

In the written part of the claim, you are typically expected to clearly describe, in a short narrative or report:

- the prior learning you are claiming for;
- the particular learning and skills that you have acquired;
- the appropriate supporting evidence (cross-referenced).

You must be aware that the learning being claimed for *must not* be the same as any learning you are claiming via APCL (certificated learning), or contained in other modules you plan to take, and it must be relevant to your proposed pathway of learning and ultimate award; in other words, you have to make sure you are not going to repeat your learning or double-claim and that your learning is appropriate for your programme.

There are two distinct ways of constructing a claim for uncertificated, experiential learning. The *first* is when you wish to make a claim for taught modules that already exist, for instance, modules from other programmes at your university. To do this, you will need to choose the modules you think you can claim for in consultation with your tutor/APEL adviser (for example, if you have negotiated a pathway towards an award in management, you might wish to look at the modules in existence at the appropriate academic level in your university's Business School or School of Management).

You will then need a copy of the relevant module details for each of these modules. This will be called something like a 'module descriptor' – some universities might have a slightly different name, but it is a printed, and usually also online, document which gives key information about the module or unit of study concerned (its aims, content, credit points value, method of assessment, and so on) and it includes the module's learning outcomes, which describe the learning that you are expected to have achieved when you pass the assessment for the module.

Having digested what the specific modules require and entail, you will then need to demonstrate that you have met the relevant learning outcomes for each module you are claiming for, through writing a claim which clearly identifies, describes and reflects on your learning, and which is cross-referenced with appropriate supporting evidence.

TIP **Share your ideas and take advice**

It is always a good idea to speak to the relevant module leader(s) to get advice from them about how you can best demonstrate that your learning encapsulates that intended by the module.

A general guide adopted by some universities (again, you will need to ask your tutor) would be to write a claim for each module which is *no more than half* of what would normally be required for assessment purposes. If your institution expects something like an assessment with a notional word count in the region of 4000 for an undergraduate 20 credit single module, then they might also expect learners writing an APEL claim for 20 credits to produce no more than 2000, plus their evidence. To produce more than this starts to feel like defeating the object of the exercise!

The *second* type of APEL claim is for learning that has been achieved in the workplace but which does not exactly match or fit existing taught modules, or which you simply do not wish to match in this way. It is now typical for the majority of negotiated WBL students claiming APEL to use this particular method. The most straightforward way to claim for prior learning in this manner is for you to treat it as a bundle of retrospective experiential learning projects or independent learning activities. Write your claim to demonstrate your achievement of learning outcomes (or associated university level descriptors mentioned above) by writing a short claim for each module, cross-referenced with appropriate evidence that can support the learning claim (see Table 2.2).

Again, it is becoming typical for students to write no more than half as much as they would for the equivalent module assessment (2000 words instead of 4000 words for a single undergraduate 20 credit module).

Level 4 Outcomes (linked to level descriptors)	Ways in which this is demonstrated in this area of learning
Ability to communicate clearly	Narrative and evidence
Ability to initiate, plan and co-ordinate programmes	Narrative and evidence
Ability to work effectively and to plan programmes and activities under supervision	Narrative and evidence
And so on for all of the outcomes at all levels, 4, 5 and 6.	

Table 2.2   Template for mapping learning outcomes for specific areas of learning

---

Exercise 2.8: Constructing your APEL claim

Make some notes under the following headings. This will help you to sort the *learning* from the *experience*.

Did I learn?	Focus on significant learning experiences
What did I learn?	Identifying your learning
How did I learn?	Your learning style and associated theory
How do I know that I've learnt?	With evidence and theory

You will need to:

- Clearly identify the skills, knowledge and abilities claimed for;
- Include reflection on how this learning was acquired, could have been approached differently, and how it has been applied since or built upon.

TIP   **Don't say it twice!**

The more evidence you have of your learning – and the more obvious it is that this evidence demonstrates the type of skills and knowledge associated with the level concerned – the less wordy your claim will need to be.

By way of example, if the main piece of evidence for a postgraduate APEL submission is a research paper that has been written for delivery at a conference, then the claim which identifies the learning and puts it in context, may be quite short (perhaps just several bullet points) as the level of academic engagement will be demonstrated by the evidence itself. However, if the evidence you assemble for your APEL submission demonstrates the *content* of your learning but not necessarily its *level* (and this is quite often the case) then the written claim part of your submission will need to demonstrate the type of skills and knowledge required for the level concerned; almost certainly with reflection on the learning achieved, supported by some academic referencing. Exactly how substantial this 'claim' part of the submission needs to be, within the suggested word count limit above – and how sophisticated academically – is an issue that should be discussed with your tutor/APEL adviser.

How the written claim is structured can vary according to the nature of the claim and the demands of particular universities. The example shown in Box 2.1 is typical.

Box 2.1 The structure of an APEL claim

Introduction
Make sure that you clearly state the general area of learning to be claimed for, the volume of credit claimed along with the level of study.

Bulleted table of the main knowledge and skills
The main knowledge and skills gained need to be identified in your area of learning and cross-referenced to module learning outcomes or level descriptors, if necessary.

A detailed elaboration of the learning processes behind the claim
- how the learning came about
- why particular approaches were taken
- what worked well and less well
- what could have been done differently and so on.

References
Cross-reference the presented evidence in the appendices:
- to relevant bodies of work
- to academic books, journals, publications
- to in-house manuals, procedures and guidance
- your learning CV

- job description
- other areas of learning you may be submitting.

Be very clear which piece of evidence refers to which item of learning. One piece of evidence can be used for several items, so this will need to be cross-referenced with clear signposting for the assessor.

Conclusion

In your conclusion consider how the learning could be applied or adapted in the future, perhaps with an action plan, if appropriate.

When constructing the written element of an APEL claim, it is vital to remember that assessors are primarily interested in your *personal* learning at work – APEL claims should not consist of extended quotations from theoretical texts about learning, or be driven by discussions of theory. By their very nature, APEL claims are concerned with learning via experience, what you have learned by actively 'doing', not just reading about. This will have already taken place. Academic theory is primarily used in APEL claims as a useful external point of reference and to contextualize knowledge. Indeed, APEL assessors will typically know when you have understood a theory when you have successfully *applied* it, rather than just described it.

What makes good evidence? – the proof

What you use to evidence what you have learned, and thereby link to what you are claiming for, is of the utmost importance. All items in your appendices of evidence should be clearly labelled for ease of reference, and an appendix contents page included. You may well ask: *what form is the evidence of experiential learning likely to take?* The following is a guide to the type of evidence typically offered in support of prior experiential learning, though it is not an exhaustive list:

- Any of your assessment material which has not led to certificated learning.
- Reports and handbooks that you have produced.
- Similarly, presentation materials like PowerPoint slides, video recordings, and so on.
- Appraisals, testimonials and reports of your performance in the workplace.

- Any correspondence that provides evidence of your involvement.
- Products and artefacts that you have made/constructed.
- Minutes from meetings with actions assigned to you.
- Budgets or forecasts that have been put together by you.
- Briefing papers that you have written.
- Drafts and plans that you have produced.
- An academic paper, or article that you may have written.
- Details of project work, procedures developed, and so on.

Exercise 2.9: Making the links

- What evidence do you have?
- Think about the evidence you have to support your areas of learning and start your collection.
- Quality is more important than quantity – but at first gather anything you think helps – you can always prune back!
- Ask your tutor – and your fellow students and work colleagues – they might think of things that you have forgotten or taken for granted.

It is important that you abide by *ethical* considerations when assembling your evidence (and writing your claim) so as to ensure personal and business confidentiality where this could be an issue. If there is any doubt, it is worth consulting with your line manager about the suitability of material you intend presenting and discussing (sometimes it might just be a matter of blanking out certain confidential information in copies of documents).

Make sure that all your pieces of evidence are *appropriate*; just because a particular document exists and relates to an area of learning in an APEL claim does not mean you have to include it. You may have already adequately evidenced the learning you are claiming for with other material. It is important that you select carefully and do not just include everything you can find – your assessor may tire of picking through irrelevant, repetitive, cumbersome material; quality is always better than quantity! Evidence should not be included just on the basis that it exists or is something you have done or produced – *its main job is to be relevant to the particular claim being made.*

Evidence must be *authentic*. Any claims you are making as to work undertaken on projects and so on in the workplace and your precise contributions to such projects needs to clearly and concisely backed up by testimonials and statements of authorship or authenticity from your line manager and/or mentor. You would do well to consider the advice of Wailey (2002) who has suggested that when putting together an APEL claim there are widely accepted criteria to adhere to; the key elements being:

- *validity* – the evidence and the learning outcomes claimed have a coherent match;
- *sufficiency* – the evidence, including reflection, has sufficient breadth to demonstrate *all* the outcomes claimed;
- *currency* – the evidence is capable of proving that the learning is of contemporary relevance or has a current application;
- *quality* – the evidence demonstrates the required *level* of learning achievement.

Both Wailey (2002) and Johnson (2002) outline and examine best practice in the field of APL and its assessment at HE level, discussing techniques commonly used to facilitate prior experiential learning claims in particular. While these texts were not primarily written with learners on negotiated WBL programmes in mind, they are definitely *recommended reading* for you as you pursue your HE level claim for prior learning.

Summary

1   APL claims help WBL frameworks to be negotiable and flexible.

2   If you have significant 'on the job' experiential learning (or certificated learning that might be difficult to 'fit' other programmes) you have much to gain from APL.

3   Even if you have commenced your study it is worth enquiring about using APL to ensure that you achieve maximum impact both for prior certificated and experiential learning.

4   Remember that you can claim for general and specific credit, but check if your general credit will be counted towards your degree or award.

5 Universities are still approaching this issue in different ways – a significant help in constructing your claim will be getting to understand your university's system and always seek advice from the tutor(s) responsible prior to submitting anything.

References

Armsby, P., Costley, C. and Garnett, J. (2006) 'The Legitimisation of Knowledge: A Work Based Learning Perspective of APEL'. *International Journal of Lifelong Learning Education*, 25 (4), 369–83.

Garnett, J., Portwood, D. and Costley, C. (2004) *Bridging Rhetoric and Reality: Accreditation of Prior Experiential Learning [APEL] in the UK* (Bolton: UVAC).

Johnson, B. (2002) *Models of APEL and Quality Assurance* (London: SEEC).

Lester, S. (2007) 'Professional Practice Projects: APEL or Development?'. *Journal of Workplace Learning*, 19 (3), 182–202.

Prince, C. (2004) 'University Accreditation and the Corporate Learning Agenda'. *Journal of Management Development*, 23(3), 256–69.

Wailey, T. (2002) *How to Do AP[E]L* (London: SEEC).

Workman, B. (2008) 'Beyond Boundaries: Value and assessing Experiential Learning Outside Module Templates' in J. Garnett and D. Young (eds.), *Work Based Learning Futures 2* (Bolton: UVAC), 72–83.

Suggested further reading

Challis, M. (1993) *Introducing APEL* (London: Routledge).

London Lifelong Learning Networks (nd) *Accreditation of Prior Learning (APL): Using Your Previous Learning and/or Experience To Enter Higher Education* [online] Available at http://www.southlondonlpe.co.uk/documents/Generic/APL%20LEARNER.PDF (accessed 3 December 2009).

McKelvey, C. and Peters, H. (1993) *APL: Equal Opportunities for All?* (London: Routledge).

Merrifield, J., McIntyre, D. and Osaigbovo, R. (2000) *Mapping APEL: Accreditation of Prior and Experiential Learning in English Higher Education* (London: Learning From Experience Trust).

Nyatanga, L., Forman. D. and Fox, J. (1998) *Good Practice in the Accreditation of Prior Learning* (London: Cassell).

Qualifications and Curriculum Development Agency (2006) *The National Qualifications Framework: Helping Learners Make Informed Decisions* (online).

Available at http://www.qcda.gov.uk/libraryAssets/media/qca-06-2298-nqf-web.pdf (accessed 3 December 2009).

Quality Assurance Agency for Higher Education (2004) *Guidelines on the Accreditation of Prior Learning* (online). Available at http://www.qaa.ac.uk/academicinfrastructure/apl/APL.pdf (accessed 3 December 2009).

Quality Assurance Agency for Higher Education (2008) *Higher Education Credit Framework for England: Guidance on Academic Credit Arrangements in Higher Education in England* (online). Available at http://www.qaa.ac.uk/England/credit/creditframework.asp (accessed 3 December 2009).

Wilcox, J. and Brown, R. (2003) on UK Centre for Material Education. *Accreditation of Prior and Experiential Learning: A Student Guide* (online). Available at http://www.materials.ac.uk/resources/library/apelstudents.pdf (accessed 3 December 2009).

3 Learning to Learn: Practical Advice for Work-based Learners

Elaine Hooker

In this chapter you will learn:

► about some of the main theories, concepts and themes of learning;
► the commonly used terms and processes, as you 'return to learning';
► how to put a Learning Contract together;
► how to develop autonomy in your learning;
► ways to cope with change;
► the value of personal development planning (PDP) and continuous professional (and personal) development (CPD).

I use the analogy of a road map to signpost the content of each section (Figure 3.1).

● Self-analysis, learning styles and some of the associated theory

> I hear and I forget. I see and I remember. I do and I understand. (Confucius, Chinese philosopher and reformer, 551 BC–479 BC)

As you embark upon your own learning journey you will need to consider your own learning style. Having been away from formal learning for some time, your perception of how you learn best may be quite underdeveloped or perhaps you cannot recall your own, preferred, learning style. When involved

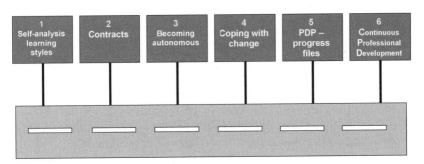

Figure 3.1　'Learning to learn' road map

with HE level learning, work-based students will find that one of their first core modules will typically discuss possible and favoured ways of learning, as well as learning theories and so on.

Learning styles are, merely, different approaches or ways of learning. Most of us have a preference and choose a particular way of taking in and processing information. The idea that students learn via individualized learning styles has gathered momentum since the 1970s and much has been written and proposed (Honey and Mumford, 1982, 1984, 2006; Kolb, 1984; Felder and Brent, 2005). The efficacy of learning styles has been questioned by some (mainly by educational psychologists – Stahl, 2002; Coffield et al., 2004 and others) but they are a useful aid to understanding learning and are certainly a valuable first step and practical start for those returning to learning. They are used widely on work-based, negotiated programmes, alongside other methods and ideas.

Learning styles can form a significant part of the self-analysis process and audit of lifelong, experiential learning that will be required as you begin any work-based programme. The reasons for you to undertake self-analysis will become very evident as you develop but a typical characteristic of work-based learning (WBL) programmes is to encourage you to become an autonomous, independent learner. As a critical stage in the learning journey, becoming an autonomous learner will see you increasingly take on responsibility for, and control of, your own learning. This is often a gradual process as WBL usually starts with lots of encouragement, support and some formal learning. However, as the learning concerns you and your work role and as your confidence and knowledge of the pedagogy and process involved with your learning matures, it will become easier to develop into a successful, self directed learner.

As your learning journey progresses, critical connection with your preferred learning style will be recommended via a variety of methods These methods of measurement, often referred to as psychometric tests, not only assess learning styles but can be used to measure personality traits, attitudes, abilities and knowledge, with different types of psychometric testing measuring the different traits. It may well be that your employer also favours similar tests. These measurements include a range of assessment techniques that can support self-analysis to determine:

- your *personality traits* (Myers Briggs Type Indicator – MBTI) with more information at http://www.geocities.com/lifexplore/;
- how you behave in a *team role* – http://www.belbin.info/;
- how you behave as an *individual* (rather than measuring your personality type), and these can gauge how you may react in a

given context using Neuro-Linguistic programming and Neuro semantics – www.neurosemantics.com/;

- how you can improve both your business performance and your behaviour through *Emotional Intelligence* at Work – www.6seconds.org/business/.

It is essential that the results of your learning style assessment (and any other similar test results) be revisited on a regular basis to evaluate the changing nature of your preferred learning style and to examine the influence of various conditions on this established style. Perhaps the most commonly used model and one that you may have heard of would be David Kolb's Model (1984), based on his experiential learning theory, which is used extensively in education and training. Learning theory is, by its very nature, a complex area and this section will unpick in more detail two models commonly used in WBL: Kolb's and Honey and Mumford's.

Kolb's model (Figure 3.2) focuses on two learning actions, perception (how you take information in) and processing (how you deal with that information).

Perception is divided into concrete experience and its polar opposite – abstract conceptualization:

- *concrete experience* uses feelings and senses, for example seeing, hearing and touching whereas
- *abstract conceptualization* uses thought processes.

When the information has been perceived, it is then processed, often in one of two ways:

- *reflective observation* – thinking about the information;
- *active experimentation* – doing something with the information.

The concrete experience part of this cycle can be any learning experience that makes you reflect on things differently, for example, information and skills gathered from working with others, reading about something or the learning that comes from many diverse sources. A good example of this is the notional learning hours attached to modules you are undertaking. The total of these hours is often in excess of 100 – causing many new students to gulp! – this almost certainly will not come entirely from time spent 'with your nose in a book'; it will be a combination of the sources of learning suggested above – and others.

At the reflective observation stage concrete experience is turned into

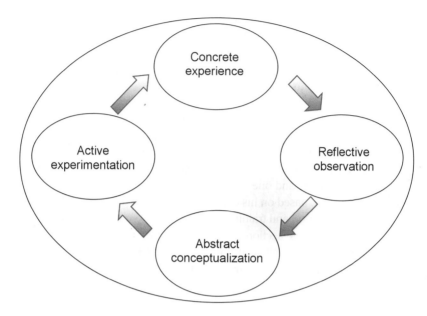

Figure 3.2   Kolb's learning cycle
Source: Kolb (1984).

learning, as you think/reflect and consider the experience by asking yourself, 'How can I use this information?' and 'How will it help with my daily work tasks or enhance my work role?' The active experiment stage is the testing stage, where you can work out (experiment with) and decide how the learning can be applied to become part of your skills and knowledge base. In essence, Kolb's cycle does not have to be used in such a cyclical manner where you follow each step, neatly, from experience to experimentation. Although Kolb's model is often reproduced with numbers from one to four (starting with one at experience and four at experimentation), the cycle is continuous, allowing you to start at any stage with testing leading on to further experience.

Exercise 3.1: Get on board with Kolb's learning cycle

Why don't you try it? Think about a new work task you have recently undertaken and reflect on Kolb's learning cycle and the different stages that you went through to finish the task and achieve an outcome

Kolb developed an assessment method so that individuals could assess and determine their own learning styles through a Learning Style Inventory (see http://www.infed.org/biblio/b-explrn.htm). This inventory places the learning in one of four styles:

- *Accommodator* – you use concrete experience and active experimentation;
- *Converger* – you favour abstract conceptualization and active experimentation;
- *Assimilator* – you use abstract conceptualization and reflective observation;
- *Diverger* – you are characterized by concrete experience and reflective observation.

Honey and Mumford adapted Kolb's ideas and further developed their own model (Figure 3.3) for assessing learning styles, which is also extensively used in education, with the help of their learning style questionnaire (see http://www.peterhoney.com/content/LearningStylesQuestionnaire.html). The questionnaire differs from Kolb's inventory by asking you to consider work-related behaviours rather than determining how you learn. Having decided

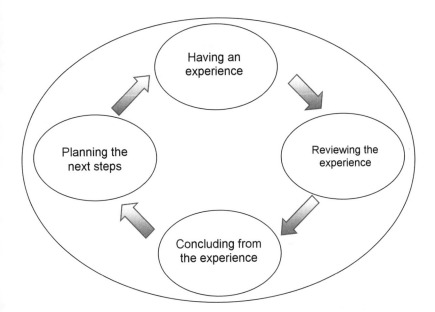

Figure 3.3 Honey and Mumford's learning cycle
Source: Honey and Mumford (1984), originally devised 1982.

your learning style you can then concentrate on the other available learning styles you are perhaps under-utilizing to encompass the learning achieved through your work experiences.

The Honey and Mumford styles that relate to the identified stages in their cycle are called:

- *Activist* – actively seeking through experience;
- *Reflector* – using thoughtful reflection to review the experience;
- *Theorist* – understanding the lessons learnt from the experience;
- *Pragmatist* – planning how to translate the experience into actions.

These styles can be changed through different experiences or through a concentration of effort. This will allow you to become an all-round learner or to at least be aware of where your learning weaknesses lie. For example, (what follows is slightly reductive but gives a flavour of the learning categories and how they function) a *pragmatist* will learn best through very practical, action type experiences – by getting on and doing. A *reflector* will learn through thinking an experience or task through, analysing the outcomes and pondering how those outcomes can be or were achieved – mostly by thinking. However, having to undertake a project that requires careful thought and planning will mean that the *pragmatist* is required to take time to think, more than just getting on and doing. Conversely, a *reflector* will be involved with tasks that involve little time to plan that require a more practical, doing role. Learning through these different styles may not always be comfortable to you, but it will make you aware of where your learning preferences are, and help you to actively seek out and learn in different ways and better understand your areas for development.

Feeling confident with your self-reflection and how to identify your individual learning style? Let us contrast this with something that may be more familiar to you as an employed learner – the process of Training Needs Analysis (TNA):

> The identification of training needs at employee, departmental, or organisational level, in order for the organisation to perform effectively. The aim of training needs analysis is to ensure that training addresses existing problems, is tailored to organisational objectives, and is delivered in an effective and cost-efficient manner. Training needs analysis involves monitoring current performance using techniques such as observation, interviews, and questionnaires; anticipating future shortfalls or problems; identifying the type and level of training required; and analysing how this can best be provided.
> (http://dictionary.bnet.com/definition/training+needs+analysis.html)

Just as you have been asked to reflect upon and identify your own learning style, a TNA reflects upon and defines the needs of the whole business or organization to implement training, but then also attempts to evaluate and determine the effectiveness of that learning/training. The delivery of any training initiative will, whether formal (involving structured training courses) or informal (involving coaching, mentoring or work shadowing), require a systematic approach where the predominant learning style of a large number of individuals will be considered against the resource (funding) available.

Understanding self-analysis and your preferred learning style can be usefully perceived as a TNA at individual level. A TNA, whether organizational or individual, will not only identify your learning needs but also help you to understand how best to take on and progress that learning (see Appendix 2, Example of questions asked in Training Needs Analysis).

● Learning contracts (also called agreements/proposals)

> If you are leaping a ravine, the moment of takeoff is a bad time to be considering alternative strategies. (John Cleese [b. 1939]
> http//www.leadershipnow.com/creativityquotes.html)

As a work-based learner you are probably over 21 years of age, and much more inclined to take a proactive approach to your own learning. Therefore, tailoring your learning experience is very important to how you learn, what you learn and in obtaining a successful outcome. It also allows you to develop a sense of ownership and responsibility for your learning which, in turn, will bring commitment, added enthusiasm and satisfaction.

The use of learning contracts in higher education and training has become common practice during the last 10 years; they can take the form of a written, therefore considered binding, contract between a tutor, learner/employee (you!), and employer (or some combination of these three); they can be printed, formal documents and/or online, interactive documents.

A learning contract will confirm:

- what you will learn;
- how you will learn;
- how you will be able to apply the learning to your job role;
- timescales involved;
- ways to evaluate and review the learning.

Malone (2003) has come up with an acronym (LORE) to recall the critical elements of a learning contract:

Learning task described
Objectives for learning
Resources needed
Evidence of achievement

There are many advantages for you in producing a learning contract – in consultation with your tutor:

- you manage your own learning and can hopefully prioritize your own preferred learning style;
- you become a self-directed, self-managed learner utilizing and enhancing your own self-reflection;
- you combine your own work experience and job role to initiate new learning experiences;
- you set very clear objectives, identified in consultation with your tutor, and a directed pathway to achieve those outcomes;
- learning outcomes are tailored and therefore more relevant than a set/formal assignment;
- it is a particularly useful tool for WBL as it uses negotiation to ensure communication between you and your employer.

Contracts/plans/agreements need to be reviewed on a regular basis to ensure that the learning taking place still matches the original course of agreed action (and indeed that the original course is still the required one!). What I have described is a general learning contract that can be used in a number of learning programmes; however, let us consider a learning agreement used in a HE work-based studies undergraduate programme. Planning your 'programme of study' may well be embedded in a formal planning and development module; usually carrying credit and usually called something like, 'Individual Programme Planning'. Whether it is part of a module or part of your own preparation when writing your learning agreement you will need to develop a constructive approach to the acquisition of knowledge based on the identification of your development needs, your career aims, the needs of your employer, and the university's criteria for an approved programme of study. Planning your programme independently in this way may feel messy and a bit scary at first but you will be guided and ultimately what you are doing will encourage your reflection and promote your independent learning.

A learning agreement is:

- a three-way agreement between you, your employer (if appropriate) and the university;
- a record of your proposed programme of study for the next level of that study;
- a description of forthcoming study which might include taught modules, work-based projects, distance learning, modules from other universities and so on;
- a reminder of when chosen modules will be offered (for example, which semester, which year) and the amount and level of credits attached to them;
- an outcome of a process of negotiation between the requisite parties;
- a statement of intent and a statement of award title sought;
- renegotiable if circumstances require or demand.

TIP **Completing a learning agreement (check your own institution's rules)**

- Remember that at least one-third of the credits you require for your target award must be obtained through the university. It is not possible to gain a qualification purely on the basis of learning credits.
- You need to check the start dates for the modules you select. These will probably be year-long starting in September. Check with the appropriate academic school as most schools run modules over a year long period but there may be some modules which start more than once a year.
- Plan any work-based projects in advance so that you can ensure that they fit in with the taught modules you have chosen. You must undertake Research Methods at either level 5 or 6 before you can undertake a work-based project.
- Remember to check which core modules your award requires you to do.
- Make sure you provide a full rationale of how your AP(E)L credits are appropriate to your award.
- Check to find out whether your chosen modules have any pre- or co-requisites. Planning in advance will enable you to take these compulsory modules.
- Remember that you can include modules from other universities, however the last module you study in your programme must be with the awarding university.

Box 3.1 is a sample of what you might choose to put in your learning agreement.

Box 3.2 is an example of a learning agreement for a whole programme.

Box 3.1: Sample learning agreement

Name: Module: Tutor:

Objectives	Resources and Strategy	Timing	Evidence	Verification
What are you going to learn?	How are you going to learn it?	Dates for completion	How are you going to know that you have learned it?	How are you going to prove that learning has taken place?
Research Methods	Enrol on and undertake research module at HE Level 6 at Summer University	September 2010	Achieving module learning outcomes. Application of the learning to job role – research and analytical skills.	Assessment and learning review
Continuous Professional CPD	Undertake CPD module Level 6	September 2010 to March 2011	Understanding theory of CPD and applying learning to job/personal goals	Assessment and updated CPD plan and log
Work-based Project	Undertaking research methods module will allow me to determine the subject for my work-based project. Will register for WBP and liaise with my supervisor regularly to undertake a WBP	September 2010 to September 2011	Using knowledge gained and actual research skills to carry out a WBP. Using both quantitative and qualitative methods to answer a research question.	Assessment, dissemination and consultation with employer re WBP. Leading to implementation of processes identified through WBP into the work place.

Box 3.2: Example of a learning agreement

Module	Level 4	Level 5	Level 6	Credits achieved	Date
APEL – areas of learning *completed*	100	100		100, 100	May 2008
Research Methods *completed*			20	20	July 2009
Returning to Learning	10				In progress
Managing own Learning			10		In progress
Planned Modules					
English module		20			February 2010
Information Handling	10		20		February 2010
English module			20		July 2010
Mentoring in practice			40		September 2010
Work-based Project			10		September 2010
Level 6 area of learning					February 2011
Total credits	120	120	120	220 / 360	Complete degree

Exercise 3.2: Planning for the future

Try and complete a learning agreement document for your proposed study route:

- State the title of your award.
- Indicate the area of focus of your study.
- Show the total number of credits required.
- Specify credit gained through AP(E)L and AP(C)L and why it is relevant to your programme.
- Specify credits gained elsewhere, for example from modules.
- Give your areas of learning a status code, for example, Completed (C); In-Progress (IP); and Proposed (P).
- Make a note of Levels, Semesters and Years.

You are now prepared with your own version of a learning agreement, and a better understanding of what one is. Hopefully this will have focused your thoughts!

● Becoming autonomous

> Give a man a fish and you feed him for a day. Teach a man to fish and you feed him for a lifetime. (Chinese proverb – origin unknown)

The ultimate aim of your learning journey is to become a self-directed learner – an autonomous learner. The fact that you are undertaking a non-traditional learning programme shows that you are comfortable with the idea of independent learning.

What is an autonomous learner? Autonomous means: self-governing; acting independently or having the freedom to do so, therefore an autonomous learner is someone who controls their own learning. We become autonomous learners as we increasingly make our own choices about what we learn and how we learn it. Consequently, you have much more responsibility for planning, organizing and 'doing' your own learning. But what does becoming an autonomous learner mean exactly? How will you know when you are one? Learner choice and control are two key concepts in becoming autonomous. You need to decide on your learning objectives; the content of that learning; be able to select methods and

techniques to learn by; choose when, where and how learning takes place and to manage the learning progression (Ciekanski, 2007). This journey (remember our map at the beginning of the chapter) will take you from dependence upon others via learning styles and formal learning models through interdependence to complete autonomy.

Still cannot decide if you are a self-directed learner?

Exercise 3.3: Steps to becoming an autonomous learner

How do you do on the following list? How many of the choices have you undertaken in your own learning journey?

- Set your own learning aims?   Yes/No
- Make choices about learning modes?   Yes/No
- Plan and organize work?   Yes/No
- Decide when best to work alone, work collaboratively
  and when to seek advice?   Yes/No
- Learn through experience?   Yes/No
- Identify and solve problems?   Yes/No
- Think creatively?   Yes/No
- Communicate effectively orally and in writing?   Yes/No
- Assess your own progress in respect of your learning
  aims?   Yes/No

(Based on Candy, 1991)

This is not a definitive list but will help to show your progress.

Hughes (2003) summarizes (from work in this area) the characteristics of autonomous learners and provides details of the support mechanisms required for learning opportunities:

Characteristics:

- Self awareness and reflection
- Intrinsically motivated
- The ability to plan and manage own learning, understanding requirements and procedures (knowing how 'the system' operates)
- Ability to formulate own questions
- Possessing the research and information skills necessary to pursue a line of enquiry

- Interdependence – the ability to work well with peers and to recognise when appropriate support and guidance from tutors and peers will be helpful
- Critical thinking
- Discipline and subject awareness – knowing how knowledge has been and is created in your subject area

Support mechanisms:

- Clear induction and guidance regarding institutional structures, guidelines and regulations so as to demystify HE
- Skills training and support
- Provision of opportunities for negotiated learning, for example through the use of learning agreements or contracts
- Project based learning
- Problem based learning
- Stand alone independent study modules
- Provision of opportunities for self assessment or self evaluation
- Provision of opportunities for group work and peer evaluation
- Learning and assessment through learning journals or diaries to stimulate reflection
- Provision of learning and assessment opportunities designed to stimulate and assess critical thinking. (Hughes, 2003)

This list is a good start but an obvious exclusion would be the use of ICT (information and communication technologies). Autonomous learning has to be supported as well as encouraged and this is often provided through technologies in ICT. Communities of learning that do not have the opportunity to come together as often as traditional students depend upon a programme that includes some blended and distance learning. The use of blogs or twitters to keep in touch with your peers becomes essential as you move from relative dependence to autonomy (Chapter 7).

Coping with change

> Change is inevitable. Change is constant. (Benjamin Disraeli, British statesman and novelist [1804–81])

If change is both inevitable and constant why do we react so differently to it? Some people are more resilient to change and enjoy the challenge, embracing the adjustments that accompany new learning experiences, or taking on

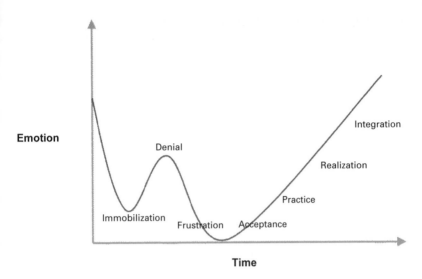

Figure 3.4 Phases of change
Source: www.trainerbubble.com

new job roles and responsibilities, while others find change very difficult and expend wasted energy resisting change and all that accompanies it. As your learning journey continues you will find yourself having to cope with increasing change and you will need to pay attention to the transitional stages of change and not only focus on the end product.

Figure 3.4 shows the various emotions associated with change.

Exercise 3.4: Coping with change

Think about the emotions that have accompanied any change that you have been through. Was this the order of your emotions when met with change or were they different?

Whether you perceive change as a threat or an opportunity depends upon how prepared for change you are.

In January 2009, the UK Government issued *The New Opportunities* White Paper (www.hmg.gov.uk/newopportunities) which explains the government's agenda for both creating and capturing jobs for the future while investing in families and communities. The paper proposes a future where there will be lots of new opportunity for Britain (conceding also that times will be tough) but that the next 10 years will see up to a billion skilled jobs created worldwide. The government's plan is to invest now to win those jobs and ensure new opportunities for everyone. We already know that job roles will change and that the workforce must keep ahead of that change by keeping their skills updated by learning. Learning is transformative and a vehicle for change; coping successfully with change and continually improving are intrinsically linked. As a work-based learner you are in a good position to see the world of work as it is now and know that although impossible to predict, the future will be better if you are equipped for change. Self-analysis, reflection and 'learning to learn' all help you prepare for change by ensuring that you become more adaptable; learning through work can help you to cope with or at least handle change.

There are five basic factors involved with change management:

1   Different people react differently to change (as previously mentioned).
2   Everyone has fundamental needs that have to be met.
3   Change often involves a feeling of loss.
4   Expectations need to be managed realistically.
5   Fears have to be dealt with.

Change is very personal but there are ways to cope with and manage change. For example, don't confine your understanding of change to books or training courses; distinguish between operational and strategic change to develop a model of organizational change which will be helpful to you (Leigh and Walters, 1998).

TIP   **Coping with change**

- Give people information – be open and honest.
- Don't let the grapevine take over! Produce a communication strategy that ensures information is disseminated efficiently and comprehensively to everyone.
- Give yourself choices to make, and be honest about the possible consequences of those choices.
- Give others time to express their views and support decision making, providing coaching, counselling or information as appropriate.
- Where the change involves a loss, identify what will or might replace that loss – loss is easier to cope with if there is something to replace it.
- Keep observing good practice, such as making time for informal discussion and feedback (even though the pressure might seem that it is reasonable to let such things slip – during difficult change such practices are even more important).

Work-based learning is compatible with the current world of work, whereby the notion of a job for life has become an unfamiliar concept to the modern workforce. You will probably strive to develop yourself to possess the skills required at that moment in time for the job role you are undertaking. If after a period of time the work role changes then you have to be able to diversify to address that need, as a multi-skilled individual. As Helyer (2007) proposes, in a rapidly changing society employees need to be adaptable and multi-faceted.

Personal development plan (PDP)

> Once I was on the programme there was no looking back, I had a clear route mapped out to achieve my goal of graduation.
> (WBL graduate)

A PDP has become an essential part of WBL, as a 'structured and supported process undertaken by an individual to reflect upon their own learning, performance and/or achievement and to plan for their personal, educational and career development' (QAA, 2001). The Progress Files Initiative was a result of the Dearing Report (1997) which recommended that HEIs develop *Progress Files* with two elements:

- a transcript recording student achievement which should follow a common format;
- a means by which students can monitor, build and reflect upon their personal development (QAA, 2001: 2).

As a relatively new process to HE, it became fully operational in 2005/06. The QAA *Guidelines for HE Progress Files* have been implemented across the HE system, for all HE awards. These timely recommendations have proved to be valuable, not only for you as a work-based learner, but for traditional graduates seeking employment as the transcripts provide employers with information about the knowledge and skills you gain throughout your study. This goes over and above the subject content of a course to include experience and learning from extracurricular activity and WBL, which demonstrates to an employer that you have the kind of employability skills that they are looking for; by providing more detail than a degree classification it makes it easier for an employer to appreciate your full range of experience and skills.

The other component, PDP, imitates something that you may have already done at school or as a Further Education student whereby you keep a 'National Record of Achievement'. The process involved in becoming profi-cient with programme planning (and by Progress Files and National Records of Achievement) will also be utilized when undertaking continuous profes-sional development (CPD), explained in more detail later in this section. PDP and CPD are frequently the subject matter of HE level modules for work-based learners; these modules encourage you to think about what you want, where you want to get to and how you will get there. Exercise 3.5 provides some (light-hearted) ways to kick start your thinking.

Exercise 3.5: Ways to develop that reflective reflex

- Think about where you want to be in 10 years' time – reflect and write a couple of detailed paragraphs about your thoughts and ideas.
- Write down several statements that begin with 'I want to ...'
- Write about 'if I had one million pounds to spend in 12 months'.
- Finally, write about how you would like to be remembered.

Completing this exercise will help you to identify your personal strengths and weaknesses and to concentrate upon your training and development needs. You are now in a better position to start on your PDP and to think of some specific aims and outcomes for your educational and career develop-ment. The primary objective for PDP is to improve the capacity of individuals to understand what and how they learn and to review, plan and take respon-sibility for their own learning. This helps you to:

- become more effective, independent and confident as a self-directed learner;
- understand how you are learning and relate that learning to a wider context;
- improve your general skills for study and career management;
- articulate personal goals and evaluate progress towards what you want to achieve;
- adopt a positive attitude towards lifelong learning.

Preparation for PDP will certainly be enhanced by the production of a portfo-lio containing your:

- Personal statement. Throughout history we have kept diaries and journals to consign to print our thoughts, feelings, memories and goals and this should be the start of your learning journey. Write a personal statement (which might well grow into a diary or journal) to describe where you have come from, in order to provide an account of how you have arrived at this time in your life and explain your ambitions for the future. Many different factors may have made you decide that this is the right moment for you to undertake a programme of study at university. Write about these factors, but also what you want to achieve from learning. This will be a useful self-analysis/self-reflection tool (see Appendix 3 for an example of a personal statement from a WBL student).
- Curriculum vitae (CV). You need to develop a learning CV which will provide an overall picture of your past learning achievements, similar to the more familiar CV that provides an overall picture of your previous job roles and responsibilities. However, your learning CV will give contextualizing information on your past learning achievements *linked* to your job role and employment. Do not forget any voluntary or unpaid work which is sure to have learning attached (see Appendix 4 for an example of a CV from a WBL student).
- Job description (JD). As with your CV, the JD should provide a clear picture of your current roles, responsibilities and achievements. You should think of the term 'job description' as one which encompasses the work you do. A formal job description provided by an employer may be a useful starting point – but you will need to add to it to ensure that it gives as full and accurate picture of your work role as possible (see Appendix 5 for an example of a job description from a WBL student).

Understanding your own strengths and development areas can also be identified through undertaking a SWOT analysis and will also assist with your ultimate goal of becoming an autonomous learner. A SWOT analysis is a self-evaluation technique which aims to identify the critical issues in any situation and to organize them in a way that enables you to come up with a sound approach to self-development planning. It is a very useful tool for WB learners and should be used as part of your personal development plan. As with most self-analysis exercises SWOT will not, on its own, give you any specific answers but it will help you to organize the information required to develop a learning plan.

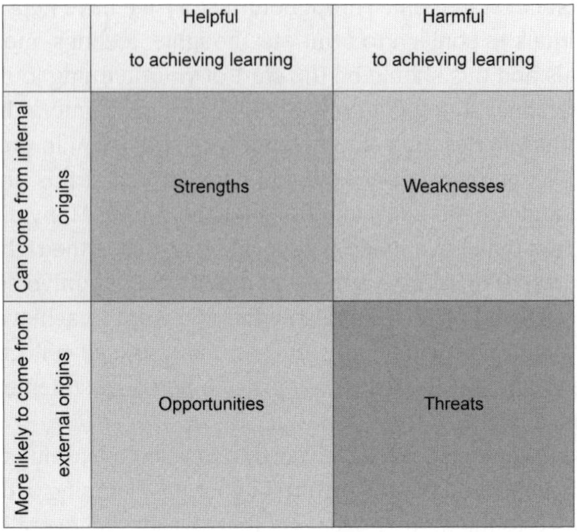

	Helpful to achieving learning	Harmful to achieving learning
Can come from internal origins	Strengths	Weaknesses
More likely to come from external origins	Opportunities	Threats

Figure 3.5   SWOT analysis chart

From Figure 3.5 (helpful to visual learners) undertaking a SWOT analysis as part of your planning will allow you to:

- Consider your **S**trengths – honestly – try to look at it from a third-party perspective, what strengths can an outsider see? How can those strengths and attributes help you to achieve your objective?
- Consider or reflect on any **W**eaknesses (it might be more helpful to use the term 'areas for development'). These will be those attributes that will be harmful or impede your performance that will, in turn, limit your skills or capability to achieve your objective(s).
- Use **O**pportunities for learning – these usually arrive from external origins, but can provide real learning opportunities. The trick is being able to identify (and seize) them when they come along. They can come from changes in our job role, secondments, promotion or participation in different working groups. Anything that gives an opportunity for learning ultimately leading to achieving your objective.
- Ensure that you counter any **T**hreats, which can be explained as anything that will stop you from achieving your objective. Generally external factors but not always, these could include time management skills, personal problems, blockages that hinder your learning.

Exercise 3.6: Be part of the SWOT team

Take a look at this example of a SWOT analysis undertaken by a group of work-based learners involved in a programme at Teesside University. It centres on the scenario of a landscape gardener with a personal goal of becoming self-employed, specializing in water gardens.

SWOT analysis example – Landscape gardener

Strengths:

- Technical expertise
- Good communicator
- Commitment to work long hours
- Able to set realistic goals
- Not afraid to ask for advice
- Researched market thoroughly
- Support of family and friends

Weaknesses:

- Limited financial accounting knowledge
- No experience of selling
- No experience of self-employment
- Lack of management experience
- Poor time management
- Technical expertise limited to a specific area – water gardens

Opportunities:

- A growing market
- University/college courses in horticulture to open up new markets
- Courses/workshops to attend to gain knowledge in other areas – finances, management
- Use home as office-saving costs
- Practise artwork for designs – even computerize them with software package

Threats:

- Competitors seeing the market opportunities and the need to be 'first to market'
- Future government legislation (Europe/local/national) might hinder plans

- Missed opportunities, if training in up-to-date methods/other areas of landscaping not taken up
- Business failure possibilities if knowledge in business/administration not widened
- Designs need to be professionally drawn – not expert in this

Now do your own personal SWOT analysis using the same format.

Having now competed a personal SWOT analysis you can combine this with your personal statement, CV and job description to help identify the skills and knowledge that you most frequently use and any gaps.

Continuous professional development (CPD)

> 'Would you tell me please, which way I ought to go?', said Alice.
> 'That depends on where you want to get to,' said the cat.
> 'I don't much care where–,' said Alice.
> 'Then it doesn't matter which way you go,' said the cat.
> '–so long as I get somewhere', said Alice.
> 'Oh, you're sure to do that,' said the cat, 'if you only keep walking.'
> (Lewis Carroll, *Alice in Wonderland*, 1865, Chapter 6)

You need to plan and think about your aims. You can be aimless and still travel, but, as the quotation suggests, you could end up anywhere!

Most WBL programmes contain a module that introduces work-based learners to continuous professional development (CPD). As a tutor on such a module I can report that the growth and development that occurs is tangible. What is more exceptional is that, for many, it is their very first introduction to the idea of CPD (despite being employed, mature students). Most WBL groups are mixed, they contain students from all walks of life, involved in a diverse range of work roles, but all with a common goal – to gain a qualification from higher level learning. Commonly the group, throughout the length of their programme, become a community of practice who support each other – also, commonly, their levels of engagement with CPD in the work place are very wide-ranging. The engineers and high-level managers, who often come from multinational, corporate companies, have a firm understanding of CPD; they know what it entails and are practising members of a professional association; membership of which improves, expands or sustains their learning, skills and knowledge, while continuously developing those personal qualities vital in their professional lives.

The other regular group involved are learners from the public sector including teaching assistants who have, up until now, had little experience of CPD; however, it has now begun to permeate the public sector and education. Practices and the benefits of CPD have created much more awareness and have changed the policy in these sectors with CPD being more widely practised. I would also like to think that the emergence of WBL has positively influenced the take-up of CPD activity. In the module those who practise CPD certainly influence those who do not, while also reaffirming for themselves the importance of something that they are already doing. As a Level 6 module it is for many learners the official end of their 'learning to learn' journey for this particular programme; however, it is also obvious from module evaluations and feedback that for all of them it is looked upon as the start of their lifelong learning journey.

CPD is defined as:

> The holistic commitment to structured skills enhancement and
> personal or professional competence. It is the conscious updating of
> professional knowledge and the improvement of professional compe-
> tence throughout a person's working life. It is a commitment to being
> professional, keeping up to date and continuously seeking to
> improve. It is the key to optimising a person's career opportunities,
> both today and for the future CIPD (http://www.cipd.co.uk/)

What might CPD mean to you? The main concepts of CPD place you at the centre of your own learning destiny; you are the one in control. It will:

- encourage you to examine any skills that may be dormant;
- build on the talent and skills that you already have in all areas of your life;
- develop new knowledge and skills and therefore develop yourself;
- help you to recognize and achieve your potential;
- help you to respond to a very changing world.

It will most certainly help with the continuing development of your self-reflection and critical reasoning skills and although it might be something that you start at university through your WBL programme, it will become a practice that you will want to continue. One of the most fundamental benefits in the challenging world of work is that it will keep you, with your knowledge, skills, experience and added awareness of possible development areas, at the forefront of your profession, which in turn will keep you employed and employable.

The benefits of undertaking CPD do not only extend to you, the individual learner/employee, but extend to the employer and more widely to the colleges and universities who are required to ensure that their curriculum encourages learners to undertake rigorous CPD and equips them with sustainable knowledge. CPD can make up for previous poor, inadequate or even non-existent career guidance. By encouraging curiosity, reflection and hence questioning the need for change, it could make you consider that you are in the wrong job. Often, in busy working lives there is neither the time nor the inclination to pause and analyse what is happening – but CPD will encourage you to find time for self-development analysis.

Employers consider CPD as part of retaining the best staff and improving performance and therefore productivity; and as a consequence of this increasingly value employees who take responsibility for their own professional development. Universities and colleges who deliver CPD, tailor this learning for the individual and ensure that you record your progress. Delivering CPD modules allows universities and colleges to improve their curriculum by providing a strong context between job role and learning.

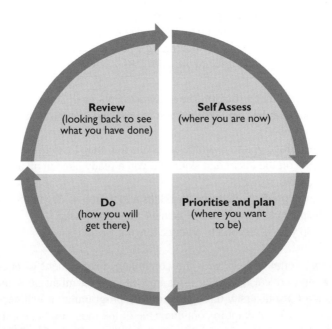

Figure 3.6 CPD cycle
Source: Megginson and Whitaker (2003).

CPD makes you consider the factors that might be hindering your development. Considering any restrictions (self-inflicted or otherwise), serious obstacles or excuses, you will become aware of your own limitations and try to deal with them as either a personal or professional development need.

Exercise 3.7: Need another cycle?

Examine the CPD cycle in Figure 3.6 and apply it to where you are now in your development or, even better, bring it to life by reflecting upon a situation where it has already been applied and consider the difference it made.

An interesting exercise and a place to start, suggested by Megginson and Whitaker (2003), would be to consider your career as a metaphor. Is it a train stuck at the station waiting for the green light? Or like being on a one-way roller coaster, climbing first up then down, feeling a bit out of control? Do you feel like a caterpillar in your job role, but that with improved skills and knowledge you could turn into a butterfly? Does your career resemble a labyrinth with lots of paths and obstacles but no clear way out?

Exercise 3.8: Where are you?

Think about your own career. What metaphor would best describe your career and where you are now?

Whatever metaphor you use to describe your career it should be able to give you an insight into where the development areas are. You will also need to spend some time thinking about actual problem areas and how they might be confronted.

As with PDP, an interesting place to start to formulate a CPD development plan is to consider where you eventually want to be, how you will get there and what you will need. A useful first step for CPD would be to start a CPD learning log, for an example see: http://www.teachernet.gov.uk/cpdtool/index.cfm?pageID=259.

Exercise 3.9: Be aware of obstacles

Spend some time identifying what may be stopping you from moving forward and list them. Can these be easily resolved and if so how?

Having identified items for your development you could include these in your CPD learning log (see below).

Written more like a diary or journal this can be narrative in style and more free-flowing than a formal CPD plan and record. It will capture your thoughts and does not necessarily have to be coherent or neat (as long as *you* can understand it). It will help you to gather the thoughts which will then translate into a development plan by considering:

- What do I want to learn?
- How will I achieve this?
- What resources will I need to help me?
- How will I measure my success?
- What time frame will I need to achieve my outcomes?

(Or referring back to Exercise 3.5 where you kick start your thinking on this.)

Having once considered these questions you will be able to create a more formal, effective development plan and also a CPD record to establish if you are maintaining progress, for an example see: http://www.cipd.co.uk/cpd/guidance/CPDrecordandplan.htm.

Becoming skilled with your own CPD will help you to become an accomplished learner. In order to recognize solutions for your development objectives you will become adept at anticipating learning opportunities; in order to seek out new learning you will be need to be more relaxed about taking risks and being creative. You will become confident at being constructively self-analytical while also being open to the thoughts of others involved in your career or learning development.

Summary

1   Monopolize on all available resources to get to know your preferred learning style.

2 Plan your learning programme using PDP and CPD (with those involved); use learning contracts as a mechanism to formalize your learning strategy.

3 Remember that you are a different type of learner from the traditional HE student; you will be working, predominantly, on your own. Maximize this opportunity to become a self-directed learner.

4 Embrace the opportunities that arise from change, be prepared to adapt by developing your own learning tactics.

5 And don't forget, revisit your exercises – you could be surprised at how much you change and develop.

References

Belbin Team Role, *Frequently Asked Questions* (online). Available at http://www.belbin.info/ (accessed 2 December 2009).

BNET, *Business Definition for: Training Needs Analysis* (online). Available at http://dictionary.bnet.com/definition/training+needs+analysis.html (accessed 22 July 2009).

Candy, P.C. (1991) *Self-direction for Lifelong Learning: A Comprehensive Guide to Theory and Practice* (San Francisco: Jossey-Bass).

Carroll, L. (1895) *Alice's Adventures in Wonderland* (London: Macmillan & Co).

Chartered Institute of Professional Development, *Development Plan and CPD Templates* (online). Available at http://www.cipd.co.uk/cpd/guidance/CPDrecordandplan.htm (accessed 2 December 2009).

Ciekanski, M. (2007) 'Fostering Learner Autonomy: Power and Reciprocity in the Relationship between Language Learner and Language Learning Adviser'. *Cambridge Journal of Education*, 37(1), 111–27.

Coffield, F., Moseley, D., Hall, E. and Ecclestone, K. (2004) *Learning Styles and Pedagogy in Post-16 Learning: A Systematic and Critical Review* (London: Learning and Skills Research Centre).

Dearing, R. (1997) *National Committee of Inquiry into Higher Education* (London: HMSO).

Encyclopaedia of Informal Education, The, *David Kolb on Experiential Learning* (online). Available at http://www.infed.org/biblio/b-explrn.htm (accessed 2 December 2009).

Felder, R.M. and Brent, R. (2005) 'Understanding Student Differences'. *Journal of Engineering Education,* 94 (1), 57–72.

Helyer, R. (2007) 'What Is Employability? Reflecting on the Postmodern Challenges of Work-based Learning', *Journal of Employability and the Humanities* (Lancashire: University of Central Lancashire).

Honey, P. and Mumford, A. (1982) *The Manual of Learning Styles* (Maidenhead: Peter Honey Publications).

Honey, P. and Mumford, A. (1984) *Using Your Learning Styles* (Maidenhead: Peter Honey Publications).

Honey, P. and Mumford, A. (2006) *The Learning Styles Questionnaire,* rev. edn (Maidenhead: Peter Honey Publications).

Hughes, P. (2003) 'Autonomous Learning Zones', paper presented to the 10th European Conference for Research on Learning and Instruction, 26–30 August, Padova, Italy.

International Society of Neuro-Semantics, The, *Welcome to the World of Neuro Semantics* (online). Available at http://www.neurosemantics.com/ (accessed 2 December 2009).

Kolb, D. (1984) *Experiential learning: Experience as the Source of Learning and Development,* (London: Prentice-Hall).

Leigh, A. and Walters, M. (1998), *Effective Change: 20 Ways to Make it Happen* (London: Chartered Institute of Personal Development).

Malone, S.A. (2003) *Learning about Learning: An A–Z of Training and Development Tools and Techniques* (London: Chartered Institute of Personnel and Development).

Megginson, D. and Whitaker, V. (2003) *Continuing Professional Development* (London: Chartered Institute of Personnel and Development).

Myers and Briggs Foundation, *MBTI Basics* (online). Available at http://www.myersbriggs.org/my-mbti-personality-type/mbti-basics/ (accessed 2 December 2009).

Myers and Briggs Foundation (http://www.myersbriggs.org/my-mbti-personality-type/mbti-basics/)

Peter Honey Publications, *The Learning Style Questionnaire* (online). Available at http://www.peterhoney.com/content/LearningStylesQuestionnaire.html (accessed 2 December 2009).

Quality Assurance Agency (2001) *Guidelines for HE Progress Files* (online). Available at http://www.qaa.ac.uk/academicinfrastructure/progressfiles/guidelines/progfile2001.pdf (accessed 2 December 2009).

Six Seconds: The Emotional Intelligence Network, *Getting Started with Emotional Intelligence* (online). Available at www.6seconds.org/business/ (accessed 2 December 2009).

Stahl, S.A. (2002) 'Different strokes for different folks?'. In L. Abbeduto (ed.), *Taking Sides: Clashing on Controversial Issues in Educational Psychology*, 3rd edn (Guildford: McGraw-Hill), 98–107.

TeacherNet, *Example CPD Log* (online). Available at http://www.teachernet.gov.uk/cpdtool/index.cfm?pageID=259 (accessed 2 December 2009).

Trainer Bubble, *Phases of Change – Business Model* (online). Available at http://www.trainerbubble.com/Products/Phases_of_Change_Model.aspx (accessed 2 December 2009).

● Suggested further reading

Bee, F. and Bee, R. (1994) *Training Needs Analysis and Evaluation* (London: Institute of Personnel and Development).

Boak, G. (1998) *A Complete Guide to Learning Contracts* (Aldershot: Gower).

Chartered Institute of Logistics and Transport (UK), *Professional Development and Training: What is CPD?* (online). Available at http://www.ciltuk.org.uk/pages/cpdwhat (accessed 2 December 2009).

Cottrell, S. (2010) *Skills for Success: The Personal Development Planning Handbook*, 2nd edn (Basingstoke: Palgrave Macmillan).

Goleman, D. (2004) *Emotional Intelligence and Working with Emotional Intelligence* (London: Bloomsbury).

Gray, D.E., Hay, D., Cundell, S. and O'Neil, J. (2004) *Learning through the Workplace: A Guide to Work-based Learning* (Cheltenham: Nelson Thornes).

Laycock, M. and Stephenson, J. (1992) 'Using Learning Contracts with Employees', in M. Laycock and J. Stephenson (eds), *Using Learning Contracts in Higher Education* (London: Kogan Page), 122–4.

Marsick, V.J. and Watkins, K.E. (1990) *Informal and Incidental Learning in the Workplace* (London: Routledge).

Moon, J. (2002) *The Module and Programme Development Handbook: A Practical Guide to Linking Levels, Outcomes and Assessment Criteria* (London: Kogan Page).

Moore, I. http://extra.shu.ac.uk/cetl/cpla/whatislearnerautonomy.html (accessed 5 December 2009).

Whitmore, T. (2009) *How to Write an Impressive CV and Cover Letter: A Comprehensive Guide for the UK Job Seeker* (Oxford: How to Books).

4 Making the Most of your Assessment Opportunities: Thinking beyond the Grade

Sue Graham and Garth Rhodes

In this chapter you will learn:

▶ about WBL assessment;
▶ why WBL needs to be assessed;
▶ that there are different types of WBL assessments;
▶ how you will be assessed; the various methods, processes and procedures;
▶ what the rules and regulations are;
▶ your roles and responsibilities in all this.

● Introduction

If you asked the majority of people what was the most worrying aspect of their learning experience, the answer would probably be assessment. Similarly if you asked tutors what concerned their learners most, again the likely answer would be assessment. Why is this? Well, the probable answer is that basically we all want to do well (or well enough) in whatever we do and as assessment is primarily about making a judgement about our performance, telling us how well, or how badly we have done, then clearly it is important.

For many adult learners, unhappy experiences of assessment at school have been one of the major factors which have turned them off learning. At some point you may have worked incredibly hard on your work, only to have your enthusiasm dashed because you did not receive a good mark or grade. There may be a number of reasons for this, for example:

● a lack of clarity in the teaching or in the instructions given for the assessed work;
● the assessment was not capable of measuring what you have learned.

Sometimes negative attitudes to assessment are self-induced. You have to stop the burden of assessment undermining the enjoyment of the learning experience. Similarly, try not to let assessment seem so unappealing that you adopt avoidance strategies, such as leaving the work until the night before; for a few this results in an inspirational piece of work, but for most of us it results in poor marks.

Exercise 4.1: How do I view assessment?

Everyone is different, but when it comes to assessment there are some clear personality differences. We have identified five broad categories. You:

a   want to be the best above everything else, no matter what;
b   want to do your best and get the most out of your learning;
c   want to do as little as possible to scrape by;
d   are happy to be average, doing as well as you can in the circumstances;
e   are so consumed by worry that you feel doomed to fail.

Consider your own attitudes towards assessment:

- Into which of the above categories do you fall?
- To which category do you aspire?
- How will you need to change and what will you have to do to achieve this?

Example: John

John is extremely nervous about his assessment after a bad experience of learning at school and expending all his energy on worrying about whether or not he will pass. He has been considering what he needs to do to move towards Category (b) above. His action plan involves him in:

- benefiting from the support mechanisms offered by the university, for example, Study Skills;
- talking about his concerns with his tutor and supportive colleagues and fellow students;
- making sure he understands what is expected by breaking down assessment tasks and criteria;
- planning and prioritizing;
- taking the opportunity to submit drafts of work for early feedback to build up his confidence.

Virtually everyone will have undertaken some form of assessment during their lifetime. If nothing else you will have 'done' homework, written essays and taken tests or 'exams' at school. At university assessments traditionally were made through examination, essay, dissertation and thesis or more recently through presentation, portfolio or even group or peer-assessed activity. If you went directly into work after leaving school or have under-taken an apprenticeship, trade tests and professional body qualifications will have been used. How does WBL assessment differ from what you might have experienced already?

● WBL assessment – the 'what'

When tutors are assessing WBL, they are looking for more than just the demonstration of your workplace skills and competencies. What they want to see is something which not only provides evidence of academic ability, but delivers a real and positive impact upon you and your working environment. In essence, what you will be assessed upon is your ability to articulate and apply high-level critical thinking and reflection (Chapter 1) within complex situations in your work, your organization or even your wider profession. In this way, the learning for which you will be assessed will, to a great extent, be unique to you. This requires a high degree of autonomy on your part (Chapter 3), as well as negotiation of both what you will be learn-ing and how you will evidence this.

> WBL programmes are designed to promote professional and personal development, and intended to benefit both learners and the work-place. Inter-personal, inter-professional, intellectual and practical skills are developed through each learner's recognition and reflection upon his or her professional development and the application of this to the workplace. (Durrant et al., 2009: 2)

For assessment your tutor will expect you to show that you have undertaken significant investigation and enquiry around key issues affecting your work-place, and drawn upon relevant theories, concepts, new research and poli-cies to support your thinking, in line with the level at which you are studying and the responsibility you hold or aspire to in your job.

**Exercise 4.2: Some key words used when
talking about assessment**

When thinking about your WBL, these words might be helpful in
ensuring that you address the requirements of university-level assessment, many of which are covered in this chapter:

Critical • Transferability • Complexity • Innovation • Application •
Summative • Enquiry • Understanding • Level • Theory • Concepts
• Reflection • Policy • Formative Practice • Evaluation • Deep-
level Thinking • Learning Outcomes

Any more you can add?
   Why not come back to these words at the end of the chapter and
see if they mean more to you!

As a work-based learner you are likely to have:

- considerable professional/occupational knowledge and
  experience;
- opportunity to engage in active learning through reflecting upon
  everyday work tasks;
- confidence in your own competence, already proven through you
  ongoing ability to do you job;
- a sense of motivation and expectation of success;
- a predisposition to engage in a meaningful learning experience
  (Walsh, 2007: 81–2).

These characteristics will help you to get the most out of your assessment.

Purposes of WBL assessment – the 'why'

WBL assessment enables you to:

- gain qualifications and provide the university with a way to judge
  your performance;
- demonstrate your learning;
- develop yourself;
- improve your career opportunities;
- improve your workplace performance.

Traditionally Higher Education (HE) has focused on the quality assurance aspects of assessment, that is, the standards of qualifications, and issues concerned with judging your performance against these. These quality aspects still remain vital and are one of the mainstays which indicate to universities your ability to perform in society and in the workplace. However, assessment is also seen as a vehicle to enable you to get the most out of your learning experience and to perform to the best of your ability. Assessment for Learning strategies are a way for you to enjoy your learning experience, gain considerable achievement and to reach your full potential.

Race and Brown (1998) suggest that good assessment, should also:

- motivate you;
- enable your progression onto further learning;
- diagnose your faults and help you to rectify mistakes;
- offer you a variety of learning experiences;
- make you 'get down to serious learning'.

Assessment strategies such as these should be an integral part of any WBL programme.

Exercise 4.3: The purpose of assessment

What, for you, should be the main criteria (as outlined above) with regard to the purpose of assessment?

Does the assessment on your chosen WBL programme enable you to meet your key criteria?

● Negotiating assessment in work-based learning

Boud and Solomon (2001: 47) identify that characteristically WBL not only focuses on the needs of the workplace, where the learning is both purposeful for both you and your organization, but also provides 'an excellent example of a learner-centred approach'. In traditional education interaction revolves around the 'teacher' determining and disseminating the content of the course (syllabus) on which you are tested. In work-based learning there is a shift with you, as learner, taking a much more proactive role. Key to this is your responsibility for the negotiation of your learning and how it is assessed (some programmes will use this negotiation much more than others, check with your course tutor). Your tutor will expect that the learning agreed should challenge you, extend you and encourage you to explore new boundaries. The idea that you have the power to negotiate much of your learning and assessment feels rather alien at first, but it gives you increased ownership which makes the assessment process far less intimidating.

WBL programmes are more flexible about the specific nature of the learning you undertake and you might often encounter what are referred to as 'generic' or 'empty box modules' (Chapter 2), which allow you to negotiate elements of your study. You produce a coherent learning contract (which in itself may be assessed – Chapter 3), which brings together the generic and specific elements of the learning and lays out the details of the focus of your programme and the details of the modules to be undertaken and assessed. You will negotiate with your tutor and sometimes with your workplace.

Areas that might be open to negotiation:

- *Aims and outcomes* of your intended programme of study – unique to you.
- *Focus of assessment* – for example, semi-structured question or unstructured?
    - Semi-structured: 'How do you think leadership and management might be improved in your own organization? Draw upon good and bad practice that you have encountered in your workplace'.
    - Unstructured: work with your tutor to agree a suitable title and scope for your assessed piece(s) of work.
- *Method of assessment* – see the section 'Different types of WBL assessment – the variety (and the diversity)' below, for many examples.
- *Level of study* – depending on previous academic learning; experience; role and level of responsibility in the workplace, and so on.
- *Size of module* – decided by complexity and scope.
- *Timescale* – flexible, but still fair to other students with fixed hand-in dates and so on.

Areas which are likely to be non-negotiable:

- University regulations.
- The overarching aims and outcomes of the programme.
- Final hand in dates (linked to university academic boards – see below).
- Word count (linked to the size/level of the module).

- Standard academic requirements relating to presentation of work, referencing and so on.
- Issues relating to confidentiality and ethics.

Linking learning and assessment

When you are planning and negotiating your study, remember the vital link between the learning process and its assessment. This is at the forefront of designing assessment used in HE and it is sometimes referred to as constructive alignment (Biggs, 1999: 27; Walsh, 2007: 79; HEA Engineering Subject Centre, 2009). There should be a clear link between the objectives of the course or module, the teaching and learning activities undertaken during the course and how and when these are assessed. You need to consider this alignment when planning and negotiating your study (see Figures 4.1 and 4.2).

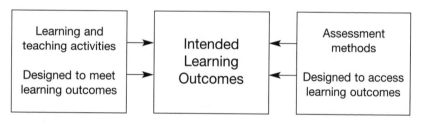

Figure 4.1   Aligning learning outcomes, learning and teaching activities and the assessment
Source: Adapted from Houghton (2004).

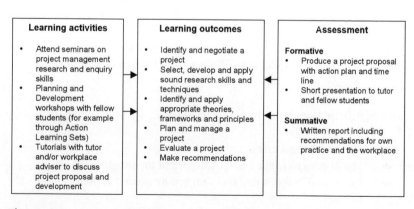

Figure 4.2   An example of Figure 4.1 in a work-based project

Level and volume of learning

All students need to know that their learning is calculated in terms of level and volume (Chapters 1 and 2); however, as a work-based learner who may be negotiating the content and assessment of your own programme it is even more crucial that you have a good understanding of these concepts. All UK HE qualifications map onto the levels used in the National Framework for Higher Education Qualifications (QAA, 2001). Table 4.1, based upon the Ufi, learndirect Learning through Work level descriptors © Ufi Limited 2001, gives an indication of the different expectations at each level.

The required facets are also listed here:

- *Context* in which you are expected to apply the learning.
- *Complexity* of the study and your *responsibility* within it.
- Depth and extent of *thinking and understanding.*
- Degree of *investigation and evaluation* you are required to demonstrate.
- Amount of *innovation* and *originality* you should exhibit.

Referring at regular intervals to these level descriptors, alongside those used by your own university, will help you to ensure that you are working at the correct level. Other examples of level descriptors in common use in WBL are NICATS (2001) and SEEC (2001).

How do we measure the amount of learning? Volume = Credits

Most university qualifications (including WBL ones) are divided up into chunks of learning (usually called modules). Each module will normally be designated a 'size', which means the number of credit points it represents. Most universities have a system of notional student workload where each credit point equates to 10 hours of learning, including attendance in classes or seminars, private/independent study, reflection in the workplace and writing up of your assessment (Chapter 2). A typical full-time undergraduate degree normally takes three academic years to complete (see Table 4.2).

Therefore a typical BA or BSc (Hons) requires 120 credits at each of three levels giving you a total of 360 credits. Each level is broken down into modules, so for example, you might do 8 modules at 15 credits to get to 120, or you might do fewer modules worth more – say 6 modules at 20 credits. All universities operate slightly different systems. Many WBL awards are much

Column 1 HE LEVEL*	Column 2 Typical higher education QUALIFICATIONS within each level	Column 3 What it means to study at this level?** LEVEL DESCRIPTOR
	UNDERGRADUATE	
4	*Certificates of Higher Education (CertHE)*	At **Level 4**, *you will:* • *be thinking through and reviewing courses of action, making informed judgements on issues which affect your work, and coping effectively with a range of unfamiliar situations and problems* • *need to be able to use your understanding of principles which apply to your work, as well as producing your own ideas and developing innovative responses* • *need to be able to carry out small-scale practical investigations, and review the appropriateness of different options*
5	*Foundation Degree (FD)* *Diplomas of Higher Education (DipHE)* *Higher National Diplomas (HND)* *Higher National Certificates (HNC)*	At **Level 5**, *you will* • *be thinking through and reviewing courses of action, including for their impact outside of your immediate work* • *be making informed judgements on issues which affect your work, and coping effectively with a range of unfamiliar situations and problems* • *need to be able to draw on a broad personal or formal knowledge-base and set of concepts which apply to your work, as well as producing your own ideas and developing innovative responses* • *be able to develop your own theories and find ways forward when faced with contradictions and dilemmas* • *need to be able to carry out small-scale practical research in relation to your work*

6	Bachelor's degrees with honours (BA/BSc (Hons)) Ordinary degrees(BA/BSc) Graduate Diplomas (Grad Dip) Graduate Certificates (Grad Cert)	*At **Level 6**, you will* • *be thinking through, understanding and reviewing different courses of action, including for their impact outside of your immediate area of work. You will be making informed judgements on issues which affect your work, and working effectively with unpredictable issues* • *need to be able to draw on a broad personal or formal knowledge-base as well as concepts, theories and models which apply to your work* • *be producing your own ideas and practical theories, and developing innovative responses in complex situations* • *be able to manage dilemmas and find ways forward in problematic situations.* • *need to be able to design and make use of practical, methodologically sound research to contribute to your work or that of your organization*
7	**POSTGRADUATE** Master's degrees (MA/MSc) Postgraduate Diplomas (PG Dip) Postgraduate Certificates (PGCert)	• *be developing thought-through courses of action which take into account alternative implications and issues beyond your immediate area of practice. You will be making informed judgements on issues which affect your work, and working effectively with unpredictable issues* • *need to be able to draw on mastery of a broad personal or formal knowledge-base relating to the area of your work and its wider context, as well as developing and evaluating concepts, theories and models which apply to your work* • *be producing your own ideas and practical theories, and developing innovative responses in complex and unpredictable situations* • *be able to manage dilemmas and value-conflicts and find ways forward in problematic situations. One of the features of this level is that you will need to consider issues beyond your immediate area of practice, and take a critical approach to the thinking and assumptions which you and others are using* • *need to be able to design and make use of practical, methodologically sound research to contribute to your work or that of your organization*

continued overleaf

Table 4.1 University HE qualification framework and level descriptors

Column 1	Column 2	Column 3
HE **LEVEL***	Typical higher education **QUALIFICATIONS** within each level	What it means to study at this level?** **LEVEL DESCRIPTOR**
8	*Doctoral degrees (PhD, D.Prof)*	At **Level 8**, you will:
• be developing thought-through courses of action which take into account alternative implications and issues beyond your professional discipline or area of practice.
• be making informed judgements on issues which affect your discipline or area of practice, and working effectively with unpredictable issues.
• need to be able to draw on critical and creative mastery of a broad range of concepts, theories and practices, as well as being aware of the assumptions underlying them from perspectives which go beyond individual disciplines and contexts
• be producing your own ideas and theories and developing innovative responses in complex and unpredictable situations; you should be able to manage dilemmas and value-conflicts and find ways forward in problematic situations, including those which go beyond your organization or discipline. One of the features of this level is that you will be taking forward an area of practice in a way which is of value beyond your organization or community of practice, and developing as a leading practitioner in your field
• need to be able to design and make use of practical, methodologically sound research which contributes to your area of practice, and which results in new understandings or approaches which extend or redefine existing knowledge or practice

*   (QAA, 2001). This document sets out the nature and characteristic of qualifications at each level.
** Based upon the Ufi LearnDirect Learning through Work level descriptors (Ufi LearnDirect, 2001).

Table 4.1 *continued*

Academic year	FHEQ level (see Table 4.1)	Credit points to study at each level	Notional student workload (hours)
1	4	120	1200
2	5	120	1200
3	6	120	1200

Table 4.2 Typical volumes of credit

shorter than a full degree, for example, you may have enrolled on a University Certificate which equates to 60 credits at Level 4. The size of programme will be dependent upon your learning needs and possibly the requirements of your employer. A Master's Award (postgraduate Level 7) requires 180 credits. The first 60 credits can be taken independently as a Postgraduate Certificate, while 120 credits make up the Postgraduate Diploma. If you are undertaking Doctoral study, this requires 540 credits (180 at Level 7, 360 at Level 8).

Different types of WBL assessment – the variety (and the diversity)

University assessment brings exams to mind; a large hall with desks neatly spaced out and three hours in which to write four essays. The good news is that exams are rarely, if ever, used in the assessment of work-based learning! Other assessments typically used at university include essays and reports, multiple choice tests, dissertations and oral presentations. These are entirely suited to the kinds of courses on which they are used and you may come across them if your course allows you to mix WBL with other more traditional taught modules. Some of these methods have been adapted to allow for innovations in learning and teaching (for example, the use of technology or take-away papers and open book exams), while other methods of assessment reflect the particular focus of the degree in question, for example, a student teacher will be assessed partly on their performance in the classroom during teaching practice, while a fine arts student will be assessed upon their final year show where they exhibit a collection of sculptures or paintings. In WBL we not only assess 'traditional academic forms of learning', we also assess 'tacit' knowledge – that is, knowledge which has been gained through the experience of work – which is often not written down anywhere – but is kept in our own heads and acted upon; tapping into this knowledge requires innovative forms of assessment. This section gives a flavour of what you might expect by describing some of the WBL assessment methods commonly used by universities – you will probably not come across all of these, and indeed your programme may utilize further approaches.

Learning contracts (also known as learning agreements and learning plans)

Chapter 3 discusses learning contracts in detail; however, as it is quite common for the construction and content of the learning contract itself to form part of the assessment process it is worth mentioning them again here. You will probably find that a standard proforma is used on which you give a written critical account of where you are now, your aims and objectives and how you intend to achieve them. Once completed, the contract is submitted for assessment, and assuming it is of an acceptable standard (it will be marked and graded by some universities), provides the 'map' for the rest of your learning journey (see Chapter 3, 'Learning contracts').

Accreditation of Prior Experiential Learning (APEL)

In your learning contract you plan ahead; with the APEL process you look back, to ascertain whether learning you have already undertaken might be useful now. In order to claim for entry to your new programme, or use it to gain exemption from certain elements of that programme, or indeed include it in the programme as relevant content, you will need to evidence the level and nature of the learning. Chapter 2 addresses APEL in far greater depth, but it is worth mentioning again here because many universities include the process in modules which are assessed, perhaps called: 'Recognizing and Assessing Learning'; 'Making your Learning Count'; or 'Evidencing Prior Professional Learning'. You will be assessed on the quality (that is, not the quantity!) of the evidence which demonstrates the learning that has taken place and the extent of your critical reflection upon this. Evidence can be presented in a variety of ways including a portfolio of evidence with commentary (electronic or hard copy) or by oral presentation. Oral evidence is usually recorded for the purposes of quality assurance (see below).

Work-based projects

This is one of the most common forms of WBL to be assessed by universities. Chapter 5 gives you all the details you need for this important area. The key thing to bear in mind is that a work-based project is a piece of real work that you are required to do, as part of your job, and upon which you reflect to show what you have learnt, hence making it assessable.

Portfolios

'Portfolio' literally means a 'folder' in which papers are carried; in assessment terms the portfolio brings together the evidence acquired and matched against the assessment criteria, to demonstrate the learning achieved. Evidence comes in a variety of formats including paper-based, artefacts and audio-visual. It is increasingly likely that you will find you are expected to complete an online/electronic portfolio, the format of this is usually provided by your university although some students design their own. Your tutor will want to see how you have illustrated the coherence of what you have learnt through analysis, critical reflection and discourse; that is, how it all links together and the thinking that has gone behind it to create a coherent submission. Portfolios are widely used in WBL assessment because of their versatility, but please don't confuse versatility with randomness – a file full of mismatched unexplained bits and pieces will never get you a good mark! Hopefully, you will be invited to develop your portfolio throughout the course, submit it for formative assessment and feedback and then submit at the end of the programme for summative assessment (see the section 'Methods, process and procedures – the "how"' below), building upon the good advice you have received.

Reflective diaries, learning journals and critical incident logs

Self-assessment is a really good habit to cultivate, by writing about how you are progressing from week to week you will maximize upon your formal assessment opportunities. As you write, either by hand or keyboard, you will find that your thoughts seem more 'real' and in turn help you to clarify what it is exactly that you are learning. This forms the basis for you to reflect upon your learning process and to begin to put your learning into practice. The more you write in your diary, journal or log the more material (evidence) you will have when it comes to analysing and evaluating your experience; this will enhance your final assignment immeasurably. This more informal approach to learning and assessment has the potential to liberate you if you feel self-conscious or inexperienced about the more academic style of writing. It allows you to show your tutor how your ideas have developed over time as you become increasingly confident and more aware of underlying theories and principles (Ramage, 2005: 102; Dunn et al., 2004: 164).

Reflective diaries

These are used to note your key work activities and allow you to reflect on what has been learnt in order to perform better in the future. Used mostly for formative self-assessment, these diaries are initially private to you.

Learning journals

Sometimes extracts from a reflective diary can be included in summative assessment as evidence of reflection upon your learning. If they are to be used for assessment there needs to be a clear mechanism for providing a public version, often called a learning journal.

Critical incident logs

Critical incident logs encourage a move way from a descriptive approach to learning. These require you to focus on a key event; often one that took you out of your comfort zone, for example, a tricky meeting, a complex report, or a difficult case; and to comment on:

- A brief description of what happened with a particular focus on your actions
- Relevant theories or concepts drawn upon
- Courses of action you did /did not take and why?
- How you would tackle a similar situation in another circumstance?
- What learning you took from the incident
- Implications for future practice. (Brown and Glasner, 1999)

Collaborative assignments and group assessments

You may be asked to work in groups to identify, address and write up a shared idea/project. This could be based on a real-life piece of work, or a hypothetical scenario – but both will require you to use many of your workplace skills. Your tutor will be looking for evidence that each individual has addressed and met the learning outcomes. Sometimes there will be a group assessment task, for example, a joint presentation, but you will often be required to submit an individual piece of work for grading purposes, demonstrating your personal contribution. However, the key here is to bear in mind that the more you put in collectively, the more you will each draw from it in the longer term; enabling you to benefit from the strengths and knowledge of others; replicating team-work in practice. There may be an expectation to use technology to deliver this collaborative work, for example through blogs, wikis, social networking sites and so on (Chapter 7).

Reports

Many WBL programmes ask you to present your substantive assessed work through a professional report. You may well be comfortable with this approach, as it is probably more familiar to you than academic-style essays. Whether you are already writing reports regularly for work purposes, or have in fact written very few, report writing is an incredibly useful skill for you to hone and develop as most workplace roles require some level of this, indeed for some employees it is a key part of their job. There are many excellent guides (online and in print) that will be able to help you structure and focus your reports (try also searching your own university's 'study skills' pages). Some key points to bear in mind are shown in Box 4.1.

Box 4.1: Report writing: Some key points to bear in mind

- Ensure you have a clearly defined objective/purpose
- Know what type of report you are writing, for example:
  - management report
  - feasibility study
  - laboratory/scientific report.
- Be concise and specific – avoid waffle and padding
- Know your readership, that is, who you are writing the report for – this will affect the style of the language used and how much technical language/jargon is appropriate. Always explain any abbreviations in full the first time you use them.
- Aim to have a set of recommendations which will emerge at the end of the report and a clear conclusion.
- Avoid including material that is extra to requirements and use tables and figures where appropriate.
- Provide clear evidence for any arguments you put forward and make your sources as relevant and up-to-date as possible. If you are reporting on your own research check your data for accuracy, objectivity, reliability and validity.
- Ensure sections and subsections follow a logical sequence:
  - Terms of reference/Acknowledgements
  - Abstract/Synopsis/Summary
  - Contents page
  - Aims /Objectives
  - Introduction
  - Method
  - Findings/Results
  - Conclusions/Recommendations
  - References/Bibliography
  - Appendices

● Methods, process and procedures – the 'how'

Formative and summative assessment and feedback

The key to understanding the difference between formative and summative assessment is to think about the purpose of the assessment. Assessment used to mean the end of course exams or tests to show how much has been learnt (or retained in the short-term memory). This is what we call *summative assessment* (that is, coming at the end of the learning process). Much more common in WBL, and much more useful as a tool for assessing learning, is what is called *formative assessment,* where feedback is used to make comments on work-in-progress (but usually not given a mark). You then learn from assessment as you progress and hopefully improve your performance. Sometimes this process is called 'feed-forward' – a useful term which prioritizes the idea that the comments you receive will help you as you move forward. Key to successful formative assessment is the feedback you receive from your tutor, your fellow learners and your workplace supervisor or mentor. Formative assessment can also be helpful to your tutor, for example if everyone is clearly struggling with the same part of the formative assignment it might signal to the tutor that they need to cover a certain point again or approach it in a different way.

You must meet the timescales set out by your tutor and not over-step the mark in how much assistance you can reasonably expect to be given. All students should be treated equitably, and given fair and equal access to the tutor's expertise and support. You should clarify what is/is not permitted with regard to formative feedback on drafts, and ensure that you make the most of every feedback and feed-forward opportunity.

Self and peer assessment

There will be opportunities to undertake self-assessments on your progress; you need to look at the aims, learning outcomes and assessment criteria of your programme and reflect upon your work, judging its appropriateness and providing an indication of your progress. Even if this is not a formal process, you should do it for yourself. It helps you to become more critical about your practice and keeps you on course towards attaining a respectable mark/grade. The flowchart (Figure 4.3) shows how you might build in self-assessment to get the best possible outcome, while Exercise 4.4 provides a checklist for planning and implementing self-assessment.

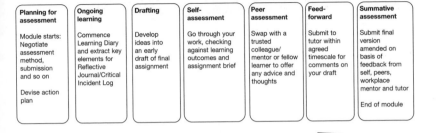

Planning for assessment	Ongoing learning	Drafting	Self-assessment	Peer assessment	Feed-forward	Summative assessment
Module starts: Negotiate assessment method, submission and so on Devise action plan	Commence Learning Diary and extract key elements for Reflective Journal/Critical Incident Log	Develop ideas into an early draft of final assignment	Go through your work, checking against learning outcomes and assignment brief	Swap with a trusted colleague/ mentor or fellow learner to offer any advice and thoughts	Submit to tutor within agreed timescale for comments on your draft	Submit final version amended on basis of feedback from self, peers, workplace mentor and tutor End of module

Figure 4.3   A formative assessment model for work-based learning

Peer assessment is where students on the same programme assess each other's work, for example, through presentations. On some programmes peer assessment can go towards the final mark. As a WBL student you are encouraged to develop informal peer-assessment arrangements with fellow students in order to network, give and receive feedback, which will enhance performance and promote reflection.

Rules and regulations – the nuts and bolts

Universities adhere to standard codes of practice; these will be issued to you in the form of a handbook (see below) of university regulations which ensure that the quality and reputation of UK higher education is upheld. You can be reassured that your programme being partly or entirely based in the work-place, and perhaps not feeling or looking like a traditional university course, does not mean that it is any way of a lesser standard; it has been rigorously checked in terms of design and delivery in line with the guidelines set out by the Quality Assurance Agency (QAA – the UK governing body). The QAA have recently published a new code of practice in which they recognize that many HE programmes are now work-based (QAA, 2007 (amended January 2008)).

Handbooks

Upon enrolment you will be given several key documents (hard copy and/or electronic), for example handbooks on university assessment regulations, your programme and modules to be studied. It is worth your while familiariz-ing yourself with these as they may offer you some useful ways of maximizing your assessment performance (alongside helpful information about other aspects of your course). See below for examples of the information you might find in your handbooks which will help you to complete your assessment,

Exercise 4.4: How do you measure up?

Self-assessment checklist for planning and carrying out assessed work

Before you start

	✔ Notes/Questions

Planning for assessment

Have you read and do you understand the:

- Student handbook;
- Module/unit/programme handbook(s);
- University assessment regulations?

Your university should issue you (hard copy or online) their equivalents of all of these. If you have not received these ask for them from your tutor or course/ programme administrator

Have you identified what help you need and accessed information on Student Study Skills and read about assessment and assignment issues?

Your university will have comprehensive student study support provision. You will find details of how to access this in your student handbooks. Don't expect to have this handed on a plate – you have a responsibility to access the support and advice you need.

Have you read and do you understand the assessment brief/instructions:

● Aims and learning outcomes;
● Marking criteria and how marks will be awarded;
● What the learning outcomes require you to demonstrate;
● Word count/portfolio size/presentation length;
● Presentational style;
● Hand in dates and submission arrangements?

At the planning stage

Have you negotiated with your tutor regarding the assignment task/brief?

Are you clear about what your tutor is wanting from your assessed work?
Do you know what you have to:

● do;
● know;
● apply;
● reflect upon;
● present?

Have you produced a Plan of Action with realistic timescales (see Figure 4.4)

Have you clarified any outstanding issues with your tutor?
Do you now feel ready to proceed with your assessed work?

✔   **Notes/Questions**

Doing the assessed work

Are you doing all the necessary reading and enquiry in order to proceed?

Are you keeping to your plan, if not have you re-scheduled your work, negotiated changes in focus/timescale/submission with your tutor?

Are you regularly checking what you are doing against the assessment brief and criteria to ensure you are on track?

Are you attending tutorials, seminars and so on and keeping in contact with your tutor?

Have you spoken to peers about the assessment and shared ideas and concerns?

Preparing for submission

Have you carefully proofread your submission?
Have you got someone else to read it?
Have you made the necessary revisions?

Have you met the requirements for presentational style?

● Front cover including title, your name, name of the module/programme and reference number – *you can be penalized for this if not done correctly, it frustrates the marker, and it could get lost*

- Contents list
- Structure – *often you will be provided with a recommended format*
- Ethics and confidentiality
- Headings/sub-headings/numbering/figures/tables – *good navigation is essential*
- Appendices

If you are doing a presentation, have you practised and ensured it meets the requirements for time and structure?

Have you undertaken a final self-assessment matching your work against the module/programme aims, learning outcomes and marking criteria?

If you need more time or have a personal circumstance that's preventing you completing your work have you

- checked the submission regulations;
- negotiated an extension with your tutor;
- completed the necessary forms, got them signed and submitted them on time?

Submission

Complete the necessary assessment submission form – submit on time – know where to submit.

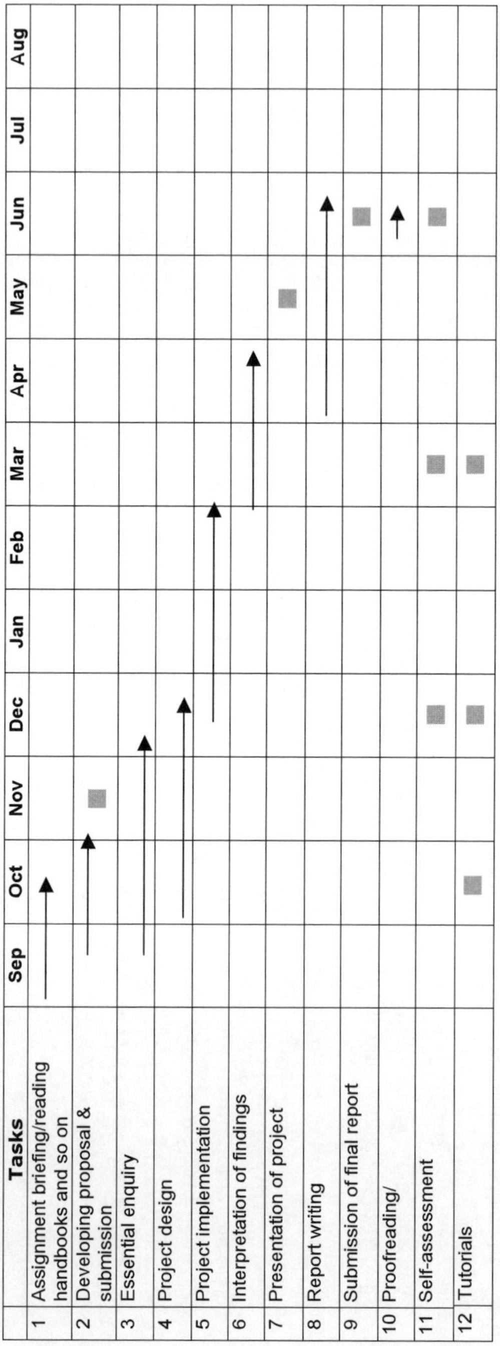

Tasks	Sep	Oct	Nov	Dec	Jan	Feb	Mar	Apr	May	Jun	Jul	Aug
1 Assignment briefing/reading handbooks and so on												
2 Developing proposal & submission												
3 Essential enquiry												
4 Project design												
5 Project implementation												
6 Interpretation of findings												
7 Presentation of project												
8 Report writing												
9 Submission of final report												
10 Proofreading/												
11 Self-assessment												
12 Tutorials												

Figure 4.4   Example of a Gantt chart showing timelines

such as the module's aims and outcomes – your assignment clearly has to address these – and also, vitally, the assessment brief and criteria, and the marking criteria.

Aims

The module's aims set out the purpose of the module (or programme) and what it is attempting to achieve (Box 4.2).

Box 4.2: Typical work-based learning module aims

The aims of this module are to:

1. Enhance the learner's individual effectiveness, employability and/or business competitiveness by locating the learning and development in his/her own organization.
2. Extend the learner's capability, promote personal development and a range of inter-personal, intellectual and practical (functional) skills and knowledge based around and demonstrated through an individually negotiated real-time work-based project that will be of benefit to their organization.

Source: Adapted from: 'Northumbria University – Work-based Project Module Descriptor Level 6'.

Learning outcomes

These provide a breakdown of what you are expected to achieve (and demonstrate) at the end of the module (Box 4.3). To do well in your assessment it is vitally important that you address these learning outcomes; they will be closely aligned to your assessment brief (see below).

Box 4.3: Typical work-based learning module outcomes

By the end of the module (*WBL project in this case*) the learner will be able to:

● Identify and negotiate a project that addresses own personal goals and organizational/professional requirement.
● Select, develop and apply appropriate practical, methodologically sound research skills and techniques.
● Draw on, apply and review considerable prior knowledge and new learning to changing situations.

- Extend a wide range of specialized technical, creative and/or conceptual skills that apply to his/her work in order to make informed judgements.
- Identify and apply appropriate theories, frameworks and principles relevant to the issues/situations addressed in the project in order to consolidate and extend a systematic and coherent body of knowledge that applies to his/her discipline.
- Plan and manage a project within an agreed framework, dealing with unpredictable situations, making informed judgements and managing dilemmas, which include those that impact outside the immediate work area.
- Evaluate a project, drawing upon concepts, models and theories to support own ideas and innovative responses through oral presentation and written report.
- Make recommendations for own professional development and that of the organization and propose a strategy for implementation.

Source: Adapted from: 'Northumbria University – Work-based Project Module Descriptor Level 6'.

Assessment brief

Fundamental to your needs as a learner is the desire to know what is expected of you:

- 'How many words are expected in this assignment?'
- 'Do I have to reference theory?'
- 'What happens if I miss the deadline?'
- 'Does it have to be word processed?'
- 'How much time do I have?'

The assessment brief (Box 4.4) is your best friend in the entire assessment process (in conjunction with the learning outcomes mentioned above); ignore it at your peril! This is what you are being asked to do.

Box 4.4: Typical work-based learning assessment brief

The summative assessment for the Module will be through the submission of a work-based project report, which should demonstrate how the stated assessment criteria have been met (see Box 4.5). This module offers 20 credit points. In order to achieve the 20 points you must successfully achieve a pass mark of 40% at undergraduate or 50% at postgraduate for the report.

You are required to submit for assessment a report which will comprise of a study report (for example, 4000 words for 20 credits) incorporating the proposal, presentation and supporting evidence.

Assessment criteria

The assessment criteria set out the requirements of the assessment brief (as described above) and identify what it is your tutors are looking for in your submitted work. It is really important that you take the time early on to understand them and to keep checking your work against them. You will need to consider them in conjunction with the learning outcomes and marking criteria for your module.

Box 4.5: Example of assessment criteria for a Level 6 work-based project

- Appropriateness of the work-based project in terms of relevance to the work role, academic level and learning and development needs of the learner.
- Use of principles relevant to the issues/situations addressed in the project.
- Ability to negotiate a project proposal (500 words, formatively assessed).
- Ability to manage under guidance, record, analyse and reflect upon the work-based project.
- Ability to demonstrate an in-depth knowledge and understanding of their immediate area of work and its relevance to the project.
- Ability to carry out small-scale practical investigations and review the appropriateness of different options, taking into consideration relevant ethical, commercial, confidential and data protection issues.
- Application of knowledge, experience and new learning to a range of workplace problems.
- Ability to make recommendations for further development of the project, which are clear, concise and realistic.
- Ability to present the project through the use of oral presentation (15 minutes, formatively assessed) and written report (4000 words, summatively assessed) in an appropriate academic format to academic assessor and line manager.

Marking criteria

This is usually a standardized university document which sets a benchmark of expectations and shows how your final marks are awarded and which parts carry more weight (see Box 4.6 for example).

Assessment success is often about going back to basics and following simple steps.

TIP   **Meeting the assessment requirements – six steps to success!**

- Read the module learning outcomes, assessment brief, assessment criteria and marking criteria carefully.
- Read them again! Make sure you understand what is being asked of you. If not, seek advice.
- Break the assessment brief and criteria down to identify key words such as verbs – that is, *what* are you being asked to *do* and any other key words and phrases.
- Use this to plan out your assessment/break it down into sections.
- Prioritize the sections and allocate your word count on this basis – that is, don't use 30 per cent of your word count on an introductory/scene setting section that doesn't address the brief, and carries 5 per cent of the marks!
- Keep referring back to your plan while you are writing (stick it on the wall in front of your desk!).

Academic misconduct

As in the workplace, trust and integrity are vital elements of any university programme and there are strict rules governing what is known as academic misconduct (cheating), from marking your work down and/or failing that particular module, to, in extreme cases, expulsion from the programme.

TIP   **Avoid these common types of academic misconduct**

- Cheating, for example, during a formal examination.
- Plagiarism that is, *unacknowledged* incorporation into your work of material derived from the work (published or unpublished) of another.
- Collusion, for example, collaborating with another student/person in the completion of work with the intention of one of you submitting that work as the work of one person.
- Falsification, for example, making up data or references.
- Impersonation of another to gain benefit in assessment.
- Ghosting, for example, submitting as your own, work which has been produced by another person on your behalf.

Submission arrangements

Follow to the letter any instructions you are given relating to the submission of your work. Failure to do so could severely jeopardize your position.

TIP   **Before submitting your work, check the following**

- *Deadline* – date/time? – aim to get it in well before the final cut-off point.
- *Where* do you hand it in?
- *Electronic submission* – is it allowed?
- *Posting* your work – have you allowed time for it to arrive?
- *Coversheet* – do you need one? Have you completed it, if you do?
- *Key information* – module code, student ID number etc?
- *Name/student number* on every page or artefact.
- *Page numbers* – usually in a footer.
- *Multiple copies* – how many required?
- *Receipt* for your work – make sure you get one.
- *Your copy* – always keep a back-up copy of your work – sometimes things go astray.

If things go wrong – don't panic!

Things sometimes go wrong and this can feel like the last straw if you are already trying to juggle the demands of a job, a family and study. If you do encounter a problem (personal, health or work-related) you must communicate this to your tutor as soon as possible, don't leave it until you have a crisis on your hands. Universities will be as accommodating as possible, and depending on the circumstances will work to try and find a way to help you to carry on with your studies. This might involve requesting that a deadline be extended or a more formal process, known as personal extenuating circumstances. The most important thing to do is to keep in close contact with your course tutor who will be able to advise you on relevant procedures.

Marking and moderation

Imagine you've finished your assessment, having followed all the advice above, and handed it in on time. You should be feeling pretty pleased with yourself and probably a little relieved. So what happens now? You might be thinking 'Thank goodness that's over – I never want to see that again'. However, you probably want to know what happens to your hard work once you have submitted it. Normally your work will be marked by your tutor, who will pay close attention to the marking criteria, assessment brief and learning outcomes. If you have handed in two copies you may find that your tutor will

Box 4.6: Example of marking criteria (Level 6)

%marks used as guide by assessor in determining final mark.	Development of topic 25%	Academic rigour 25%
Outstanding work. Logical, analytical well structured 80–100	Innovative use of knowledge and principles which progresses the topic.	High level of integration showing originality and well-substantiated argument.
Excellent work with detailed analysis 70–79	Imaginative development of knowledge applied to the question.	Detailed analysis and sustained level of argument throughout. Questioned the work of others
Good work sound knowledge and understanding 60–69	Highly relevant use of knowledge and application of principles to the question.	Evidence of critical approach, incorporating some logical argument. Incorporated the work of other authors.
Clear pass knowledge and understanding could be developed 50–59	Clear evidence that each area of the question has been addressed.	Engaged in discussion and development of ideas/topic.
Pass content limited 40–49	Evidence that each area of the question has been given some consideration.	Descriptive account. Basic level of knowledge and understanding.
Poor clearly inadequate 30–39	Limited evidence of addressing the areas of the question.	Evidence of error, or limitations, in knowledge which shows lack of familiarity with topic.
Unacceptable clear lack of knowledge and/or understanding 0–29	Inadequate development of topic/failure to answer the question.	Very superficial showing poor use of knowledge.

Reflective practice 35%	Use of work-based & literary resources & Referencing 10%	Presentation and Structure 5%
Logical development of theory/practice links.	Extensive use of resources appropriate to topic. Supported by sound referencing.	Logical development. Fluent and engages reader. No flaws in language, grammar and spelling. Accurate academic style.
Clear development of theory/practice links.	Well rounded use of resources. Referencing appropriate.	Well structured, clear development of ideas. Majority of work is expressed clearly. Grammar and spelling accurate
Clear and appropriate theory supporting practice development.	Good use of resources. Referencing sound.	Clear and appropriate structure has been adopted. Most ideas expressed clearly. Only minor error in grammar and spelling.
Some limitations in theory informing practice development	Balanced selection of resources. Minor Referencing errors.	Structure apparent but has some limitations. Language mainly fluent. Grammar and spelling mainly accurate.
Provides basics of integration of theory and practice in reflective activity	Adequate use of resources. Some referencing errors	Basic structure provided. Use of language not always fluent. Meaning apparent although, grammatical and spelling errors.
Poor integration significant errors and/or omissions in theory in practice development.	Inadequate use of resources. Many referencing errors	Poor structure. Language, grammar and/or spelling poor. Errors affect meaning of work.
Inadequate attention to theory in practice development	No evidence of reading around the subject or reference to work-based sources. Numerous referencing errors	Little care evident in relation to structure, use of language, grammar, and spelling. Badly affects meaning of work.

write comments in the margin, and that copy will be returned to you. Normally they will also complete some form of summary sheet which will give you overall comments and a percentage mark, grade or pass/fail – depending on the grading structure of the module in question.

Once your tutor has completed the marking they will pass a sample of assignments to an academic colleague who will second-mark this work, checking against the marking criteria. This will normally be followed by a meeting between the two markers to discuss the work and possibly agree to amend marks either upwards or downwards. If they are unable to agree then a third marker, or moderator, is asked to give an overall opinion. Once this process has taken place you may get your work returned to you with a 'provisional' mark.

External examination

Universities are very proud and protective of their autonomy because it means that they are able to design, develop, deliver and award university level qualifications themselves. This autonomy relies on a system of self-regulation, whereby universities undertake to maintain standards between themselves, using among other things, a system of external examining. Each university award (including WBL ones) has an external examiner from another HEI who provides a neutral, unbiased (but expert) point of view.

Once internal marking and moderation has taken place, a sample of work will be sent to the external examiner who will again check that it is of a correct level and standard to merit the mark or grade that it has been awarded.

Exam boards (modular and progression/award)

The final piece of the jigsaw is the exam board. This is a formal committee. At the module exam board all marks for people on your module or course are considered and confirmed. This is followed by the progression and award board which will look at your individual profile and determine whether you continue onto the next stage of your course or, if at the end of the course, whether you are awarded the qualification. Once these exam boards have met, the results will normally be posted up in a public place (for example, course notice-board or virtual learning environment). You will also be sent, or given access to an electronic version of, a transcript detailing your marks and/or final award.

Fails and appeals

If you fail a module or any part of your award your university will have procedures in place to deal with this. Depending upon your marks you may be allowed to re-sit the assessment or sometimes required to re-sit the actual learning process or module – which obviously will take longer. You will not be allowed to re-sit sections as often as you wish – there will be rules (individual to your institution) and a cut-off point after which time you will be seen as having failed the course/route/award.

If you have a complaint against the university or wish to appeal against a decision, there are set procedures to enable you to do this. These should be available to you and normally posted on the university website. If you feel that you have been treated unfairly, you might wish to seek advice from the National Union of Students, who will have a local branch at your university.

Your roles and responsibilities – the bottom line

You are in the driving seat. Much of the responsibility for your learning and for ensuring you meet assessment requirements rests with you. While you will be provided with a great deal of information and support, don't expect to be spoon fed. *'I wasn't told about this'* is rarely accepted as an excuse about assessed work. If you don't know something then it's up to you to find out!

Summary

1   Know clearly what the programme and the tutor expects of you.

2   Negotiate with your tutor/workplace on the assignment task and presentation for assessment.

3   Choose an area that is important to you and excites and interests you.

4   Make sure it is realistic and feasible. Don't be over ambitious.

5   Plan and pace yourself (Figure 4.4 provides an exemplar timeline).

6   Keep to the rules regarding word count, submission, presentation, referencing and so on.

7	Don't go off on a tangent.
8	Don't waste words on endless description; keep it succinct and to the point – your tutor would rather see analysis and reflection.
9	Consult with your peers, share your ideas about your assessment, ask for their comments.
10	Draw on work colleagues and workplace advisers for support, to bounce ideas around and 'open doors'.
11	Be clear on the marking criteria.
12	Don't cheat or plagiarize. You are likely to be found out and the penalties are severe!
13	Maintain an ethical and confidential stance in your work.
14	Proofread your work thoroughly and get someone you can trust to be honest with you to read it too.

References

Biggs, J. (1999) *Teaching for Quality Learning at University: What the Student Does* (Buckingham: Society for Research into Higher Education and Open University Press).

Boud, D. and Solomon, N. (2001) *Work-based Learning: A New Higher Education?* (Buckingham: Society for Research into Higher Education and Open University Press).

Brown, S. and Glasner, A. (1999) *Assessment Matters in Higher Education: Choosing and Using Diverse Approaches* (Buckingham: Society for Research into Higher Education and Open University Press).

Dunn, L., Morgan. C., O'Reily, M. and Parry, S. (2004) *The Student Assessment Handbook: New Directions in Traditional and Online Assessment* (London: Routledge Falmer).

Durrant, A., Rhodes, G. and Young, D. (eds) (2009) *Getting Started with University-Level Work Based Learning* (Middlesex: Middlesex University Press).

Houghton, W. (2004) *Engineering Subject Centre Guide: Learning and Teaching Theory for Engineering Academics* (Loughborough: HEA Engineering Subject Centre). Available at: http://www.engsc.ac.uk/downloads/resources/theory.pdf (accessed 25 February 2010).

NICATS (2001) *The NICATS Generic Level Descriptors* (online). Available at http://www.nicats.ac.uk/about/prn_tlevl_descriptors.pdf (accessed 22 June 2009).

Quality Assurance Agency (2001) *The Framework for Higher Education Qualifications in England, Wales and Northern Ireland* (online). Available at: http://www.qaa.ac.uk/academicinfrastructure/FHEQ/EWNI/default.asp (accessed 29 November 2009).

Race, P. and Brown, S. (1998) *The Lecturer's Toolkit: A Practical Guide to Teaching, Learning and Assessment* (London: Kogan Page).

Ramage, C. (2005) '"It's Hard Work!" An Analysis of the Concept of "Hard Work" as an Experience of Engaging in Work Based Learning', in K. Rounce and B. Workman (eds), *Work-based Learning in Healthcare: Applications and Innovations* (Chichester: Kingsham Press).

SEEC (2001) *SEEC Credit Level Descriptors* (online). Available at http://www.seec-office.org.uk/creditleveldescriptors2001.pdf (accessed 22nd June 2009).

Ufi/Learndirect (2001) *Learning through Work Level Descriptors* (online). Available at http://www.sld.demon.co.uk/ufilevels.pdf (accessed 22nd June 2009).

Walsh, A. (2007) 'An exploration of Biggs' Constructive Alignment in the Context of Work-based Learning'. *Assessment & Evaluation in Higher Education*, 32 (1), 79–87.

Suggested further reading

Assessment Standards Knowledge Exchange (2009) *Feedback: Make it Work for You!* (online). Available at http://www.brookes.ac.uk/aske/documents/StudentFeeback_makeitwork.pdf (accessed 2 December 2009).

Becker, L. and Van Emden, J. (2004) *Presentation Skills for Students* (Basingstoke: Palgrave Macmillan).

Boud, D. (1995) *Enhancing Learning through Self Assessment* (London: RoutledgeFalmer).

Bowden, J. (2008) *Writing a Report: How to Prepare, Write and Present Really Effective Reports*, 8th edn (Oxford: How To Books).

Cottrell, S. (2006) *The Exam Skills Handbook* (Basingstoke: Palgrave Macmillan).

Ghaye, T. and Lillyman, S. (2006) *Learning Journals and Critical Incidents: Reflective Practice for Health Care Professionals*, 2nd edn (Dinton: Quay Publishing).

Godfrey, J. (2009) *How to Use Reading in Your Essays* (Basingstoke: Palgrave Macmillan).

Greetham, B. (2008) *How to Write Better Essays*, 2nd edn (Basingstoke: Palgrave Macmillan)

Marsen, S. (2007) *Professional Writing: The Complete Guide to Business, Industry and I,* 2nd edn (Basingstoke: Palgrave Macmillan).

Moon, J. (2006) *Learning Journals: A Handbook for Reflective Practice and Professional Development*, 2nd edn (London: Routledge).

O'Sullivan, T., Rice. J. and Saunders, C. (1996) *Successful Groupwork: A Practical for Students in Further and Higher Education* (London: Routledge).

Payne, E. and Whittaker, L. (2006) *Developing Essential Study Skills*, 2nd edn (Harlow: Financial Times Prentice Hall).

Race, P. (2007) *How to Get a Good Degree: Making the Most of Your Time at University,* 2nd edn (Buckingham: Open University Press).

Zubizarreta, J. (2009) *The Learning Portfolio: Reflective Practice for Improving Student Learning*, 2nd edn (San Francisco: Jossey-Bass).

5 Work-based Projects: What They Are and How to Do Them

Barbara Workman

In this chapter you will learn:

- ▶ how to design, plan, implement and write up a work-based project;
- ▶ about the characteristics of a work-based project;
- ▶ how to structure a project proposal;
- ▶ about the key points to consider when undertaking a work-based project;
- ▶ about the ethical issues to be considered;
- ▶ about supervision and support.

● What is a work-based project?

You will find that worked-based (WB) projects form the core of most WB programmes. They provide you with the opportunity to learn from your work activities in a structured way which brings a rigorous academic approach to meeting the needs of the workplace. Such projects are usually focused upon the real-time work demands of your job and will contribute new knowledge and learning to reflect work developments. You can undertake WB projects at any academic level, but they are almost always used to consolidate learning at academic milestones within or at the end of a programme, in much the same way that more traditional degrees culminate in a large dissertation. Figure 5.1 pulls together some of the major characteristics of work-based projects.

WB projects offer you a great opportunity to transform a workplace activity into a meaningful learning experience, which will benefit the workplace, you as a learner and the university. They reflect a project cycle of activity – planning and development; implementation and delivery; monitoring and evaluation – while also meeting academic research requirements. A WB programme may include several projects at different stages, or various academic levels, building up towards a final large WB project to complete an award. For example, you might choose to write a project entitled, 'Designing an action plan' and this will be your preparation for a bigger piece of work. This smaller, initial project will involve reading around a subject to gain understanding of factors influencing the larger project. Another interim project might be 'Implementing the Action Plan', which is finally revisited in

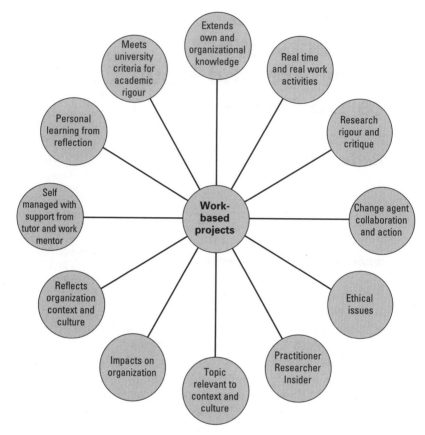

Figure 5.1 Characteristics of WB projects

the larger piece of work which evaluates the effectiveness of the total project. This approach encourages you to build a coherent programme which clearly shows your progression.

A WB project will include data collection, usually within a 'research' methodology framework, where a formal structured methodology of collecting information and appropriate inquiry is undertaken. This chapter does not discuss specific research methodologies in great detail as these can be found in many general research texts, some examples are listed at the end of the chapter. Most WB programmes include a research methods module which will help you to understand appropriate research approaches for the workplace, and the requirements of your programme.

What this chapter will do is guide you through the project processes. Studying at university will include learning to use appropriate evidence, which may be academic research literature, or in the case of WB projects, evidence from practice, or a combination of both. Practice evidence may include local, national and possibly international documents, policies, guidelines and directives. WB projects help you to become a 'scholarly practitioner' who is able to construct a case for your actions and decisions with a rationale. Do not be daunted by the term 'research'; you are probably quite happy to research a holiday destination or investigate and organize a major expenditure. These inquiry and planning skills are very similar to those needed to investigate your WB project and these skills can be transferred. Once you have undertaken the first project, subsequent ones become easier as your repertoire of information sources, helpful people, critical reading, writing and project management skills grow and develop. With academic support from your tutor you will learn tools and techniques to investigate your work, both now and for the future.

Armsby and Costley (2000) provide a useful summary of what a WB project is and does:

1 Develops your critical awareness of research and inquiry
2 Monopolizes on this to enhance practical competence
3 Collaborate with an expert tutor and/or work colleagues, and beyond
4 Differs from a dissertation – more practical and often leads to a product
5 Develops your personal and professional knowledge
6 Uncovers and shares knowledge which is intuitive and embedded in practice (often called 'tacit' knowledge – Eraut, 2001)
7 Contributes to the organization's knowledge and intellectual and human capital (Garnett, 2005)
8 Usually explores some degree of 'change'
9 Enhances communication, negotiation and dissemination skills
10 Contribute to career development
11 Provide academic recognition and facilitate addressing differing audiences.

Example: Margaret – progression via multiple projects

Margaret identified that her organization needed to update its training programme for users of specialist equipment. She knew that there was information from a government department that needed to be incorporated into the training as well as new research about how to manage the equipment for clients and staff. Her first project gathered a wide range of information about the equipment and specific training requirements from which she devised an action plan to design and implement the training programme. She then designed a new organizational policy to support the training, which became her second project. A year later she concluded her degree in a final project which evaluated the training programme to see if it met the needs of staff and clients, and adhered to government and work regulations.

This example shows how WB projects are focused on daily work activities, are relevant to work practices and update knowledge by helping to solve problems. Studying relevant topics at the same time offers new knowledge options to choose from.

Choosing a project topic

The choice of project will be directed, to some extent, by the programme requirements and your learning needs. Factors concerning size, academic level, focus of content and inquiry method are usually discussed with your tutor, and formalized in a learning plan/contract/agreement, depending on your individual programme requirements (see Chapter 3, 'Learning contracts'). The learning plan may cover the entire programme from the beginning, or each project separately. Ideally your employer or manager will be involved throughout as WB projects should be explicitly relevant to your workplace, and permission to undertake them agreed in advance. The final WB project at level 6 is usually the most significant and draws together key aspects of learning and application from the overall programme.

There are a number of types of projects that can come from work; for example, a project may be triggered by asking a question about practices, trying to solve a problem, needing to improve practice, or an area of interest that you have always wanted to investigate. Your manager may direct you to a project, particularly if sponsoring you on the programme, and may assign you to a project which also develops your knowledge and skills. When considering a project ask:

- Is it related to current work practice or arising from a work issue?
- Does it build on an area of personal interest and expertise? This will sustain you through the difficult times to 'live' with it for the duration.
- What will be the product or outcome at the end? Be specific, for example a report, a new way of working or specific skills.

- Does it form part of a larger work project that you are involved with? (Ensure it is relevant to you – this is important.)
- What learning do I need? A key learning outcome for your academic programme will be reflective learning from the project process to help with bigger, more complex projects in the future. It will be a bonus if there is a product or outcome that works well and contributes to the organization.
- To what extent is change involved? You will need some authority at work to introduce and manage a change project.

How do WB projects differ from dissertations?

WB projects differ from dissertations in that:

- dissertations are orientated to theory rather than practice;
- dissertations tend to be purely desk-based with no field work;
- ethical issues are less prevalent in dissertation work;
- personal learning is not explicitly included in a traditional dissertation;
- it is customary for a dissertation to reflect the conventions of its subject discipline, rather than those of a workplace;
- the format of a dissertation is usually an extended narrative – or long essay in sections – which would be an unsuitable format for a WB project;
- a dissertation is unlikely to include change strategies – although it will be original, provoking thought and challenging opinions;
- a dissertation may have little immediate relevance to actual work practices.

Who is learning from your experience?

You are unique in that the knowledge you bring into the university is generated from your real work experience. Sometimes university will seem to be an alien environment where tutors talk in a foreign language. It will take time to understand what is expected of you academically, but similarly tutors may find that some ideas from your workplace are just as innovative and challenging, particularly the notion that new knowledge is created from practice. Some academics may consider that new knowledge should be researched by the university before dissemination to other learners in the same subject discipline, rather than transmitted reciprocally between workers in a particular organization. You will be introduced to new academic theories and knowledge that may explain why or how your practical experience works. Some academics may not value your practical knowledge as much as your workplace does, but somehow an understanding must develop as to how these two different perspectives can, and do, complement each other. This can be particularly powerful for both parties; academics may not have been in the workplace for a while but may find it revitalizes their teaching and gives them examples that are appropriate for both you and their more traditional students. Your WB projects will make your practice knowledge explicit, but furthermore will enhance, support and analyse this knowledge with academic theories and research evidence. You will also analyse new knowledge from both perspectives. 'Teaching' you therefore, is not just about transferring knowledge from university to the workplace, but also about you bringing your knowledge and expertise into the learning environment. In your work-based study classes you will often be the expert in your field and this enriches the experience for all involved – you, your tutors and your student and work peers.

Planning a project

A successful project requires careful consideration of these four stages:

- Definition – what are you doing?
- Planning – how and when will you do it?
- Implementation – project activity (see the section 'Writing your project proposal' below).
- Completion – monitoring and managing successful outcomes.

These stages are further illustrated in the project cycle in Figure 5.2. Questions and activities are identified at each of these stages to guide you.

What will your project do?

Choosing a suitable project will depend on your work role and opportunities within your workplace. Successful projects are usually related to your current work practice and should capture your personal interest as you will be 'living' with it both at and outside work. The best planned project can still be far from straightforward; the trick is to try and tackle the difficulties as challenges rather than problems. Remember, you will learn more from dealing with the complexities of this than you would if everything was 'plain sailing'. Your manager and/ or colleagues may influence the size, scope or even the subject of your project. Small is beautiful when it comes to scoping your project; too big and it will overwhelm you and become unmanageable, yet it must be 'big enough' to extend your learning and meet organizational and academic requirements (Raelin, 2008).

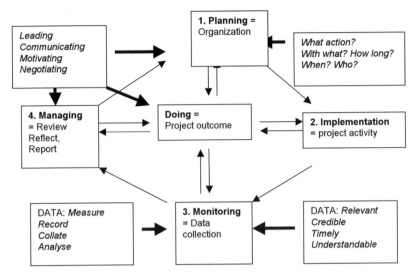

Figure 5.2 Example of a project cycle
Source: Adapted from Baguley (1999).

Everything you do at work will not automatically be suitable content for a WB project which is to be part of your work-based degree/qualification. If the project only requires some desk/internet research it is probably not substantial enough to sustain an entire project.

To define the boundaries of the project answer the following questions:

- Why undertake this project?
  - What is its relevance to you, your work and your study?
- What are you going to achieve?
  - What is the 'product or outcome? For example, a machine, a policy, improved practice.
- What are your aims and how will you achieve them?
  - For example, 'This project aims to explore the clients' level of satisfaction with our product'.
  - The objectives are the steps to achieve the aim: for example (1) undertake a literature review of measures of client satisfaction, (2) design and pilot a client satisfaction questionnaire, and so on.
- Who should be involved?
  - You may be doing the project alone but other people at work should be aware of what you are doing so they can assist and support you.

- What is the timescale of the project and when must it be completed?
  - You must balance work alongside an academic timetable.
  - 3 months is adequate for a small project within a university term.
  - 6–9 months is a larger piece of work which may straddle 2 academic years.
  - You will have to choose when to stop recording details for academic hand-in deadlines – despite the real project's potentially ongoing status.
  - Projects can be written up retrospectively.
- Will there be any cost involved?
  - Consider costs to you of travel, photocopying or time, but also the cost implication for others, such as their time helping you.
- What boundaries or limitations are there?
  - These may be imposed upon you by the project requirements and from Terms of Reference which state exactly what is (and therefore also isn't) expected.
  - Other constraints may be access to data, limited time frame, current safe practice, available finance and so on.

Some common problems – a quick reality check

- *'Is it do-able?'* Realistically is there time, authority, resources, access to knowledge and skills to undertake this or should you scale it down?
- *Will resources be wasted because it is too complex or fraught with internal problems?* Internal politics, lack of support from key individuals, late consent from managers or ethics committees or lack of understanding from colleagues can be unforeseen problems.
- *Does the project lack definition? For example, is it too wide to be achieved within the time frame?* Discuss out loud with your tutor/colleagues/yourself! Do the written aims get across what you have in your mind and have explained in your conversation? Have you captured that idea accurately?
- *Have you chosen an area with insufficient resources, for example lack of expertise, insufficient funds?* Investigate who might assist you.
- *Have you negotiated the topic with your line manager? If not then you may encounter resistance when local support or access is needed.* Discuss your WB project with your manager and get permission before you plan too far; include this in your learning plan/contract/agreement (Chapter 3).

- *Have you chosen to collect appropriate and accessible data?* Inappropriate and unnecessary data will not fulfil the project requirements, could mislead the results and distract you from the main focus of the project.
- *Have you anticipated the result before carrying out the investigation?* One of the commonest faults in planning a research project is to anticipate the findings. You cannot be sure what you will find, so leave your options open.

Example: Marie – Prepare for your projects to change and evolve

Marie worked as a self-employed fitness instructor in two private health clubs. She wanted to investigate how to encourage members to keep up their fitness regimes and memberships. She decided to interview all the members in both clubs as well as all the staff to find out their perceptions as to why people dropped out and get their ideas of how to retain members. However, because she was self-employed and not employed by the health clubs, this proved too difficult to get permission from the club management. She had to scale down her project and just focus on one club, and instead of interviewing everyone, she had to target specific individuals exercising there on the specific days that the management agreed to. Gaining permission to access the club membership involved a lot of meetings and letters to the group management of the health club, and was very time consuming. She spent so long getting permission and negotiating access to her participants that she had to reschedule her project timetable and missed the first academic deadline for submission as she hadn't anticipated that this planning stage would take so long. Then during the data collection process, she discovered that one interview generates a lot of information and she had to work out how to analyse and categorize the data from ten interviews. She also discovered that transcribing the recordings takes several hours, for each interview. On reflection afterwards she acknowledged that her original plan was too ambitious and as a lone researcher it would have been far too difficult and time consuming to gather and analyse data from everyone as originally planned.

Quantitative approach

Used to answer a particular question or 'hypothesis' which is worded in a way that is then proved or disproved by the findings. It uses large numbers of participants to determine the relationship between different data sets.

Some types of quantitative approaches
Surveys, experiments, quasi-experiments
Random controlled trials

Data collection includes
Questionnaires, surveys
Numbers, statistics and percentages

Focus is on:
Group properties, identification of patterns and processes within those groups
Facts supported by statistical evidence

Researcher: Objective, training in statistical analysis or access to statisticians

Does not: reflect people's behaviour or preferences in depth, but may summarize their attitudes or expectations

Qualitative approach

Guided by research questions rather than a hypothesis, so is not necessarily going to prove or disprove anything. Useful for exploring 'how' and 'why' things may be occurring or providing explanations for a phenomenon. It uses small numbers of participants.

Some types of qualitative approaches
Case study, ethnography, grounded theory, phenomenology, biography

Data collection
Interviews, questionnaires, documents
Focus groups, observation

Focus is on:
Individual experience and perceptions
In-depth analysis of a situation
Description of phenomenon

Researcher: Aware of own influence on the data, that is, subjective, recognizes themes and interprets narrative and documents

Does not: collect large numbers of participants or statistics, but may have several sources of data

Mixed approaches
Action research and evaluation are two approaches that use mixed data collection tools from both quantitative and qualitative research approaches

Action research A collaborative and participative approach, involves others in generating data and taking action. Used to enable social or group change Often led by a practitioner researcher	**Data collection tools** May include all forms of data collection	**Focus is on:** Changing something and trying it out – uses a spiral approach of 'plan, do, review and act' to capture data and progress
Researcher: a practitioner inside the study to lead the change and involvement from all stakeholders.		**Does not:** transfer easily to other situations as may be context specific
Evaluation: Evaluation can be 'process' or 'outcome'	**Data collection tools** May include all forms of data collection	**Focus is on:** whether the intervention is fit for purpose, its effectiveness or for improvement
Requires: Can be evaluated internally by a practitioner researcher or by an outsider depending on the degree of objectivity required		**Does not:** always count as original research when seeking ethical approval as it is an exploration of current practice

Table 5.1   Summary of research approaches to aid choice for WB projects

How will you carry out the research needed?

Deciding on a research approach is an essential part of planning a WB project; you need to choose a research approach which is most appropriate for the project, rather than opting for the one most familiar to you. Robson (2002) and Bell (2005) both provide comprehensive and readable guides to research approaches; your tutor may suggest others, specific to your subject discipline. You should study 'Research Methods' before starting on a big WB project.

There are some common research approaches to WB projects which lend themselves to the workplace because they are flexible in design, cater for the human element of work research and the individual nature of the projects. These include case studies, action research and evaluations, but any type of research approach may be valid depending on your research question. Research will help you deal with a problem of logic, but not a logistical problem, so combine a project plan with your research approach. Table 5.1 provides a brief overview of research approaches to direct your early research thoughts.

TIP   **Successful project research**

- *Explore* different research methodologies to make an informed choice.
- *Identify* the methods which will answer your research questions by asking 'how' and 'why' when choosing.
- *Investigate* how a variety of differing research methods can inform data collection and analysis – this will equip you for future projects.
- *Analyse* aspects of change management via the research needed for your project – this may help to introduce the project into your organization.
- *Acquire* skills and strategies that can be used elsewhere at work, via your new-found research methods expertise.
- *Reflect* on what you are learning and keep a reflective diary or journal.

● Writing your project proposal

Your project proposal will combine both your project plan and your research approach and it should clearly communicate what you are proposing to your tutor, your manager and your colleagues. It should be structured as follows:

a   Working title
b   Introduction

c   Main aims and project significance
d   The worker/researcher role and your relevant expertise
e   Your main research questions and objectives
f   Identify a rationale for the research approach
g   State rationale for data collection and analysis, and how it will address the research questions
h   Project feasibility, timescale, resources, ethical issues
i   Project report and target audience
j   Strengths and weaknesses of research proposal
k   References

See Appendix 6 for an example of a project proposal.

Choosing a working title for your project

The project focus should be relevant to your overall academic award. The title should encompass the project as a whole, rather than as a question, for example *'An Evaluation of Littletown services …'* rather than – *'What did the clients think of …'.* Keep the title short and focused.

Examples of project titles:

- Improving communications between departments
- Developing a team to improve behaviour and performance
- Evaluating a training programme for support workers
- Identifying the education and training needs of the staff in a department
- Developing a risk assessment policy
- Developing and introducing a new automated system for pharmacy dispensing
- Designing new technology to increase production rates for packaging and distribution of fresh foods

Introduction

- Brief overview of the background and context.
- Explain your rationale; why this project is important and relevant. How will it contribute to the organization, yourself and the university? Brief reference to publications and policies which set the context and relevance.

Main aims of the project and its significance

- State your chosen research design and justify this with supporting references, for example: 'an action research approach will be used to explore the clients experience because it is participatory and will involve all those who use our services' (Waterman et al., 2001).

- State the purpose and aims of your project with brief rationale.
- Include a short critical review of the key literature in terms of themes or issues that are appropriate, for example 'Smith's (2006) previous survey of users suggested that the best way to include clients would be by internet survey. This project will involve clients who contact us through the website'.
- The target audience – who will the outcomes be relevant to and why?

The worker/researcher role and relevant expertise

- How might your position of influence/power affect the project?
- Why are your skills and knowledge particularly suitable?
- Do you have access to the required data sources? Or will permission from others be required?
- What aspects are directly related to your insider role? How will you approach them?
- Consider your resources – time, finance, equipment, experts at work and within subject area, access to data; and negotiations to all of these.

Your main research questions and objectives

- State key overarching research questions of your project; these will influence your chosen research design. These questions concern the overall project (not small details from individual participants), for example *'What are the client's perceptions of the barriers and benefits of the service?'*
- State objectives (the steps of your project), for example undertaking a literature review, designing a survey, getting permission to access participants and data, gathering data, analysing it, producing a product, writing the report.

Identify a rationale for research approach, considering and excluding alternative approaches

- Discuss your chosen research method, justifying your choice using supporting references, for example *'a survey methodology was considered but will not give the full picture of the client's preferences, whereas a case study approach could give a multifaceted perspective ...'*
- If it is part of a bigger work project that you are already involved in explain how it fits into the bigger picture.

State rationale for data collection, analysis of data and how will this address your research questions

- How will you collect and analyse data? Is this appropriate? If you are using a survey, is it quantitative or qualitative and why?
- Justify your sampling methodology with a rationale. How many and who will be your participants? How does this represent your project population?
- What about validity and reliability? Consider whether the data you aim to collect will answer your question(s) and make your research plausible.
- Will your data be triangulated? If you need data which gives different perspectives how will you do this?
- Do you need help/support/training with data analysis? For example, SPSS.

Project feasibility, time scale, resources, and ethical issues

- How achievable is this project given the constraints of time, resources, and your other work? This is an important reality check.
- How will you protect your subjects' confidentiality and do no harm? If you expose sensitive information how will that be addressed within your organization? Who do you need to seek ethical approval from?
- Can your realtime project fit into the academic timetable? Try including a Gantt chart or timeline (see Table 5.2 and Figure 4.4).

Project report and target audience

- How will findings be of use at work? And how they will be shared?

Strengths and weaknesses of research proposal

- Reflect on the constraints of multiple (conflicting?) timetables.
- Are the data collection methods chosen for expediency or appropriateness?
- Does being work-based mean your project has strengths and/or weaknesses? What are they?

References

- All your choices of research design, data collection, analysis, ethical decisions and supporting rationale should be academically referenced. Local policy documents may be used to support your decision of project subject, but also include current research wherever possible.

Activity	Wk 1	2	3	4	5	6	7	8	9	10	11	12
Lit search	■	■										
Questionnaire design		■	■									
Pilot questions			■									
Send out survey					■							
Return survey							■					
Data analysis survey								■	■			
Focus groups-FG						■						
FG analysis					■	■						
Draft first 3 chs.			■	■								
Draft ch. 4							■	■				
Draft chs. 5 and 6									■	■		
Submit drafts to tutor						■			■	■	■	
Final writing										■	■	■
Submit												■
Study time needed					■		■	■	■	■	■	■
					2 days		2 days	2 days	2 days	3 days	3 days	1 day

Table 5.2 Example of a Gantt chart showing timelines

TIP **Further ways to achieve project success**

- Outline a structured, linear breakdown of the project's component parts.
- Create a summary sheet that allows you to track progress of all project components, include responsibilities for each activity if you are relying on others to contribute to your data.
- Identify measurable objectives or milestones – some people find SMART targets useful: Specific, Measurable, Achievable, Realistic, Time bound (http://www.jiscinfonet.ac.uk/tools/smart-targets).
- Be realistic with time:
  - Include time for: piloting data collection tools, recruiting partici-pants, gaining approval from ethics and management commit-tees.
  - Allow at least 10 working days for tutor response.
  - Allow time for a social life – your family and friends still want to see you!
  - Include thinking and reading time, although the project is around work activity you still need to allow extra time to encompass your HE level study.
  - Allow time for drafting, re-working, printing and handing in – also for contingencies.

Your own boss – you need to 'do' the project *and* manage it

Within WB projects the role of the practitioner/worker/researcher, some-times also called the 'insider researcher', puts you in a dual role (Workman, 2007: 152), perhaps altering the dynamics at work. You are lucky because you are familiar with the context, the work culture, the subject and the people. However, there can be conflicts between your different roles and your colleagues may see you as a 'mole', pursuing your personal agenda by investigating your own organization. On the positive side you will have access to privileged information and insider knowledge which will help you to predict and circumnavigate potential difficulties as well as identifying champions to support you. You will find it easier than an outsider to negoti-ate access to meetings or individuals as well as having the knowledge to fit in with the peaks and troughs of demands on your colleagues.

Context

Inevitably how you record and report information is always through the lens of your own understanding and experience, with all the assumptions that come along with this. Sometimes prior knowledge will help you and on other occasions it may hinder, for example it may stop you from questioning something that a neutral researcher would question. Our own perspectives influence how objective or subjective we are (even unconsciously) and it is very difficult to claim that any data is completely bias free. Acknowledging this from the outset means that your perspective is accounted for and therefore potential limitations are explicit for your audience. It is healthy for you to generate a questioning approach as a practitioner researcher and to state your position in the organizational context, this might encompass: your power; connections; networks; level of influence; your assumptions – and any other factors which may colour your interpretations and explain your decisions.

Exercise 5.1: Map your position

To get an understanding of those who influence you, and who you influence, draw a mind map (see Figure 5.3) of your position in the organization and identify those things that affect your role; for example your job position, gender, level in the organization, networks, department and so on. Discuss with your tutor or a colleague how this affects your position and how the work context can influence your project.

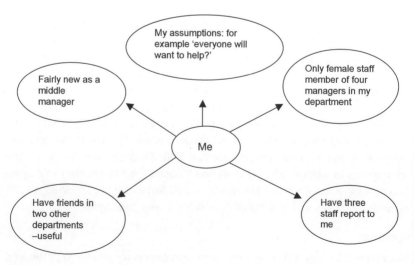

Figure 5.3   An example of a mind map

Your manager may try to dictate your project's topic and style – this represents something of a challenge to your position as a practitioner/researcher as you still have to work under their authority. Being aware of the internal influences on your project is crucial. Critical reflection (Chapter 1) will help you to interrogate your actions and data and to interpret situations realistically. Keeping a reflective journal of the project offers you an alternative lens through which to interpret your findings. It will help you to analyse the tensions around being 'piggy in the middle', while juggling organizational, personal, professional and academic contexts and priorities.

Insider/outsider researcher

In terms of WB research the position of a practitioner researcher is present whatever research methodology is used but in varying degrees. Herr and Anderson (2005) identify a continuum of 'insider to outsider' in action research, where the level of involvement with others in the project process ranges from studying your own practice (number 1 in Table 5.3), to a situation where an outsider studies it (number 6 in Table 5.3), with various degrees of collaboration and participation along the way. Table 5.3 shows who that involves and the types of research that might be used for each approach. An important consideration for you is to decide how one of these approaches could contribute to your knowledge or that of your workplace. If it is appropriate to your study, you should reflect on the impact your position makes upon the research findings. Whatever your research approach and position on that continuum you need to maintain the trust and rapport with colleagues as you still have to work with them beside and beyond the project and collegiality can be crucial to its success.

You may be required to undertake a 'change agent' role as a practitioner researcher, where you have to lead an initiative attempting to implement change, and this will require a number of practical and relationship skills and knowledge around managing change, using change strategies and understanding how people react to change. Using analytical frameworks such as Strengths, Weaknesses, Opportunities and Threats (SWOT) or Political, Ethical, Sociological, Technology, Legal and Ecological (PESTLE), or a Force Field Analysis (FFA) (Iles and Sutherland, 2001), as change tools will help you understand the context. These tools will help to analyse the current situation and influences. They will help to assess the level of change required for your project, and reveal sticking points in the organization. For example, an FFA will identify the drivers for change, such as financial imperatives or government directives, which outweigh the resistance to change, such as lack of resources or appropriate expertise.

Position of researcher	Contributes to:	Type of research
1 Insider, studies own self and practice	Knowledge base, improved critiqued practice, self and professional transformation	Practitioner research, autobiography, narrative researcher, self-study
2 Insider in collaboration with others inside	As above, including organizational transformation	Feminist consciousness raising, inquiry/study groups, teams
3 Insider(s) collaborates with outsider(s)	As above	Inquiry study groups
4 Reciprocal collaboration	As above	Collaborative forms of participatory action research that involve equitable power relationships
5 Outsider(s) in collaboration with insider(s)	Organizational development and transformation	Mainstream change, consultancies, organizational learning, community and radical change
6 Outsider(s) study insider(s)	Knowledge base	University based academic research on action research

Source: Adapted from Herr and Anderson (2005).

Table 5.3 Knowing your position

Ethical considerations

Your colleagues should know what you are doing in your project and you will need their informed consent when you use data from them. Access to organizational information must be agreed by your manager and may raise ethical issues with regard to ownership of intellectual property, or issues of commercial sensitivity or security. This differs from sector to sector but anyone working with children or vulnerable adults or in a position of power over others should gain permission from participants or ethical committees to ensure that practice is considerate, open and trustworthy. If you have connections with a professional body then you should be conversant with their ethical guidelines (www.apa.org/ethics/ or http://www.onlineethics. org/).

You must keep your sources confidential. This is difficult in a small team, making careful reporting essential. Instead of identifying colleagues by gender, and making the only female manager very conspicuous, you can call them respondent 'A', 'B' or 'C', for example. It is easy to make your colleagues anonymous for the university, but your own manager may well identify individuals. Information you uncover might reveal inappropriate practice, hence confronting you with an ethical dilemma about what to do with that information. Your tutor and key colleagues will help you to think through the consequences of your findings, and your reflective diary will help you to analyse the implications. Very occasionally the ethical stance of the company may become completely at odds with your own and you may have to entirely rethink your job role (Workman, 2007: 154). There are an increasing number of texts available which explore the delicate issues facing the practitioner researcher, such as Fox et al. (2007) and Coghlan and Brannick (2005, particularly Chapter 6).

Intellectual property

Intellectual property refers to ownership issues around a wide range of products which are the outcomes of new ideas, whether from work activities, inventions, research, literature, performances or copyright of written and artistic works. If you intend to publish the outcomes of your project you are advised to record the identities of and gain permission from those participating in the project, as part of their informed consent. Usually research from work becomes the property of the organization in which it was created, particularly if it has commercial implications, but this may vary depending on your organizational practices. The government website http://www.ipo.gov.uk/ offers practical advice about protecting intellectual property. Additionally you should check the terms of the Data Protection Act (1998) to ensure that the data you access and use does not breach the rights of others.

Exercise 5.2: How ethical are you?

Investigate the ethical issues that relate to your area of work. What are your organizational practices regarding the Data Protection Act, Intellectual Property or informed consent? Do you have a professional ethics code of practice that you have not been aware of? Whose property is the information you deal with on a day-to-day basis? Find out what you can about these and reflect on them. Discuss them with your colleagues or fellow students. How might these things affect your project? Does this new information affect how you practise? If so, how?

Example: Tony – some projects are ethical minefields

Tony worked in a prison, where he was responsible for staff working with offenders with addictions and mental health problems. He wanted to review current practice to see where improvements could be made in the management of the health issues presented by these offenders. As offenders were considered to be vulnerable adults he was not allowed to gather any data directly from them and so had to consider alternative ways of assessing current practice. After some deliberation and discussion with the prison governor and the chief medical officer, he was granted permission to audit notes recorded from consultations with offenders, but could not use any other data other than minutes from staff meetings. He decided to trace some offenders' journeys through the system using the routine paperwork as a way of monitoring their progress and management. Gaining ethical permission even to do this proved very problematic and slowed the project significantly. However, the audit demonstrated some major gaps in the documentation that could be amended and consequently improve communications and alert staff to health issues. His position as a member of staff with access to senior managers who could grant or deny access to information, proved to be very important as he was known within the organization and had the trust of his colleagues which enabled access to information which would not have been available to an outsider. Additionally, the project extended his understanding of internal politics, thus developing his professional networking skills.

As a practitioner researcher you will develop your leadership and project management skills, including monitoring the project's progress against its objectives. Managing a WB project involves others, communicating next steps and progress, networking and building relationships, and negotiating with colleagues for their time, skills and knowledge. This is where the project plan (discussed above in the section 'Planning a project') keeps you on track. You will need to review progress at regular intervals, reflect on findings and actions so far, and report on interim stages and the final outcome. Furthermore, you will need to monitor the progress of data collection, analysis and interpretation of results. The complexity involved in these stages will vary according to the project size and your role, but delivering a product will help to focus your actions.

On completion consider how to disseminate and activate any issues that have arisen, and identify who should be responsible for addressing any issues. This may mean that follow up is required, such as discussions with your manager about next steps or finding an internal or external forum to share your findings.

Supervision and other guidance

During the project you will need help from:

- *work colleagues* – they understand your context;
- *friends* – to listen and read drafts;
- *family* – enlist help with domestic responsibilities;
- *university* – access resources and general information, for example hand-in schedule and so on;
- *tutors* – get feedback and guidance and make sure you follow it up;
- *fellow students* – compare and discuss your ideas and project activities;
- *mentors* – they will encourage and stimulate you;
- *your manager* – negotiate time out for thinking.

Be prepared to be flexible, grateful and to help them in return when they need you to!

Academic input

From the tutor's perspective, there are a number of ways to support WB projects. Although each learner is doing something different, workplace discussions or online forums through Virtual Learning Environments provide learning opportunities (see Chapter 7). Groups with similar work disciplines can be managed through learning sets as everyone can share and ask questions of a common example, or individually present their project ideas for peer feedback and discussion (see, for example, www.bond.org.uk/pages/action-learning-sets.html). Posting online the aims and objectives of a project for others to critique and question can be a good learning exercise to ensure they have an example to work from. Many WB programmes advocate using a reflective diary and a selected extract could be shared online to discuss research methodologies. Problems centred on the practicalities of the workplace are good shared learning points because of the commonalities in any work situation, such as engaging colleagues when introducing new ideas. Some universities can accommodate the submission of joint or group WB projects and usually the elements of the project reflecting each individual's contribution should be identified. Additionally, there may be learning points from collaborative projects that make good discussion activities.

Rhodes and Shiel (2007) found that WBL learners often spend a disproportionate amount of time on the practical aspects of the project to the detriment of the academic written component, particularly those learners who lack academic confidence. Facilitation around developing a written argument and sustaining the story and sharing sections with other learners can help learners to see omissions in other's work that they might not see in their own. The use of a formal framework to write up a project helps to make short, achievable chunks of writing, as chapters, or 'mini' essays, and can be compared with or presented to others in small groups or online for critique and discussion. Other learning strategies can develop academic skills alongside the practical project skills. Oral or webcam presentations are particularly useful to assess individual progress and understanding; preparation for these can provide a structure on which to base a written report. It is also a good opportunity to invite employers or managers along, especially if held in the workplace, as it can stimulate discussion regarding the implications of the project and the learning achieved by individuals as well as having a celebratory atmosphere (Raelin, 2008). Rhodes and Shiel (2007) suggest a presentation framework consisting of 'theme, scope and outcomes' of the project, as giving sufficient guidance without being too rigid. Other presentation factors to consider are the work context, inquiry approach and the ability to answer questions authentically. Terminology from the work discipline should be integrated into the subject discipline so that the learners can communicate to both audiences.

Example: Health care project managers – WB projects can make a real difference

A group of health care project managers were involved in modernizing the NHS cancer services across the UK and undertook a WB project as a final part of a Master's award. They had peer and tutor support through occasional study days, personal emails and telephone calls, particularly where their projects had some elements in common. Their projects were designed to improve cancer services through speeding up waiting times for tests or treatment, evaluating video-conferencing diagnostic discussions, improving information for service users, and reorganizing a department to maximize staff cover. They presented an outline of the final project to each other for comments and feedback during the programme and the final outcomes to their sponsor at the end. Their sponsor was so impressed with the effectiveness of the projects that she encouraged them to publish in the national newsletter to share the outcomes.

Summary

1 Stick to the word count – too long or short and you will be penalized.

2 Make sure you know the hand-in date – and stick to it.

3 Follow instructions with regard to layout – you will lose marks if you don't.

4 Include an introduction, middle and end; is an abstract or summary needed?

5 Acknowledge your sources by using correct academic referencing techniques (check university guidelines) – plagiarism carries heavy penalties.

6 Secure all the parts of your project carefully; you will not get good marks if sections are messy or missing altogether.

7 Proofread your project and read it out loud.

8 Find a buddy to share the learning journey and encourage you.

9 Make sure you understand the academic terminology used, for example, 'analysis', 'critically evaluate', 'bibliography' and so on.

10 If the assessment requires an oral presentation allow time to practise it beforehand, anticipate questions that could be asked, and plan some answers.

11 Share the project's outcomes with colleagues who helped you by writing a report or discussing at a meeting; thank them for their help.

12 Celebrate your success with all those who have supported you!

References

American Psychological Association, *Ethical Principles of Psychologists and Code of Conduct 2002* (online). Available at http://www.apa.org/ethics/code2002.pdf (accessed 28 November 2009).

Armsby, P. and Costley, C. (2000) 'Research Driven Projects', in D. Portwood and C. Costley (eds), *Work Based Learning and the University: New Perspectives and Practices* (Birmingham: SEDA Publications Paper 109).

Baguley, P. (1999) *Teach Yourself Project Management* (London: Hodder Education, Teach Yourself series).

Bell, J. (2005) *Doing your Research Project,* 4th edn (Maidenhead: Open University Press).

Bond, Action Learning Sets (online). Available at http://www.bond.org.uk/data/files/resources/463/No-5.1-Action-Learning-Sets.pdf (accessed 28 November 2009).

Coghlan, D. and Brannick, T. (2005) *Doing Action Research in your own Organisation,* 2nd edn (London: Sage Publications).

Eraut, M. (2001) 'The Role and Use of Vocational Qualifications'. *National Institute Economic Review,* 78, 88–98.

Fox, M., Martin, P., and Green, G. (2007) *Doing Practitioner Research* (London: Sage Publications).

Garnett, J. (2005) 'University Work Based Learning and the Knowledge Driven Project', in K. Rounce and B. Workman (eds), *Work Based Learning in Health Care: Applications and Innovations* (Chichester: Kingsham Press), 79–86,

Herr, K. and Anderson, G.L. (2005) *The Action Research Dissertation: A Guide for Students and Faculty* (London: Sage Publications).

Iles, V. and Sutherland, K. (2001) *Organisational Change: A Review for Health Care Managers, Professionals and Researchers.* NCCSDO. London (online). Available at http://www.sdo.nihr.ac.uk/files/adhoc/change-management-review.pdf (accessed 27 November 2009).

Intellectual Property Office (online). Available at http://www.ipo.gov.uk/ (accessed 28 November 2009).

JISC infoNet, *Smart Targets* (online). Available at http://www.jiscinfonet. ac.uk/tools/smart-targets (accessed 27 November 2009).

Online Ethics Centre for Engineering and Research (online). Available at http://www.onlineethics.org/ (accessed 28 November 2009).

Raelin, J.A. (2008) *Work-based Learning: Bridging Knowledge and Action in the Workplace,* new and rev. edn (San Francisco: Jossey-Bass).

Rhodes, G. and Shiel, G. (2007) 'Meeting the Needs of the Workplace and the Learner through Work-based Learning'. *Journal of Workplace Learning,* 19 (3), 173–87.

Robson, C. (2002) *Real World Research: A Resource for Social Scientists and Practitioner Researchers,* 2nd edn (Oxford: Blackwell Publishing).

Watermann, H., Tillen, D., Dickson, R. and de Koning, K. (2001) 'Action research: A Systematic Review and Guidance for Assessment'. *Health Technology Assessment,* 5 (23).

Workman, B. (2007) 'Casing the Joint: Explorations by the Insider-Researcher Preparing for Work Based Projects'. *Journal of Workplace Learning* 19 (3), 146–60.

● Suggested further reading

Biggam, J. (2008) *Succeeding with your Master's Dissertation: A Step-by-Step Handbook* (Maidenhead: Open University Press).

Bryman, A. and Bell, E. (2007) *Business Research Methods,* 2nd edn (Oxford: Oxford University Press).

Campbell, A. and Groundwater-Smith, S. (2007) *An Ethical Approach to Practitioner Research: Dealing with Issues and Dilemmas in Action Research* (London: Routledge).

Fink, A. (2009) *Conducting Research Literature Reviews: From the Internet to Paper*, 3rd edn (London: Sage).

Greetham, B. (2009) *How to Write Your Undergraduate Dissertation* (Basingstoke: Palgrave Macmillan).

Grix, J. (2004) *The Foundations of Research* (Basingstoke: Palgrave Macmillan).

Jupp, V. (2006) *The SAGE Dictionary of Social Research Methods* (London: Sage).

McNiff, J. and Whitehead, J. (2000) *Action Research in Organisations* (London: Routledge).

Mullins, L.J. (2007) *Management and Organisational Behaviour*, 8th edn (Harlow: Financial Times Prentice Hall).

Pallant, J. (2007) *SPSS Survival Manual: A Step by Step Guide to Data Analysis Using SPSS for Windows (Version 15)*, 3rd edn (Maidenhead: Open University Press).

Pedler, M. (2008) *Action Learning for Managers*, 2nd edn (Aldershot: Gower).

Punch, K.F. (2005) *Introduction to Social Research: Quantitative and Qualitative Approaches*, 2nd edn (London: Sage).

Punch, K.F. (2006) *Developing Effective Research Proposals*, 2nd edn (London: Sage).

Ridley, D. (2008) *The Literature Review: A Step-by-Step Guide for Students* (London: Sage).

Robson, C. (2007) *How to Do a Research Project: A Guide for Undergraduate Students* (Oxford: Blackwell).

Senior, B. and Fleming, J. (2005) *Organizational Change*, 3rd edn (London: Financial Times Prentice Hall).

Wisker, G. (2009) *The Undergraduate Research Handbook* (Basingstoke: Palgrave Macmillan).

Wood, M. (2003) *Making Sense of Statistics: A Non-mathematical Approach* (Basingstoke: Palgrave Macmillan).

6 Support for Work-based Learning Students: From University, Employer and Self

Jenny Naish

In this chapter you will learn:

▶ about the support available to you as a work-based learning student;
▶ how this might differ between institutions and companies;
▶ what a workplace mentor might do for you;
▶ the role of the tutors on work-based programmes;
▶ the potential triangulation of employer – employee – university;
▶ what resources you need to support yourself as a work-based learner;
▶ questions to ask yourself to ensure you are prepared for the journey ahead;
▶ how to develop, enhance and motivate yourself.

● Support from your university (academic, pastoral, cultural and infrastructure)

Campus resources include:

- Sophisticated, state-of-the-art libraries with extensive online facilities staffed by information retrieval and knowledge management experts who can guide you to the search mechanisms you need. All universities offer an induction to their learning resources which you should take advantage of.
- An extensive ICT infrastructure, normally offering the full suite of up-to-date Microsoft software and also highly specialist software relating to your area of study. You will have your own university email account and access to a virtual learning environment (VLE), for example Blackboard or Oasis (see Chapter 7).
- There are very good student discounts for lots of software (including MS Office) and normally on-campus and online tutorials for software that you might need during your studies such as SPSS (Statistical Package for Social Scientists – for quantitative analysis of data); NVivo for note taking and Harvard, the standard UK academic referencing system.

- Subsidized child care – but often with a waiting list.
- English language support – and the opportunity to learn a wide range of modern foreign languages.
- In-depth support for people with learning and other disabilities from dyslexia to visual impairment and physical disabilities.
- Counselling and other pastoral support.

Example: Amanda – share your details with the right people

Amanda is undertaking a Doctorate in Professional Practice and has dyslexia. She forwards to her tutor a copy of the private assessment done by her local education authority's Educational Psychologist team. This is held in her file on a confidential basis but enables her tutor to be able to note this in terms of possible extenuating circumstances at assessment. Amanda's employer is also an HEI which means she can apply for funding for specialist software to support her specialist learning needs. Her application is successful and Amanda rapidly establishes her expertise in specialist graphic software to aid her research.

You, like many other WBL students, may rarely go onto campus, but don't worry, you will be given information about how you can access some of these facilities remotely. All universities who provide WBL programmes that are delivered off campus will make reasonable provision for learning resources to be available to you. You should make the most of this and ask whether your university's library enables you to order books, journals, articles and so on, online and if these can be posted to you direct. All HEIs in the UK operate reciprocal 'reading only' rights to students at other institutions, this means that you can make the most of the library facilities if you are working away from home, for example, in another town with a university. Although arrangements to obtain material at a distance are sometimes a real life saver there is also much to be said for you physically engaging with the campus experience and what it really feels like to be a student at a university, so please take advantage of any opportunities you can to 'be' there.

If your organization is sponsoring you in your studies there is likely to be some formal contractual relationship between your organization and the university at which you are studying and you will have access to information about that and the person in your organization who is co-ordinating that. However, it is very important to understand that the university also has a contract with you as a student and when you formally complete the enrolment procedure you will normally sign a form acknowledging your responsibility to adhere to university regulations. In so signing the university also commits to its own responsibilities to you as a student and that includes a 'duty of care'. That covers things such as confidentiality and your access to support services. You may never need these, but the knowledge that you have access to free counselling, information, advice and guidance *beyond* your employer is an additional resource to you, especially if you do not wish your employer to be aware of, or involved in, such support. Many WBL students find that their university's Careers Advisory Service can help them to better understand their range of options and opportunities; for example, they can arrange for you to have some job interview practice, which might help you to change job or to successfully apply for a promotion within your organization. Gaining the confidence to put yourself forward for promotion not only enhances your workplace activities, it could well lead to your employer suggesting, even sponsoring, further study, such as a Master's degree.

Another way to view the various university support mechanisms available to you is to think of them as additional layers to your networking resources both professionally and personally and, as such, make the most of them!

Support from mentors or buddies

Mentors can be drawn from your colleagues, line managers, HR directors – the number and position differs from organization to organization. Study buddies can offer similar support in all areas of a study programme. Buddies are preferably students who have also undergone a work-based study route but have either already completed their studies or are at least a couple of years ahead of you, and therefore able to offer empathetic advice and guidance.

If your university has a buddy system you will almost certainly be assigned to a buddy from the outset and probably with clear guidelines about their role and responsibilities. Your buddy will be someone who has more experience of the university and HE than you and can provide valuable support during your first few weeks and months as you find your way around. However, a buddy may not always be someone on a WBL programme so you may only get generic support from them. A mentor is rather different.

Who are your learning gurus or mentors?

These might be tutors or teachers from the past or other learners whose stamina and achievements you admire. They may even be historical figures. My learning gurus are two very different people who I worked for at different times in my life (Rosemary and Sam) and one historical figure. But if I think of the people who have influenced my learning and how I have changed then the list is longer and very much linked to what I call learning transitions; by which I mean key 'tipping points' in my professional development where learning fast and applying that learning was critical for me to progress. Thinking about the characteristics of these people is likely to enable you to think about the additional strengths you could develop to add to your intellectual agility and motivation. When you undertake any formal learning, understanding your own motivation for doing so is important in acknowledging what support you need from yourself to meet those aspirations. You must acknowledge that there are key differences between the motivation you put into the public domain – 'I've always wanted a degree', for example – and the context for why that motivator is your key driver – 'I didn't do well enough at school to go to university when I was 18'. The deeper drivers are likely to remain unspoken and may even be subliminal. You will find further information about thinking about your learning gurus later on in this chapter, in the section 'Supporting yourself'.

Support from your tutor

In WBL programmes your relationship with your tutor is unconventional in comparison to the tutor/student relationships on traditional degree programmes; communicating as equals in the learning process is key (see 'Learning conversations', below), even though you probably have no experience of traditional higher education I am sure that you have ideas, and images in your mind which sum it up for you (see Exercise 1.2 in Chapter 1). A major aspect of WBL programmes is your negotiation of your programme with your employer and the university. Supporting this process requires high levels of teaching skills from your tutor, which are applied within sensitive organizational environments to ensure academic rigour, while simultaneously meeting your organization's needs. This is almost always underpinned by a formal learning agreement/plan/contract (see Chapter 3 for a full discussion of these).

A quick summary of some of the typical characteristics of a work-based tutor:

- Provides a first rate academic service to you.
- Assists in maintaining positive and purposeful relationships with your managers and senior staff (some of whom may well be looking for tangible proof of your success/progress).
- Unlikely to hold qualifications in or by WBL.
- Likely to have a diverse academic and professional background.
- Will tend to 'facilitate learning' rather than adopt 'directive teaching'.

- Feels more like a peer/colleague with different expertise to yourself.
- Will regard you as an expert in your own field and respect your existing knowledge.
- Will support you in the articulation of that knowledge (help to make it explicit).

Telling stories

A good way to build rapport with your WBL tutor is to think about the professional 'stories' you could tell each other to illustrate your approaches to your job, and your experiences of WBL. Storytelling within a professional context is a powerful tool. It is often used to help teams to bond and to create a 'vocabulary of change', used to describe how small changes in ideas can bring about transformations for you, your team and your company.

Exercise 6.1: Using 'storytelling' in day-to-day activities

- Think of the stories you might tell to introduce yourself in a new group.
- Not just your title and job role, try to talk about why you are there.
- To further this, try referring to yourself in the third person – introduce yourself as that other person.
- Once you begin to think about yourself by your name – rather than as 'I', you will want to also say something about personality, motivation, likes and dislikes – the richer picture.
- 'Telling your own story' is good background work for writing the personal statement that you would put in an application form, or in your WBL portfolio (see Chapter 2).

TIP   **What storytelling does for you**

- Builds your credibility, confidence and perspective.
- Helps with bonding.
- Enables you to say not just who you are, but why you are present.
- Can provide a vehicle for your hopes and expectations about WBL.
- Brings structure – a plot, a protagonist, a journey and an ending.
- Can give a framework (and some distance) for exploring difficult and controversial topics.

A major emphasis of your WBL programme will be for you to critically reflect (see Chapter 1) on your learning. This critical reflection encourages an analytical style of narrative and gives you an opportunity to tell the 'story' of your learning. Your reflective narratives will provide your tutor with a wealth of information about your professional knowledge and give the kind of context that enables your tutor to learn about you quickly. This knowledge is invaluable as it enables your tutor to support you, or very occasionally accept that they cannot! In these rare instances they will find you a more suitable tutor.

Feedback from your tutor

Like most other students you probably dread feedback and align it with being told off and criticized? Good feedback is not about telling you off but rather building you up and supporting you. Both giving good feedback and acting positively upon receiving feedback are talents well worth developing. Your tutors will give you feedback on your draft work throughout your studies (the amount of feedback and the timing of it will be pointed out to you). All university WBL programmes are slightly different in terms of how and when feedback is given but it will be through some of the following:

- Comments written directly onto your work.
- Feedback via email on soft copies you have sent.
- Spoken feedback in tutorials at pre-arranged times and locations.
- Feedback placed on a protected area of a virtual learning environment (VLE) (for example, Blackboard).
- Group feedback in an actual or virtual seminar setting (for example, a discussion group on Blackboard).

This is far from an exhaustive list. There is further discussion around feedback in Chapter 4, which focuses on assessment.

Learning conversations

You should be getting the picture by now that communication is vital to your relationship with your WBL tutor(s). Much of this communication could be termed 'learning conversations' (Naish, 2006, building on Pedler et al., 1991). I developed the notion of learning conversations when I was working with groups of mature master's level WBL students. These students were highly intelligent, capable people, with vast amounts of expertise in their own areas. We worked together in many ways, but always as equals, not in traditional 'teacher' and 'student' roles. Learning conversations, which made it explicit that we were talking about learning, made it possible for me to learn as much about these students' contexts as possible. This in turn meant that I was able to facilitate their learning processes and their acquisition of further knowledge. Figure 6.1, using the parent, child and adult metaphors from Transactional Analysis theory, provides a way of looking at and understanding learning conversations. These can take many forms, including:

- formal lecture;
- workshop;
- master-class;
- distance learning materials both in hard and soft copy (for example, on a VLE);
- group discussions and seminar (actual and/or virtual);
- your own reading.

In thinking about these learning conversations (which also include those with your student peers) you might want to think about yourself as a professional adult who is also in a learning role. How you and your tutor(s) and/or supervisors communicate with one another has an impact on the support you seek, and on your achievements; the term 'learning conversations' is very much based on the equality of these conversations, adult to adult while acknowledging that you and your tutor are likely to have differing levels of expertise on different subjects/topics/processes and so on. Traditionally the relationship between tutors and students is not one of equality but rather the tutor 'teaching' the student things they 'need' to learn. This is very different from the 'facilitation of learning' style that works best for WBL.

Understanding the dynamics of your relationship with your tutor can be illustrated if you look at what happens when you adopt a role that is not

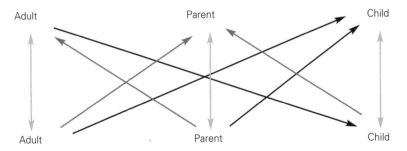

Figure 6.1 Power lines – power relations

fully that of an adult learner? To help you get to grips with the idea of 'power relations' I am going to use the metaphor of 'adult', 'parent' and 'child', to create a model based on Transactional Analysis (see Figure 6.1).

Figure 6.1 shows the 'ego' states of child, adult and parent, based on Berne (1964). Berne suggests that when 'child to child', parent to parent, and adult to adult transactions are taking place (the light grey lines) they are normally of an equal nature, whereas parent to child transactions normally imply an unequal relationship based on the power inherent in the role of parent over a child. This would be characterized as the parent 'telling' the child for instance. A major point that Berne makes is that while we are all technically 'adults' it is sometimes too easy for someone occupying a role as tutor to slide over into a 'parental' role, therefore moving you as a student into a 'child' role; conventional teaching is characterized by the teacher 'telling' you what they think you need to know. Your relationship with your WBL tutor is likely to be more effective and successful if you both inhabit 'adult' roles and use adult transactions. If we translate the different shaded directional arrows in the figure into 'traffic light colours', this illustrates the power of this way of thinking: red (black lines) = 'not ok', amber (dark grey lines) = 'sort of ok' and green (light grey lines) = 'definitely ok'. Again, an excellent WBL tutor will be very aware of *your* existing knowledge and expertise, which is often going to be very different from their own, and will not only be keen to learn about you, but also *from you* as the more in-depth understanding they have of your specialisms and environment the more effective they can be in supporting you.

If you and your tutor are occupying unequal power relationships this will influence the way support from your tutor is communicated. At its best it will be:

- constructive;
- supportive;
- challenging;
- informative;
- inspirational;
- catalytic.

If you feel the support you are getting is prescriptive you must ask yourself why that might be. Your learning journey includes developing yourself as an autonomous learner (see Chapter 3). Work out how best to appropriately question your tutor (as part of your learning conversations) about their rationale for the support they are providing. This should result in a truly 'adult to adult' transaction which will assist your own learning development. You can find out more about Transactional Analysis at http://www.businessballs.com/transactionalanalysis.htm.

Figure 6.2 combines some of the thinking about having meaningful 'adult to adult' learning conversations with some of the features of Transactional Analysis. It maps both ideas onto the four common stages of WBL programmes; namely, the accreditation, learning agreement, research methods and project phases. The nature of your learning conversations will change and evolve during your WBL programme and may not be linear; for example, the emerging autonomy of the learning agreement phase probably transforms into a more conventional learning relationship during the taught research methods phase. Have a look at the suggested Transactional Analysis modes in the grid and consider whether or not you agree with them – there are many different permutations of teacher, pupil, facilitator and learning that might appear here. Take this grid and populate it with your own experiences so far on your WBL programme. Analyse this experience so far and the factors that might be prohibiting you from moving to the Facilitator/Learner (FL) mode. If you want to you can share this with your tutor, their perception will be useful. By being explicit about what modes of communication are currently going on you are taking a major responsibility for changing them. Good luck!

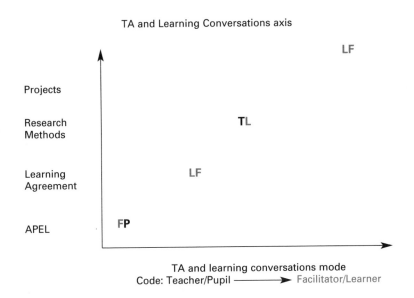

Figure 6.2 Where does your experience lie?

Support from your project/dissertation supervisor

Apart from your academic tutors, mentors, buddies and other colleagues who are helping you along the way you will also normally be allocated at least one supervisor for each work-based project that you undertake. Their support for you will be crucial in what is not only the most important part of your studies, but also the one that is most personal to your plans and aspirations. Some university WBL programmes appoint multiple supervisors for projects and where this is the case your supervisory team will have been carefully identified to ensure that they provide complementary expertise and support. Your WBL tutor may take on board the role of supervisor, an added advantage as you will have an established relationship with them and they will have an understanding of your university work so far as well as your professional context. Irrespective of how many supervisors you have, your university will issue clear guidelines at project stage, including:

- contact details for your supervisors;
- confirmation of whether contact is initiated by you or them (usually you);
- how many supervisory sessions/number of hours time you have with them;
- at what stages in your project work you should seek feedback on draft work and arrange tutorials;
- if you have more than one supervisor whether you get feedback from them both.

One of the things you may wish to clarify with your supervisor(s) is their support to you if you are given contradictory feedback and/or (also see below) if the comments you are getting from colleagues at work appear to contradict feedback from your supervisor. This is entirely normal: we all bring our own perspectives to work-based projects and part of your learning is always going to be weighing up those differing messages and feedback and making your own decisions about how to value them when attempting to achieve your aims and outcomes.

Autonomous learning

It may not be made explicit in the guidelines you have from your supervisor or university but, as mentioned in Chapter 3, one of the distinctive features of WBL programmes is the intention to develop autonomous learners. This is a complex topic which is substantiated by theory, for instance Kolb (1984). The support your project supervisor gives you will be designed to encourage you to become more autonomous, and that might feel as if they are becoming increasingly 'hands off'. You might notice them not giving you a specific answer to your questions; giving you a range of options that may not always be clear cut; returning the question to you and asking you what you think the answer is and so on. This feels quite uncomfortable at first, especially as in the early phases of WBL programmes you are likely to have experienced quite a lot of very 'hands on' and almost directive support from your tutors. You should see this as being a transition into an exciting new phase of your learning. The type of support that works best to facilitate a transition to greater levels of autonomy is what you might at first class as discomfort! (This is why expressions such as 'getting out of your comfort zone' are frequently used in discussions about learning, stretching and self-development.)

Upping your game

Usually work-based projects are the final pieces of work you would be expecting to complete for your award, and by that stage in your programme you are likely to know all the assessment grades or marks you have achieved so far. Therefore you are also likely to know what kind of grade or mark you need to achieve to get the award classification (first class, 2:1 and so on) you are aspiring to. This may make you feel anxious; this is entirely normal and the support your supervisor can provide here is crucial. They can advise you about what kinds of approaches you would need to take in order to aim for a realistic classification within the scale and scope of your capability. When my students ask specifically for support in this way I encourage them to develop what I call a 'personal voice'. By this I mean encouraging a new wave of confidence and to strive to develop not only as an autonomous learner but also as an autonomous thinker. Try to express your views and opinions more assertively as your growing data and evidence enables you to be more courageous in your analysis and interpretation. You will find that your confidence grows alongside your ability to back up your findings.

Some universities will enable you to look at the graded work of previous students (under controlled conditions) and where this facility is available to you it is well worth taking advantage of the chance to see the diverse range of writing styles, content and context for work-based projects. Also you will see the attention to detail in terms of vocabulary, referencing, data collection and analysis.

As the deadline for submitting your project looms, the pressure will increase and you will be tired, but hopefully exhilarated that you have almost completed your work and the final couple of weeks should all be about 'perfecting' it (while at the same time acknowledging that perfection is unattainable but excellence is!). At this time the support you should seek from your supervisor is about the 'readiness' of your work for submission against the assessment criteria that will be used to judge its merit. The findings of WBL students' work are often taken up and used by their employers. It is therefore worth making the best attempt possible with your assignments.

Example: Employer benefits from high quality informed research of employees

A major food retail company sponsored 20 of their managers to undertake postgraduate WBL programmes. Candidates made presentations of their final projects to a group of senior managers and their tutor. The senior managers felt that the projects were of a vastly improved calibre to the equivalent work of external consultants because the managers' insider knowledge of the detailed context of their work brings in-depth understanding and analysis.

Support from your employer

The role your employer may take in supporting your WBL can be diverse and range from the official support of funding or part-funding your studies, through to helping you to get the most out of your studies in terms of project advice or even co-supervision. The amount and quality of the support you receive from your employer will depend on a number of factors, but especially on the nature of any agreement your employer has with the university at which you are studying. A lot of university WBL programmes for individuals are established as partnership agreements between the university concerned and the employer. Where this is the case there will be some form of formal contract between the employer (often through the Human Resources and/or Staff Development department) and the university and this should specify the rights, roles and responsibilities of people in your organization in terms of what support is available for you as part of your studies.

Example: Meena – be joined up

Meena is taking a WBL Masters that is sponsored by her employer and is part of a group of managers from her organization. Because of Meena's senior role with the organization she undertakes to be the lead co-ordinator for the programme with the university. She forms an excellent professional relationship with the programme tutor which enables the university to gain in-depth insight into the company which in turn makes the programme more organizationally relevant. Meena and the programme tutor are also able to 'trouble-shoot' the few infrastructure gremlins very quickly because they know precisely who to talk to in their organizations.

TIP   Managing your employer's involvement with your WBL

- Find out if your employer will pay all or part of your fees.
- If so how will this happen? 'Up front' or through pay roll?
- What are the implications of them paying? Some employers will ask you to sign an agreement confirming that you will reimburse any fees paid if you leave the organization within a set period of time.
- If your employer is involved in a partnership with the university then administrative arrangements for your admission, enrolment and the delivery of the programme are probably made on your behalf – you need to check.
- Partnership arrangements usually mean that your timetable is known well in advance and the programme may be delivered within your own workplace, again, check – your personal time management will be helped by this.
- If your employer has 'sent' you on this WBL programme it is important to know why. Have you been chosen or nominated? Is the course compulsory to your job role? You need to understand your employer's expectations of your studying.
- If you *do not* know why you've been sent then your human resources or staff development teams at work are your best first point of contact via your line manager.
- If you are part of a group of students from the same company there will probably be a designated member of the group who acts as the programme liaison officer with the university – make sure you know who this is.

There is also a wide range of ways that your employer might support the academic side of your WBL, and your line manager is central to this. Irrespective of whether you have been nominated for your WBL programme or have applied for it and been successful in your application, your line manager will have played a key role in supporting and agreeing to your application. It is important for you to understand what your line manager's hopes, expectations and aspirations are for your role in undertaking this programme, and equally important for you to have a chance of exploring with them how they might support you, and the level of formality that support might take.

You can safely presume that your line manager will take a keen interest in what you are doing, how well it is going and give you advice and guidance where appropriate. What it would not be appropriate for your line manager to know (directly from the university at least) would be what actual assessment marks or grades your academic work had been awarded, and while *you* are at liberty to let people know (to celebrate your success), that information would normally be confidential between you and the university you are studying with.

Learning agreements

All WBL programmes are designed to help you develop professionally within the context of your work role, enabling you to contribute more fully to your organization achieving its objectives. In order to facilitate this, most universities running WBL programmes require students to complete a learning agreement/contract/plan (Chapter 3) in which you will negotiate the specific learning you intend to do, usually with both the university and your employer, but definitely with the university. As your learning agreement may have to be signed by your line manager or other senior person in the organization (this isn't always the case) who understands your programme then allowing time for that process within the framework of deadlines from the university is important for you to manage.

As part of a learning agreement you would need to discuss (normally with your line manager) the content of any work-based projects you are planning to do as part of your programme to ensure that as well as meeting your learning needs they are going to be of benefit to the organization. This is a vital and very dynamic interaction between you, your employer and the university and it is very important that not only do you consider this very carefully but also that you initiate the discussions to progress this and take the lead in the decision making (Chapter 5 further considers work-based projects).

Planning your WBL project

Your line manager will be able to give you advice on the context for your work-based project and all sorts of suggestions about who else in the organization might offer you support and assistance in terms of deciding the scale and scope of what your project is about. A work-based project is not just about *what* you are planning to do, but what the outcomes or 'products' might be and how those are going to be beneficial to your own professional development while also meeting organizational needs.

Some (often larger) organizations hold databases of previously undertaken projects so if this is the case in your organization find out what kind of work might have already been completed, as not only do you not want to duplicate that, but you could look at the recommendations coming out of previous projects to see if there are any that you wish to take forward in your own work. However, 'second generation projects' within organizations can be an especially important way of developing larger initiatives to implementation stage. Their propensity to progress issues may make these kinds of projects more likely to win support.

> **TIP** **Accepting support and guidance – while avoiding railroading!**
>
> - Your projects should be very largely your decision, in negotiation with your organization and the university.
> - Avoid undertaking projects for your employer's convenience – it could be a project from their ongoing (and maybe old) list – it has to engage you and be current. This isn't the same as taking on a project you are both enthusiastic about.
> - Some of your learning comes from going through the process of deciding on a suitable project, so embrace this process.
> - Your motivation and feelings of ownership towards the activity are significantly higher if the project you are doing is one of your choice.
> - If your line manager and/or other people in your organization are directing you towards a project topic that doesn't appeal to you, talk to your work-based tutor and/or supervisor at the university.
> - Early topic ideas often have to be refined and even discarded until all parties agree on a suitable topic – look at this as formative and useful.
> - Your university will have guidelines for you to support you in the process and possibly even guidelines for your employer or at least some you can share.

Your line manager will play an important role in supporting your early planning for your project and you should normally expect them to help 'open doors' for you to access any reasonable additional resources you will need. Early on in your planning your supervisor will encourage you to produce an action plan (or even a formal Gantt chart perhaps, see Figure 4.4 and Table 5.2), showing what you need to do, and by when, to produce your project report. This will include things such as your schedule for data collection and where this includes conducting questionnaires, focus groups or interviews for instance, it is important that your line manager knows about and supports this. For example: What time do you need to undertake interviews? Where are they going to be held? and so forth, are all questions to consider and might need explicit support from your line manager to make happen. In my organization, I have two colleagues who wish to interview the Vice-Chancellor as part of a piece of research they are currently working on. In my role, not only am I able to encourage them that this is both feasible and desirable but I can also act as an initial liaison person with the Vice-Chancellor's office to ensure they understand the rationale behind this, and why the Vice-Chancellor is the only person in my university who can answer some specific key questions to inform the research.

Doing your project

Once your project is underway your line manager may effectively become an informal supervisor alongside your academic supervisor, some WBL programmes even make this a more official role. Where that is the case there will be clear written guidelines as to how this works, provided by the university. Where that is an informal arrangement then it is up to you, and the relationship you already have with your line manager, to decide how you wish to involve them and keep them informed as to your progress. Regular updates and no untoward surprises would be the general rule of thumb!

Undertaking the research for a work-based project (Chapter 5) and writing it up will be time consuming and possibly a quite intensive experience, and while a vast amount of the research will be necessarily done in work time (and that is part of the planning support to be talked through with your manager) it is very unlikely that the writing up is likely to be undertaken in anything other than your own time. However, do remember to check with your line manager and organization whether you are entitled to any 'study leave', and make the most of that. This is generally more likely to be available in public sector organizations and large private sector ones which have a graduate intake and actively encourage further professional development.

When you are approaching the final phases of your project/dissertation; namely when you reach the stage of writing up your conclusions and recommendations you will definitely appreciate the support from your line manager.

TIP **Your line manager's support – questions to ask**

- How can they support (and guide) the dissemination of your recommendations?
- Can they ensure that you have access to personnel at the optimum level in the organization to do so?
- What are the protocols for getting in front of the right people and distributing appropriate details arising out of your project?
- What is the organization's preferred format for writing an executive summary and/or presentation about your project? These are busy senior people.
- How is your line manager going to celebrate your successful completion of your WBL programme when you get your qualification and share your achievement with the rest of your colleagues? With a special event?
- Employers and/or line managers often attend formal university graduation ceremonies.

Example: Fred and Harriet – support via celebration

Fred, Harriet and their colleagues are all due to graduate from the WBL programme. In liaison with their university, it is arranged that senior managers from their organization who have sponsored the programme are invited to graduation. At graduation there is a corporate photo-call with their tutors and managers which goes into the in-house magazine and forms part of an application for an industry-specific training award.

Supporting yourself

You have now considered the range, scale and scope of the support available to you from the differing stakeholders who have a role to play, and a vested interest in your success as a work-based learner. This section draws them together by two related means; *first,* by asking you to explore how, holistically, you can maximize the combined strengths and opportunities of your stakeholders; and *secondly,* by exploring what range of resources already exist (internal and external, psychological and practical), which enable you to support yourself.

Exercise 6.3: Consider your potential stakeholder group

What do we mean by stakeholder, and who will this involve?

Everyone's stakeholder group is different and never static; your personal stakeholder group (employer, tutor, buddy/mentor, supervisor and so on) represents just a few of the influences and therefore supporters of your WBL. There will be others, fellow students, fellow workers and a diverse group of professional others. Not forgetting your family and friends. You will find it beneficial to think carefully about the level, extent and quality of influence these different groupings of people have on you and indeed how much you choose to be influenced by them. In doing so you will probably

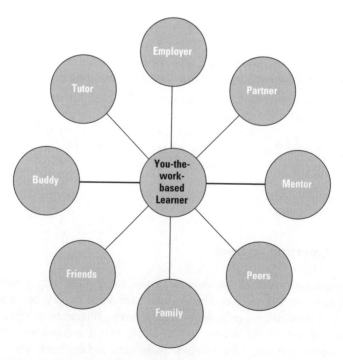

Figure 6.3 Your potential stakeholder group

find it helpful to remind yourself of the multiplicity of professional and indeed personal roles you occupy in your life; friend, partner, employee, student, learner, for instance. And be very mindful that the dual role of being both an employee and a learner within your own organization may bring with it a number of advantages and disadvantages. How you make yourself aware of any tensions and/or dichotomies the dual role of worker and learner may bring and your management of them could be crucial in your learning journey, especially once you are planning for and engaged in work-based projects.

A major advantage of being a learner within your own organization has to be your in-depth knowledge of the organization itself and your proficiency in your own job, together with the specialist knowledge which comes with that. One of your key characteristics as a WBL student will be your existing expertise; however, it is not always straightforward how you will draw on this. Are you too close to the issues and/or influenced by the values that come with them to see your work environment critically and analytically? You are likely to have close working relationships with colleagues who are highly supportive of what you are doing, but just suppose that through your studies an evaluation of your work environment is academically critical of that environment; how might you manage that, and would it be a tension for you? Thinking through the duality of your rights, roles and responsibilities as both a learner and a worker in your organization, and both a student and an expert, and how you might support yourself is perhaps one of the most vital elements in preparing to deal with the duality of your roles in an analytical but also reflective way.

Your personal stakeholder group

Take some time to draw up your own stakeholder group, and consider the direction of power and influence (it is unlikely to be solely one way). What does this look and feel like to you? Is the influence 'authoritative', for instance, or is it 'personal' or 'expert', and most importantly how does your stakeholder group change over time? Exploring this and revisiting it at various times during your study (but especially when you are doing your project) will enable you to consider the shifting dynamics of the group in relation to yourself and therefore how you can make choices about how to gain the support you want from the stakeholder group members.

Figure 6.4 might give you a helpful framework for this as it shows some of the different stakeholder groups, with arrows to indicate that the relationships and influences will be two-way.

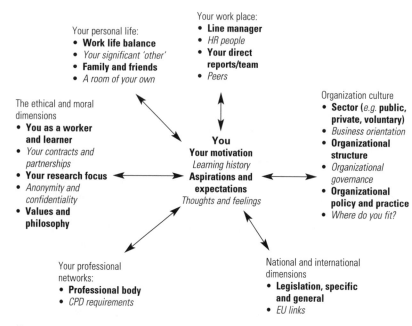

Figure 6.4   Your personal stakeholder group

Exercise 6.4: Try to quantify the influence

Think about the quality and quantity of influence in these relationships; it will be uneven and not necessarily linear. You also need to consider the extent to which the 'power' components feel comfortable for you.

TIP   How much do you know?

Consider what you know in relation to the above figure, but use some different ways of thinking about knowledge to do so:

- Know what?
- Know why?
- Know how?
- Know when?
- Know where?
- Know who?
- Know the context?
- Know for what purpose?
- Know with what consequences?

Key to this list of tips is 'know the context', because if you know the context (which as a work-based learner you are in a strong position to) then you can usually answer the other 'knows' even if only in outline and it is useful to acknowledge the varying degrees of knowledge that you have for different events/occasions/scenarios and to ask yourself – 'is this sufficient?'

Example: Managers in the retail section – support yourself with what you know

A group of managers working in the retail sector were all embarking on their work-based Master's level projects. Each one was different but all within the context of food retail. As these were experienced managers they could use their contextual knowledge to short-cut a number of the 'know' questions. Some of the managers were doing projects related to training and development with a high-level strategic objective of reducing food wastage on the shop floor. This is a fundamental character-istic of food retail through factors such as:

- sell by and use by date;
- damage;
- deterioration;
- faulty packing.

Because these managers knew the context they also knew 'with what consequences' food wastage might be reduced and the significant impact this would have on product turnover and consequently on bottom line profit and loss, as well as on stock management. They also knew that the 'know where' had impli-cations at store level, backstage storage, regional distribution centres and centred on intelligent use of electronic point of sale product ordering. You may find it helpful to think about your own work-based project in the terms of what is the question you are seeking to explore and then asking yourself the 'know' ques-tions starting with 'know the context'.

You, the work-based learner

Finally in this section, I want to turn to the heart of WBL, and that heart is you, the person, the learner, the student, the employee. You will want to get the most out of your WBL programme and only you and those closest to you will know what 'most' means in terms of what does it look and feel like when you have got there. In thinking about this the experience of WBL is often profound, motivating, non-linear and can be life-changing. All in the best possible way, but you will wish to ask yourself how you feel about such powerful statements and their reality for your own professional and personal development. Some very practical questions will help you with this. WBL means that a lot of your studies will be taking place at work and possibly not in lecture rooms. However, while a lot of the thinking, listening and planning can take place in this way, the actual writing up of your work will have to take place in your own time and own space. Have you got that space organized and the most up-to-date ICT equipment you can afford? If you have to share that equipment with anyone else what deals have to be done for equitable sharing? Virginia Woolf addresses the issues around writing needing 'A Room of One's Own' – what are you doing to meet that need for yourself? The majority of work-based learners report a huge learning curve with ICT. Help yourself by pre-empting that learning curve and getting the latest software that you need and by also attending in-house/university IT courses (with some HEIs they will be free once you are a registered student).

Intellectual agility and stamina

Under what circumstances (state of mind and mental alertness) are you at your best for real hard reading, thinking and writing? If your best 'brain time' is early in the morning, then do all you practically can to ensure that when you have a big piece of work to do you can block out morning time to do it. How used are you to concentrating for long periods of time, reading, note taking and writing for instance? You will need to build up that intellectual stamina and that will include your own inner resilience and perseverance for writing, rewriting and rewriting where necessary to ensure you are doing full justice to your capability and potential. The university will have all sorts of practical and motivational ways of supporting and guiding you – make the most of them and above all raise your levels of self-awareness of what works for you and equally, what does not!

How do your previous experiences of formal learning influence your hopes and expectations of WBL? Do you know what your preferred 'learning style' is or indeed if you might have any 'blocks' to learning effectively and successfully that you need to address? You can find out your learning style by undertaking the Honey and Mumford Learning Styles Questionnaire which you will find at http://www.peterhoney.com/content/LearningStyles Questionnaire.html.

Further aspects of learning styles are discussed in Chapter 3, and all students work in different ways. It is therefore very useful to know what your likely strengths and weakness may be as a learner and prepare for that. So, for instance, if your preferred learning style is that of an activist (see Chapter 3) then you are likely to find the reflective requirements of WBL programmes more challenging and if your preferences are for more theoretical learning experiences you are likely to find approaches to research methods within the workplace much easier. Given the emphasis within WBL on reflective practice I would always recommend that you actively develop your reflective abilities (Moon, 1999; Walsh, 2008) as reflection on learning and then being able to apply that learning to your practice is one of the essences of WBL (more on reflection in Chapter 1).

Summary

1 Be proactive – ask about the full range of support available to you from your university and your employer.

2 Make SMART (Specific, Measureable, Aspirational, Realistic and Timely) *choices* about how, why and when you need to make use of this support.

3 Remember that you might wish to use university support with some employer-related matters and vice versa.

4 Help your tutor to support you – turn up on time for tutorials; send work in advance if you expect feedback; be clear about what you need.

5 Have upfront negotiations with family and friends – don't just presume they are there to support you.

6 Support yourself by networking effectively within your stakeholder group.

References

Berne, J. (1964) *Games People Play: The Psychology of Human Relationships* (New York: Grove Press).

Businessballs, 'Eric Berne's Transactional Analysis – TA Theory Development and Explanation' (online). Available at http://www.businessballs.com/transactionalanalysis.htm (accessed 1 December 2009).

Honey, P. and Mumford, A. (2006) *Learning Style Questionnaire*, rev. edn (Maidenhead: Peter Honey Publications).

Kolb, D. (1984) *Experiential Learning: Experience as the Source of Learning and Development* (London: Prentice Hall).

Moon, J. (1999) *Reflection in Learning and Professional Development* (London: Kogan Page).

Naish, J. (2006) 'Application to the Higher Education Academy for a National Teaching Fellowship', unpublished.

Walsh, A. (2008) 'What Is Distinctive about Work-based Knowledge and Learning?' in *Workforce Development: Connections, Frameworks and Processes* (York: The Higher Education Academy).

Suggested further reading

Becker, L. (2004) *How to Manage Your Distance and Open Learning Course* (Basingstoke: Palgrave Macmillan).

Brennan, J., Little, B., Connor, H., de Weert, E., Delve, S., Harris, J., Josselyn, B., Ratcliffe, N. and Scesa, A. (2006) *Towards a Strategy for Workplace Learning: Report to HEFCE by CHERI and KPMG* (Bristol: Higher Education Funding Council for England).

Cottrell, S. (2008) *The Study Skills Handbook,* 3rd edn (Basingstoke: Palgrave Macmillan).

Jamieson, C. (2008) *Managing Dyslexia at University* (London: Routledge).

Lizotte, K. and Litwak. B.A. (1995) *Balancing Work and Family* (New York: AMACOM).

McDury, J. and Alterio, M. (2003) *Learning through Storytelling in Higher Education: Using Reflection and Experience to Improve Learning* (London: Kogan Page).

Moore, L.J. (2007) 'Ethical and Organisational Tensions for Work-based Learners'. *Journal of Workplace Learning*, 19(3), 161–72.

Nixon, I., Smith, K., Stafford, R. and Camm, S. (2006) *Work-based Learning: Illuminating the Higher Education Landscape* (York: Higher Education Academy).

Quality Assurance Agency (1999) *Code of Practice for the Assurance of Academic Quality and Standards in Higher Education: Section 3 – Students with Disabilities* (online). Available at http://www.qaa.ac.uk/academicinfrastructure/codeOfPractice/section3/COP_disab.pdf (accessed 1 December 2009).

Raelin, J. A. (1999) *Work-based Learning; The New Frontier of Management Development* (Reading, MA: Addison-Wesley).

Scevak, J. and Cantwell, R. (2007) *Stepping Stones: A Guide for Mature-Aged Students at University* (Victoria: ACER Press).

Stewart, I. and Joines, V. (1987) *TA Today: A New Introduction to Transactional Analysis* (Nottingham: Lifespace).

Zachary, L.J. and Fischler, L.A. (2009) *The Mentee's Guide: Making Mentoring Work for You* (San Francisco: Jossey-Bass).

7 The Technology Revolution: Online Support for Work-based Learning

Kerstin McClenaghan and David Young

In this chapter you will learn:

► how to get the best from your university's Virtual Learning Environment (VLE) and maximize your off-campus opportunities;
► about blended learning;
► what e-learning is;
► the role of online tutors;
► what Web 2.0 tools are, and how they can aid your learning;
► about tagging, wikis, blogging and much more.

● Off-campus opportunities for supporting WBL

Your WBL can be supported through paper-based methods – the postal distribution of learner handbooks, study guides and the like. However, in recent years, such support has inevitably had a significant electronic dimension, often including the use of a virtual learning environment (VLE). The nature of technology is that it is always further developing and this means that VLEs are no longer the last word in electronic support for you, even though they may have been not so very long ago. One of the challenges you might experience as a WBL student is forming mutually supportive relationships with other students; learning often occurs in a community and this is hard to recreate on a remote study programme and difficult to maintain if you are a part-time student, not often on the campus. However, e-learning, which incorporates Web 2.0 services and applications, has the potential to facilitate membership of learning communities for you, with all of the opportunities which come with that; including collaboration and networking, even under remote or time-restricted circumstances.

VLEs, PLEs and getting the most from them

The notion of a dedicated VLE to support WBL seemed the answer to providing meaningful remote support for students like you, undertaking work-based higher education study as recently as 2000. A decade on, VLEs are still useful for content-based delivery as they provide you and your tutors with a mutual 'virtual' place where all relevant information for learning can be stored and accessed. Furthermore, most VLEs also incorporate, to a varying degree, tools enabling you to interact and collaborate, such as discussion boards, blogs and wikis (more detail later!). The advantage of such tools within a VLE is that they have been pre-selected by a team of professionals (for example, an 'E-learning Team') with the focus on supporting your learning for a specific module.

As a WBL student, much more so than for a full-time student, one of your daily tasks is to self-organize your learning. Whichever institution or route you choose for your study programme, no-one can manage self-organized learning *for* you. The only thing they can do is to create an environment for you in which you can organize your own learning. VLEs, dedicated or not, do not allow for customization and individualization and only offer a very small part of the technology that is available online today. Therefore, there is a general shift away from this 'funnel' style of learning towards personalized learning spaces which allow you to create your own learning environment. This might mean more personalized curriculum profiles with resources and support aggregated and channelled to your specific interests and requirements – you decide what content you need for your learning and which format you prefer, which tools you require and which networks you use to collaborate with other people – in short; how to make your learning space your 'own' (Wheeler, 2009).

Most universities are not yet totally at this position in supporting WBL online or through a Personal Learning Environment (PLE) or similar, but the process of internet evolution is leading in this direction. The section on Web 2.0 tools for learning in this chapter gives you more details on how current technology can be used to support, manage and organize your learning on WBL programmes. Meanwhile, there is still a huge resource available to you now from your university's VLE, so make sure you get the most from it:

TIP   **Embrace your programme's Virtual Learning Environment**

- Use the electronic library. You will know that material on there is from reputable sources which, particularly in your early days of HE learning, is important as you start developing your critical perspectives.
- Browse, delve and browse again. You will almost certainly find useful advice on searching information sources.
- Explore and use all the course and study resources to which your password gives you access; don't just stick to a narrow range.

● Blended learning

Blended learning, as the name suggests, does not rely on a single style, method or approach, but rather seeks to provide a range of resources and tutorial support for you to access at a time and place of your choosing. The stress is on 'easy access' and the possibility of you accessing learning at different times and in different locations. Often, the term 'blended learning' seems to be used simply to refer to the combination of teaching or instructional processes and to resources and facilities which are available to you and provided by your tutors or institution.

However, blended learning on negotiated WBL programmes means a blend of the whole learning process. In such a model, you are encouraged to create a personalized blend, not only of learning materials and resources, but also of the various elements of the curriculum itself. So, when you are in such a partnership with your university and WBL tutor(s) you can propose what you want and need to learn and achieve, suggest how your achievements might be assessed, and what kinds of support you need to accomplish this.

Example: Tom – an individual programme of blended learning

Tom, an engineer, developed the following WBL programme with a specific professional and technical focus in his company.

Beginning with a credit-bearing learning contract, and supported electronically with his tutor, he planned and undertook a programme which blended APEL, taught university modules and a substantial work-based project studied independently with electronic and face-to-face tutorial support.

Tom's choices:

Element	Focus	Mode	Support	Assessment
APEL	Professional engineering design	Directed independent study	• WBL tutor • Engineering tutor • Line manager	• Presentation to panel • Reflective portfolio
Learning contract	Professional reflection Programme planning	Electronic distance learning module	• Online resources • Electronic tutorial	• Programme rational and plan

Element	Focus	Mode	Support	Assessment
Mathematics	Partial differential equations	Taught evening module (face to face)	• Face-to-face lectures • Tutorial	• Coursework • Examination
Computing	Programming in Java	Electronic distance learning module	• Online resources • Electronic tutorial	• Online examination
Work-based project	Professional engineering design project, with direct outcomes for the company	Independent study	• Electronic and face-to-face tutorial	• Project report/ dissertation

● E-learning and social learning

Most universities will offer e-learning provision in the form of modules, courses or programmes of study where you access the whole of your learning and its resources online and you do not – or very rarely – attend lectures and tutorials on campus. E-learning provision can range from short modules to full degree programmes and you will find that you can probably pick up e-learning modules with a specific subject focus as part of your negotiated WBL programme.

E-learning divides opinions. While it may be an exaggeration to say that you either love it or you hate it, there are definitely students who really appreciate the flexibility of being able to study at a time and in a place which exactly suits them, while other students regret that there aren't more opportunities to learn as a part of a physically present community or group. This has been true with e-learning for the last 15 years or so and it is worth you noting how your personal responses to e-learning map across to any work you have done so far on your general learning styles and preferences (Chapter 3).

However, the evolution of e-learning means that Web 2.0 tools are now available. Web 2.0 refers to a second generation of web services which focus on collaboration and sharing. It is also known as social learning because there is an emphasis on communities and networking; the focus is on you sharing information and knowledge (Centre for Learning and Performance Technologies, 2009a).

But before we explore the possibilities of Web 2.0 technologies for your learning on a WBL programme, let's have a look at the main outcomes of two studies about online tutorial exchanges between WB learners and their tutors. You might find yourself in a similar situation – on a remote WBL study programme where your main form of communication is via e-mail; what kind of issues do other WBL students discuss with their tutors? Perhaps you'll recognize some of it from your own experience.

● Online tutorial exchanges – some examples

Bosley and Young (2006) and Young and Stephenson (2007) studied the actual transcripts of almost 2500 online tutorial exchanges between WBL students and their tutors through the Learning through Work (LtW) VLE (http://www.learningthroughwork.org/).

Although dialogues could be initiated by either party, the majority of the dialogues studied (undergraduate and postgraduate WBL students) were initiated by the students. This is not usually the case in classroom or tutorial situations, where the teacher tends to control the agenda and is therefore the instigator of questions. It is an indication that WBL students consistently take the initiative in interacting with their tutors.

You can see from Table 7.1 that the online dialogues replicate the processes of face-to-face academic tutoring; therefore, if you and your tutor

Learners	Tutors
Ask questions	Respond to learners' questions
Seek feedback	Give feedback
Give feedback to tutors	
Report and reflect on their plans and progress	Advise and suggest
Explain and elaborate
Disclose feelings about their studies, plans and progress	Encourage and reassure
Signpost/refer

Table 7.1 Tutorial functions: shared features of online and face-to-face approaches

are able and willing to engage in online dialogue, the functions of a conventional tutorial can be achieved (or even surpassed?) in the context of remote online learning.

The following themes and categories are based on Young and Stephenson (2007) and give you examples of the tips above.

Focus on work

WBL programmes are built on and respond to workplace opportunities and problems:

> I have discussed with my manager which kinds of modules and workplace projects could be built in to the programme.

Workplaces are rich in higher level learning opportunities, but realizing these opportunities is not always straightforward for busy WBL students:

> Work is hectic at the moment and I am struggling to get quality 'thinking' time!

But, at the same time, the WBL approach offers you the chance to allow your study to respond to your evolving work situation – to the benefit of both:

> We have had some news at work that may affect the research component I have been working on. I want to discuss a possible change of direction within this module ...

Learner control, initiative and empowerment

You can be proactive in the design, direction and content of your programme of study; take the initiative and articulate your own learning intentions – you will feel empowered!

I propose to critically analyse the effect that some of my and senior management's decisions on my customers and staff have had over the past two years.

You will begin to take responsibility for the short and longer-term planning of your WBL activities:

My tasks for the coming week are to ensure that: a. something is written in each relevant section of each component, b. The appropriate level indicators are checked-off.

However, you will also look to your tutor for reassurance:

... am ready to start collating 'evidence' and get on with the programme if you think I'm about ready.

Seeking reassurance and clarification

It is fine to ask your tutor to check things – to make sure you are on the right lines:

Please could you let me know if there are areas that I need to improve?

It is normal to want to be reassured that you have the ability to succeed in higher education. Students often get over-anxious:

You will guide me as to the amount and level of work I need to produce to meet the required credits, won't you?

As you know, working, learning and having a life can be tough:

Thanks for your support and guidance at present; I really needed those words of encouragement.

But seeking help, advice and support is always worth it:

Thanks so much for the result and feedback. Just sitting in the office telling all!! Can't believe I did so well.

HE culture and expectations

As a WBL student you need to engage with and understand HE levels and credit, academic writing and the whole idea of critical reading, thinking and referencing as a defining characteristic of university level study. Use your online conversations to improve:

> I have particularly noted your observations concerning the poor Harvard referencing and a lack of academic style in my writing, both problems I feel I can overcome with your help.

Like every other student you need to be realistic and self-critical about your work:

> Although the grade wasn't as good as my first assignment, I think that it accurately reflects the problem that I encountered in balancing an outline of the background with the 'change project' and analysis!

Your skills and confidence will build:

> Thank you for your continued support, I feel a bit more positive over this assignment. I am learning a lot and feeling more confident in my role because of it.

Social/affective

Your studies come first, but online contact also offers opportunities for season's greetings, jokes and information about domestic events, holiday dates and so on. Lightness of tone probably characterizes these exchanges from the more serious ones:

> I did a Belbin exercise last week, and worryingly should avoid co-ordination and monitor/evaluator type roles, so I'm expecting the sack any day!

These student messages were drawn from almost 2500 online exchanges – communicated between about 40 learners and 10 tutors over a three-year period. Some patterns clearly emerged:

TIP Online exchanges

- You are not a passive recipient of knowledge! You can shape and manage your own university programme – online facilities emphasize this two-way street.
- Get online when you need to – it is more flexible and readily available than a lecture or seminar schedule.

- Writing is good! It helps to formulate your thoughts – leading to focused and productive exchanges – especially if you don't like to shout up in a class situation!
- Speak first! It is allowed – encouraged even.
- If you do initiate a conversation sustain it for its useful life.
- More casual online exchanges give you the chance to discuss your pride in your achievements, not always so easy to place in a formal assignment.

Exercise 7.1: Learning from online conversations

- Look at the themes of the online conversations discussed above.
- Identify examples of these themes in your own WBL programme.
- Could increased use of online technologies help you with the issues you have listed?

Theme	Example from within your own programme
Focus on work	
Learner control, initiative and empowerment	
Seeking reassurance and clarification	
HE culture and expectations	
Social/affective	

Web 2.0 tools for learning

Let's move on from looking at how e-mail dialogues and basic VLE functions can support your WBL programme to how you might engage with more advanced current technologies. Having appropriate technology is now an expected standard for entry to the arena of distance support for WBL. Having said that, a good – or a great – learning experience still relies on what you, as student, put into the technology – how you back it up with your human interactions, either virtually or in the 'real' world. Despite constantly changing technologies, the case for providing tutorial support for you, if you are working remotely from your university campus, is strong and will remain strong for everyone working on such programmes. However, if you are more often than not unable to attend tutorials or meet up with other WBL students for collaboration and support and you want something more than simply email support, the use of Web 2.0 tools can offer a real alternative to you (JISC, 2009).

So, what are Web 2.0 tools? Web 2.0 tools are also called social tools and are about people, about human interaction, about sharing knowledge and information, working and learning collaboratively. Some of these tools are now household names and you will probably have heard of them – blogs, wikis, RSS, podcasts, social bookmarking and social networking sites such as Delicious and Facebook, YouTube, Twitter and so on.

The main categories for these tools include:

- communication (for example, Skype);
- collaboration (for example, Wikipedia);
- networking (for example, Facebook);
- sharing (for example, YouTube).

So, why should you use Web 2.0 tools in your WBL? Don't be mistaken – using technology for your studies might not free up precious time for you to do other things; on the contrary, while you are trying to get your head around new tools it might even be more time consuming in the first instance! However, when selected wisely and used appropriately, Web 2.0 tools can help organize and manage your learning, whether you are on a negotiated learning route, taught on-campus modules or pure e-learning modules. Moreover, as the emotional impact is vital for all kinds of learning but harder to create and come by in remote study programmes, the collaborative aspect of some of the Web 2.0 tools might provide you with a deeper learning experience – despite not being able to physically be on campus on a regular basis.

The following sections will provide you with an overview of some of the currently popular Web 2.0 tools and offer you some examples on how you could use these tools in different learning situations. Even though the popularity and use of technologies rises and falls quickly, and some of the services and applications mentioned might not be around in a couple of years, most of the tools described have a good chance of being further developed in the future and used in similar ways. The learning skills stimulated by engaging with Web 2.0 technologies – communication, participation, networking and sharing – are also seen as the twenty-first century employability skills (JISC, 2009). You might only ever want to use one of the tools discussed in this chapter, none, or a whole range of them – in the end, it's not really about the technology but rather about how you can improve and deepen your learning experience. The good thing about these tools is that there is really no set way in which you have to use them; a blog can be a learning log, a place where you collect information or just simply a platform where you stay in touch with others. The priority is whatever suits you and your purpose – as the boundaries between formal learning (structured and in a classroom for example) and informal learning (occurring at work, when you talk to people, read the news, listen to podcasts – anything you learn outside of a structured learning situation) are blurring, you might start using some of the tools for both your social and professional life, alongside your study.

Exercise 7.2: Researching Web 2.0 tools

Find and collect information about:

- Google Scholar
- RSS Feeds
- Google Reader
- Pod/Vodcasts
- Delicious

Google Scholar

Google Scholar is a topic-specific search engine that makes searching for academic literature easier.

What does it do?

It allows you to search for published material including books, journals, peer-reviewed papers, articles, abstracts, citations and any other types of academic publications.

How can you use Google Scholar for learning?

Google Scholar is a more appropriate starting point for research than Google itself as it is aimed at Higher Education and therefore makes it easier to find relevant material for your studies at this level. However, a word of warning – as with all searching tools, don't use Google Scholar as your only (re)search

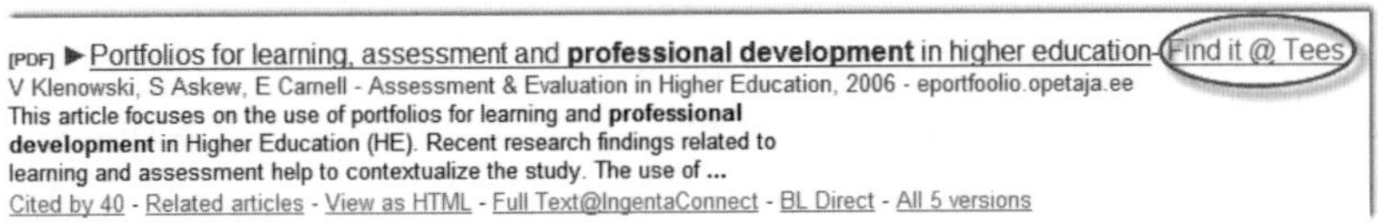

[PDF] ▶ Portfolios for learning, assessment and **professional development** in higher education ⟨Find it @ Tees⟩
V Klenowski, S Askew, E Carnell - Assessment & Evaluation in Higher Education, 2006 - eportfoolio.opetaja.ee
This article focuses on the use of portfolios for learning and **professional**
development in Higher Education (HE). Recent research findings related to
learning and assessment help to contextualize the study. The use of ...
Cited by 40 - Related articles - View as HTML - Full Text@IngentaConnect - BL Direct - All 5 versions

Figure 7.1   Example of a Google Scholar link

tool. Some important publishers of academic journals are not included and sources that might be available through the Learning Resource Centre/Library of your university, for example through subject specific databases, might provide you with a far better range of material. But with the sheer volume of information available on the net, this specialist search engine makes a good starting point!

How to get started?

Access Google Scholar by going to http://www.google.co.uk/ and click on the little arrow next to 'more' on top of the website. Or you can go directly to http://scholar.google.co.uk/. You don't need to subscribe to use this service.

TIP   Using Google Scholar

- If you are using Google Scholar on campus at your university, a link will appear (for example, Find it @ Tees for Teesside University – see Figure 7.1) if the item is included in one of the library's paid subscriptions.
- If you are using Google Scholar from home or generally off campus, you can select your university by clicking on Scholar Preferences from the main Google Scholar page. You will need to check with your library about how to get valid certificates on your computer to access your library resources away from the campus.

RSS

You have probably come across these initials before. They stand for Really Simple Syndication feed and it is, simply put, a universal subscription mechanism. RSS readers are a piece of software that checks the feeds that you have subscribed to, collects them, and displays them for you to read, listen to (podcasts) or watch (vodcasts) in one location. RSS readers come in many different versions, some you need to download, other ones are web-based so you can access your feeds from any computer with an Internet connection.

What does it do?

By clicking on the orange button (which could also read RSS or XML), you subscribe to a service which automatically informs you when there is new content published on the website you have taken the feed from. You can get the latest headlines from news pages, the latest blog entries, podcasts, videos – anything really that interests you, delivered to one place as soon as they are published, without you having to check each single website.

Google Reader

Google Reader is a free web-based RSS feed reader.

What does it do?

It helps you to collect and manage all the feeds you subscribe to on the web. You can access Google Reader from any computer with online access and it also works on any mobile phone with a browser.

How can you use Google Reader for learning?

The most obvious answer to this is to keep up with the things you want to read or listen to/watch. It makes it easy to collect all the information on the web that you are interested in by pulling it together in one location, and saving you from having to go to each website, blog and so on to check whether anything new has been added. You can follow news feeds, blog and social bookmarking feeds, feeds from online forums and discussion boards – anything you can think of really, or better, anything you can subscribe to.

Figure 7.2   Signing into Google Reader

How to get started?

You need a Google account in order to use this service (see Figure 7.2). You can go to any Google website (for example http://www.google.co.uk/) to sign up for an account. Once you have created your account, go to http://www.reader.google.co.uk and log on with your Google account details.

Podcasts and Vodcasts

The term *podcasting* comes from a combination of the words broadcasting and iPod (Apple MP3 player). A *podcast* is an audio file that you can download; you can listen to it on your computer, your MP3 player or iPod, your mobile phone – any device that plays audio files (usually MP3 or WMA format). A *vodcast* (vod = video on demand) is a video podcast which you can download and watch.

What do they do?

Pod and Vodcasts can be on any topic. They can last for only a minute or for an hour. They can be informative, like interviews, talks, lectures, panel discussions or just be about nothing, someone in front of a microphone or camera talking about the weather or last night in the pub. Anyone can create podcasts and vodcasts; you just need a microphone, and/or a camera and preferably something to say! You can either manually download single pod/vodcasts, or you can subscribe to both podcasts and vodcasts series. If you subscribe to series (RSS feed), new episodes and updates are automatically downloaded for you.

How can you use podcasts and vodcasts for learning?

Podcasts and increasingly vodcasts are a popular tool on study routes which include online delivery or self-study aspects. It's also a more personal way to stay in touch and some lecturers put podcast announcements or instructions on their VLE, especially when they don't see their students on a regular basis.

How can you find free educational podcasts and vodcasts on the net?

There are many educational podcasts and increasingly vodcasts available on the net. You can find them by just using a search engine like Google, and add 'podcast' or 'vodcast' to your key word.

How to get started?

Below are some providers who offer free content:

- Palgrave offers a series on study skills (podcasts) which are free for you to download. http://www.palgrave.com/skills4study/mp3s.asp
- LearnOutLoud.com has sourced over 2000 free audio and video titles from the internet which include lectures and audio books. http://www.learnoutloud.com/Free-Audio-Video#directory
- iTunes U (by Apple) offers free lectures from educational institutions, among them Oxford University, Stanford University and the Open University. Apple claims there are more than 200,000 educational audio and video files available. You need to download iTunes to be able to access iTunes U. To download iTunes: http://www.apple.com/uk/itunes/download/. To access iTunesU: http://www.apple.com/uk/education/itunesu_mobilelearning/itunesu.html

Delicious

Delicious is a free social bookmarking tool and currently the most popular and well known of these services. It has been ranked number 1 in 2008 and 2 in 2009 under 100 top tools for learning by over 200 learning professionals (Centre for Learning and Performance Technologies, 2008).

What does it do?

Delicious provides you with a virtual place where you can store and manage your bookmarks and share them with other people. It might not have the greatest variety of functions among the social bookmarking services, but it is very easy to use and has a strong community, which means it has an enormous collection of bookmarks for you to search.

How can you use Delicious for learning?

It is very easy to get lost in the huge amount of information that is available via the Internet. Using a service that not only allows you to intelligently manage the information you find on the web but also gives you access to other people's bookmarks is just like having your own little research assistant. You could start by using Delicious to expand on a module's reading list. By sharing it with other students you will quickly discover what other people find around a subject will add value to your own information base. You could also use Delicious as an alternative to Google to search what people with similar interests have bookmarked as the tags (labels) make it easy to narrow your search down.

Also, as people can add notes and comments to their bookmarks, this might give you a quick indication as to whether something is interesting to you or not. As with most Web 2.0 tools, you can combine this service with other tools such as subscribing to RSS feeds of people's bookmarks that you find interesting, which makes it easy to keep up with their new entries.

TIP **How to tag**

In social bookmarking, you *tag* your online bookmarks; which means that you label and categorize them. Tagging is much more flexible than putting bookmarks into folders. You can use as many or as few tags as you like – your bookmarks will automatically form categories according to your tags and sort themselves into these categories – how's that for service?

Exercise 7.3: Setting up a Delicious account

- Go to http://delicious.com/
- Set up an account with Delicious.
- Read and follow the instructions on getting started. If you get lost, click on 'Help' to get back to the section 'learn more about Delicious'. Try to read all information in that section, it's time wisely spent!
- Install the Delicious 'bookmarklets' (buttons) on your browser's toolbar.
- Import your bookmarks from your computer.
- View your bookmarks on Delicious.
- Save some new websites and add your own tags.
- Browse some of the popular or fresh bookmarks.
- Search Delicious for something you are interested in. Check out what tags other people have used for that topic. How did you find their tags? Confusing? Useful? Why?
- Try the same search in Google or any other search engine – how do the results compare?
- Subscribe to someone else's bookmarks and follow their new entries.

Collaborate and reflect
- Wikis
- Google Docs
- Blogs

Wikis

A wiki is a group of web pages which can be used as a collaborative writing space where users can add and edit content.

What does it do?

You can add written content, documents, links, embed videos and sound. The term 'wiki' comes from the Hawaiian word for 'quick' and most wikis use a relatively simple technology and are indeed easy and quick to create and use. Wikis are an ideal place to consolidate a project in one place – users can build up a whole pool of information around a specific topic or theme.

How can you use a Wiki for your learning?

At its simplest, you can use a wiki 'passively', as an online reference point for a quick access to information (for example, Wikipedia – but keep in mind that information on it might not be correct). Wikipedia is the best-known example of a collaborative wiki on the web – it is the largest digital encyclopaedia in the world. Its biggest plus point is at the same time its biggest downfall – nearly all articles can be edited by anyone and it is a constant work in progress – including errors and unfinished articles. However, the real strength of wikis for learning lies in the fact that they are a valuable tool for group learning and assessment, and as such they are increasingly used in Higher Education, for example for:

- group work or presentations;
- project development and management – you could consider using one for your WBL project;
- archive for group discussions and group activities;
- data collection during a module, for example reference, background information;
- editable base for a collective glossary or FAQ.

If you have been involved in any group work before, be it professionally or as part of your studies, you know that contribution – or the lack of it, can sometimes be an issue. This won't be the case with wikis, the usage statistics will list the history of every single modification and show who edited what and when; this makes it easy to acknowledge each individual's contribution. Each time an individual makes changes to a wiki page, this revision becomes the up-to-date version of the document, and as older versions are stored they can be compared side by side and reversed if necessary.

The screen shot in Figure 7.3 shows an example of a wiki which was used in a WBL Research Methods module on the topic 'hypothesis'.

History of Hypothesis

Modified By	Date of Change	Revision	
Mike Bell	Wednesday, 14/10/2009 3:20 PM	Latest (version 3)	View Diff
Christine McDermott	Wednesday, 14/10/2009 1:15 PM	Version 2	View Diff
Allan Fitzgerald	Wednesday, 14/10/2009 1:00 PM	Original (version 1)	View Diff

Figure 7.3   Example of a wiki
Note: Student names have been altered.

How to get started

Everyone can start a wiki on any subject they like. Wikis are now very often a part of universities' VLEs but there is also a whole range of wiki tools available on the web which include free hosted services and free software which you can download to your computer. The following three tools are currently among the most popular wiki tools:

- Wetpaint: www.wetpaint.com/
- Wikispaces: www.wikispaces.com
- Mediawiki: www.mediawiki.org/

Example: Wikis in action

In a WBL Research Methods module at Level 4 and 5, a wiki was used to build up an information base on all important parts of the module, for example how to write a hypothesis, literature review, quantitative and qualitative research methods, questionnaires and so on. After having discussed a topic in class, students had to summarize the content, with each student being able to comment on, add to or revise what had been written.

The WBL students on the module liked the fact that they were able to build up their own knowledge base and could add sources and revise entries as their understanding grew throughout the module; they also found it an invaluable source of information once they started writing their research proposal.

The webpage in Figure 7.4 shows student collaboration.

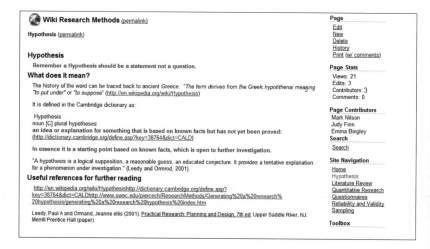

Figure 7.4 Student collaboration on a wiki

Note: Student names have been altered.

Google Docs

Google Docs is a free hosted service which allows you to work on documents collaboratively. It's a neat online alternative to MS Office and the like.

What does it do?

Google Docs enables you to import, create, store and share documents, spreadsheets and presentations. You can simply save the documents you create or send them as emails, as well as publishing them, to the web for everyone to see or just for a selected group of users.

How can you use Google Docs for learning?

Do you need to prepare a group presentation or project and can't keep up with all the e-mails and attachments of latest versions from your group members? With Google docs you can easily edit documents online with whomever you choose, view the documents' revision history which shows you exactly who changed what, and if necessary you can roll back to any earlier version.

How to get started

Go to http://docs.google.com/

You need a Google account to use this service (please refer to section on *Google Reader* in this chapter for more details).

Blogs

A *blog* is, simply put, an online writing tool. The term 'blog' comes from 'we**b log**', the activity of writing a blog is called *blogging* and someone who keeps a blog is called a *blogger*.

What does it do?

It allows you to publish information online. You can use a blog as your private and personal diary or a collaborative space where you share your entries and allow comments from other people. A blog is normally displayed in a chronological order with the most recent entry on top. Older entries are archived on previous pages and can be easily accessed via links on the most current page.

On the web, there are blogs on basically any topic you can imagine. Try it – think of a topic, type it into a search engine and add 'blog'; you will be surprised how many hits you will have. Blogs are used in many different ways; people use them to write about their personal experiences, share information with like-minded people, for example on hobbies or interests, or use them as a platform for professional exchange.

How can you use a blog for learning?

Reflection plays an important role in your WBL studies and blogs offer a good tool for developing this skill. You can use a blog as a reflective journal or a learning log as it offers plenty of room for you to express yourself and grow in understanding. It is quite common now to use blogs or online journals as part of modules which means that your journal is open for comments between you and your tutor or your fellow students and you can learn from each other through discussion and feedback.

Blogs are frequently a tool within your university's VLE; besides being used in the ways already mentioned, they might also be used to share information and stay in touch with your tutor and peers.

How to get started

There are many different blog tools available. Check out a few; if you are thinking of using a blog it is important that you like the 'feel' of it. There are generally two kinds of blogging software, hosted ones which are web-based and free, such as www.blogger.com and installed ones which usually offer more functionality, such as http://wordpress.org. Choose a service, if applicable, download the application, and create an account.

Example: Real life blogging at Teesside University

In a Research Methods module for WBL students at Teesside University, blogs have been used over the last few years as an assessed learning tool at Level 5 and 6. Students use it in the form of a reflective journal to sketch their research ideas, develop a research question, collect information, share thoughts, and generally keep track of their learning during the module. The journal is set up online so that the tutor and all fellow students from the module can view the entries and provide feedback. In sharing their experiences, students are given the opportunity to learn both by example and critique.

Below are some blog entries which show both posts and comment from students. You might notice a difference in tone and style. The guidance for using the blog was to use it in a way that personally suited the student.

Note: Names of students have been altered.

Post on May 14 2009, 19:07 PM by Mike Walters

felt so much better turning up with an idea for my proposal, ideas for my main question and the hypothesis. found the session very informative and was happy to see a full listing of the contents and requirements for the portfolio. The literature review information was great, have never done one and although slightly daunting to do i think i will find the reading of the articles i wish to review interesting so should find it ok to write about them. on going to the library found the input into the university site and the methods for searching for and viewing literature brill. [...]

Comment on May 18 2009, 08:07 AM by Matthew Slider

Hi Mike, I can only say again that I think the working from home topic is very interesting – and very current. BBC 4 did a radio series on this last January (if I remember right), you might be able to find the podcast on their website.

~~~~~~~~~~~~~~~~~~~~~~~~~~~~

Post on June 1 2009, 10:03 AM by Emma Jones

*My preliminary reading of culture suggests that to enquire
about the organisational culture, a questionnaire (quantitative/
qualitative) and interviews (qualitative) should be carried out as it
gives an overall picture at a certain point in time and allows you
to get insights. [...] As we have covered the goals and objectives
and methodology (I still am not sure how to write that. What is
being looked for? I am getting a little frightened there seems to
be a lot to do and there is limited time. It takes me a while to
work out what things mean and I find translating it to a report
hard. In the journal entries using the way the writers put things
down helps me to collect my thoughts but I do not have confidence in the way I put things down) the planning and designing
of the survey needs to be thought about now.*

Comment, June 2 2009 12:11 AM by Brian Miller

Hi Emma

*As always I am extremely impressed with your research journal
and find it quite amazing that you seem to have such a good
grasp on the theory side of it all and have applied it very well to
your research area yet you say you lack confidence in the way in
which you put things down!*

*When it comes to the theory of research I have switched off
completely. I find it painfully boring and time consuming and
would rather read 20 of those high brow Leadership Journals
than just one chapter of Saunders' book on the theory of
research methods!*

*I do not think you have anything to worry about. You seem to
always doubt yourself and push yourself to the limit and yet
always achieve at the end of the day so why should this be any
different? Why not try taking a week off the theory and analysing
everything and just ponder your research question and
objectives. You may find you want to change them or that you
refine them to make sure that everything you research directly
relates in some way to the research question. If it doesn't then
leave it out. Task 3 should help to clarify your thoughts on your
points above.*

Create and share

- SlideShare
- YouTube and YouTube Edu
- Flickr

SlideShare

SlideShare is a social file sharing service which allows you to host and share presentations.

What does it do?

It allows you to upload and share your PowerPoint presentations, Word documents and PDF files. You can add images and graphics, embed videos and synchronize audio to your slides to create so-called SlideCasts.

How can you use SlideShare for learning?

You could use SlideShare if you are working in a group where several people need to add and edit a collaborative presentation. You could also use it if you are looking for comments or feedback from other people, for example your mentor or your tutor. Besides that, it is generally a comfortable place to store and archive your presentations online, and if you don't want other people to view them, just choose the privacy option while you are uploading your work. If you are looking for inspiration, you could join groups about interesting topics or browse other people's presentations to reflect upon your own practices while learning a thing or two about presenting your work. There are some really excellent presentations from academics and specialized people on SlideShare, so it's well worth browsing some of the categories.

Exercise 7.5: Creating an account on SlideShare

- Go to http://www.slideshare.net
- Create an account.
- Watch the QuickTour 'What is SlideShare?'
- Start browsing
  - by 'Categories' that sound interesting, such as Business and Management, Career, Entertainment, Pets;
  - by 'popularity' (most viewed, most downloaded, and so on).
- Found something that you like? Check out the presenter's details, for example: Location? What's their profession? How many other presentations have they added? How many people 'follow' them? (that is, get automated updates on new uploads of that person).

- If you think it is useful, find the little button to follow them as well.

Now you are a part of the SlideShare community. When will you add your first presentation?

YouTube

You probably know YouTube as a video repository site where you can watch music videos, comedies and millions of private videos. In 2009, YouTube launched a new site, called YouTube Edu, where they bring together the best lecturers from (so far) about 200 US and Canadian institutions, including Yale and Harvard, as well as about 45 institutions from Europe (including Cambridge, Leeds and Edinburgh – October 2009).

How can you use YouTube Edu or YouTube for learning?

YouTube Edu caters for educational topics, hence you can search for lecturers or educational contributions in specific subject areas. On the other hand, on YouTube you will probably find videos on virtually any subject. There are also instructional videos on how to use blogs, twitter and so on which might come in handy if this section caught your interest. Or you can get inspired by other people's work and embed topically valid videos, for example talks by top-notch professionals, in your group wiki, blog or any other kind of presentation to enhance your work.

How to get started

Go to http://www.youtube.com/ or http://www.youtube.com/edu and start browsing (for example by university, by subject, most viewed and so on).

Flickr

Flickr is a photo sharing site by Yahoo and at the same time an online community platform.

What does it do?

It is currently one of the most innovative places to store and manage your photos; you can edit your photos, tag (label) them, stick virtual post-it notes on the pictures, create photosets and slideshows, and share your pics with others. You can set privacy levels for each of your photos so it's up to you who you share your pictures with – keep them private, share them with a small selected group or the whole global Flickr community. Flickr also lets you decide on usage licence for each image so your copyrights are protected;

for example when you choose 'attribution licensing' for pictures you allow other people to use these specific photos as long as they give you credit for them. This also works the other way round – if you are searching for photos that have the attribution licensing, Flickr will only display images that you can rightfully use in your presentations.

How can you use Flickr for learning?

Are you always looking for pictures to make your presentations that bit more original? You can use tags to search Flickr for images to enhance your presentations or insert them into blogs and other applications. If your job involves creating digital presentations, you could use Flickr as a way to open up an online discussion as you can use the notes function (virtual post-it notes) to comment on specific images or parts of images.

Exercise 7.6: Creating an account on Flickr

- Go to http://www.flickr.com/
- Create an account.
- Upload some of your photos, 'tag' them with descriptors and annotate them if you like.
- Use tags to search for other people's pictures or browse some of the categories.

Meet, tweet and network

- Skype
- Twitter
- Facebook
- LinkedIn

Skype

Skype is a VOIP (Voice over Internet Protocol) service that allows you to chat both via messaging and internet phone (headphones with microphone) for free.

What does it do?

At a basic level you can use Skype as a text-based chat facility and send files and links. Skype-to-Skype calls are free, so provided you have headphones with a microphone or loudspeakers and a built-in microphone on your computer, you can speak to any people who are on Skype and undertake conference calls and video calls for free.

How to use Skype for learning

Skype is good for both individual and group conversations and tutorials where you're looking for something more immediate than the asynchronous exchanges through a VLE or e-mail. Some tutors use it for drop-in sessions to answer questions. The recently added free feature of screen sharing makes Skype a real winner as you can show your Skype contact exactly what you're looking at by sharing all or part of your screen which could be useful when you are working on a group project or want some immediate feedback.

How to get started

Go to www.skype.com, download the application and set up an account.

Twitter

Twitter is a free micro-blogging service which allows you to write and read messages.

What does it do?

Twitter lets you send and read micro messages which are limited to 140 characters and known as tweets. You can build up a network of people and follow what they say and people can follow you and what you say. Don't get paranoid; this is what you are trying to achieve with twitter – get information from one person to many people in a blink of an eye. It is therefore a good tool for people with common interests, for example communities of practice, professionals, and like-minded people (Galagan, 2009). Don't be put off by trifling tweets such as: 'I just walked my dog' or 'I am going to order pizza' – once you build up your own network it should be easy to follow what interests you.

On the web, twitter is used for social and professional networking, for example to keep in touch, to share expertise and information and get inspired by others. If you use the hash key (#) in your searches, you will find tweets about key topics or events which make it easier to follow specific information. There are many additional applications and tools available which help you to manage and monitor your tweets or to interlink them with other tools such as instant messaging or your mobile phone.

How can you use twitter for your learning?

On the emerging list of the top 100 tools for learning 2009, twitter has been voted the Number One tool for teaching and learning by over 230 learning professionals (Centre for Learning and Performance Technologies, 2009b). For many, the key aspect of twitter is its immediateness; its quick collaboration on the fly.

> **TIP** **How Twitter can help you**
>
> ● With group work – giving quick updates and information exchange.
> ● To share your thoughts, resources, links.
> ● Connect and network with like-minded people.
> ● Get inspired! by those who are doing something similar to you, or are experts in your subject.
> ● Ask questions.
> ● Stay in touch, up-to-date and informed.

Lecturers might use it for brainstorming, feedback, for opinion polls, or announcements such as a reminder for your project due date or a room change.

How to get started?

Currently twitter (http://twitter.com/) is the most popular micro-blogging service, but there is also Jaiku (http://www.jaiku.com/) or Edmodo (http://www.edmodo.com/), the latter being a private communications platform for teachers and students. You sign up, create a profile and start sending short messages.

> **Example: Twitter as a learning tool**
>
> At the University of Waikato, New Zealand, twitter was used in 2009 as a pilot tool for reflection during student teacher training practices. The trainees were asked to tweet at least three times a day answering a set number of questions such as 'what are you learning right now?', 'What are you going to do next?' At the time of writing, the results as to what difference using Twitter has made to reflective writing have not been published but students have been very enthusiastic about the project with a general comment being that it forced them to think about what was happening at a specific point in time. Using twitter, and the fact that they had only 140 characters to report with, made them refine their ideas into essentials and think hard about what they really wanted to say. (N. Wright quoted by N. Robertson, e-mail correspondence, 13 October 2009). This gives an indication as to how twitter will be used for learning and teaching in the near future.

Facebook

Facebook is currently one of the leading social networking sites with over 250 million users (October 2009). Social networks are websites that focus on connecting people. They allow you to build your private, social or professional network. Facebook is free and anyone can join. As with many of the Web 2.0 tools, there are applications which let you interlink services, for example Facebook and Twitter.

How can you use Facebook for learning?

You could use Facebook to create study groups and exchange information and updates. Some universities use it to support you during your first weeks to make sure that you find all the information you need and to provide a platform for you to meet other students. However, as security and privacy is an issue around Facebook, some universities prefer to use secure spaces for social networking within their own VLE.

How to get started

Go to http://www.facebook.com/ and create your user account. If you wish, you can then create as many groups as you like, for example a study group, groups for friends, one for professional acquaintances, and so on. You can set groups to be open for everyone to join, or to be joined at your invitation only.

LinkedIn

LinkedIn is a professional network with currently over 50 million members worldwide and over 11 million professional members in Europe alone (October 2009).

What does it do?

LinkedIn in lets you create and manage your professional identity online, enables you to connect with professionals around the globe and extend and keep track of your contacts. It also provides you with a platform to seek out expertise in specific subject matter areas.

Exercise 7.8: Creating an account on LinkedIn

- Go to http://www.linkedin.com/
- Create an account.
- Explore the other profiles you find.

- Can you find anyone you know?
- Anyone from your industry or professional field who sounds interesting?
- Can you find someone who has done a WBL degree?
- Check out other features such as groups and open Q&A.
- If you are brave and ready for it, create your own profile.

How to use LinkedIn for learning?

Even though LinkedIn is not specifically for learning, it still has its place in this chapter as it has the potential to be a great tool which could enrich your personal and professional development. You could use LinkedIn to start networking with people who have been in a similar situation to you, and have done, or are doing, WBL, to learn from their experiences. Or you could use LinkedIn to post questions to other people in your professional field and therefore network with people to advance your career. One learning professional who put LinkedIn on his 'Top 10 tools for learning' list, sums it up like this; 'Ultimately, learning is all about people. Building and maintaining a professional network is important not only for one's career, but for leveraging the human talent pool. I've hired consultants via LinkedIn based on searches for specific skills' (Anderson, 2008).

Which tool for which purpose?

Table 7.2 gives you an overview of all the tools and applications described in this section. It also gives you an indication for which tasks, or in which learning situations, you could use them. However, as pointed out in the beginning, there are no right and wrong ways to use Web 2.0 tools for learning; so if you come up with a different function for a tool, good on you!

	Search/Collect	Create	Share	Reflect	Communicate	Collaborate	Network
Google Scholar	x						
RSS	x						
Google Reader	x						
Pod/Vodcast	x	(x)	(x)	(x)			
Delicious	x		x		(x)	(x)	(x)
Wiki	x	x	x	x	x	x	(x)
Google docs	(x)	x	x		x	x	
Blogs	x	x	x	x	x	x	x
SlideShare	x	x	x		x	x	x
YouTube/YouTube Edu	x	(x)	x				
Flickr	x	x	x		(x)	x	(x)
Skype					x	x	
Twitter	x	x	x	x	x	x	x
Facebook			x	(x)	x	x	x
LinkedIn			x	(x)	x	x	x

Note: (x) in the table indicates that you could use this tool or application for a task but it would probably not be your first choice. For instance you could create a video and put it onto YouTube, create podcasts and share them or search Google Docs for documents that other people made available to everyone, but none of that might be a top priority to support and improve your learning.

Table 7.2 Which tool? At a glance

Summary

1   Get to know your university's VLE – the better you know your way around it, the more you will get out of it.

2   Use your university's electronic library – if it offers an online tutorial on how to search literature, go for it! It will make your life so much easier.

3   Be proactive – if you need information, clarification, or just a word of support from your tutor, drop them a line. They are there to help.

4   Set some time aside to explore the potential of Web 2.0 tools for your learning – the skills that you are learning might also come in handy in your professional (and most certainly) private life, as well as enhancing your study.

5   If you are interested in using a tool or a selection of them, make sure you spend time reading or watching the instructions – knowing about the little things can make a huge difference.

6   And last but not least – online support is not primarily about technology but about your learning experience. So whatever your goal, enjoy the journey!

References

Anderson, G. (2008) on Centre for Learning & Performance Technologies. *Gabe's Top 10 Tools* (as at 26 February 2008) (online). Available at http://c4lpt.co.uk/recommended/gabeanderson.html (accessed 27 November 2009).

Bosley, S. and Young, D. (2006) 'On-line Learning Dialogues in Learning through Work'. *Journal of Workplace Learning*, 18 (6), 355–366.

Centre for Learning & Performance Technologies (2008). *Top 100 Tools for Learning and Teaching 2008* (finalized 31 October 2008) (online). Compiled by Jane Hart. Available at http://www.c4lpt.co.uk/recommended/top1002008.html (accessed 27 November 2009).

Centre for Learning & Performance Technologies (2009a). *A Quick Guide to Social Learning.* (online). Available at http://c4lpt.co.uk/handbook/social-learning.html (accessed 27 November 2009).

Centre for Learning & Performance Technologies (2009b). *Top 100 Tools for Learning and Teaching 2009* (as at 30 October 2009) (online). Compiled by Jane Hart. Available at http://www.c4lpt.co.uk/recommended/index.html (accessed 27 November 2009).

Galagan, P. (2009) *Twitter as a Learning Tool. Really* (online) for The American Society for Training & Development (ASTD). Available at http://www.astd.org/LC/2009/0409_galagan.htm (accessed 26 October 2009).

JISC (2009) *Higher Education in a Web 2.0 World.* (online). Available at http://www.jisc.ac.uk/media/documents/publications/heweb20rptv1.pdf (accessed 27 November 2009).

Wheeler, S. (2009) *It's Personal: Learning Spaces, Learning Webs* (online). Available at http://www.slideshare.net/timbuckteeth/its-personal-learning-spaces-learning-webs (accessed 27 November 2009).

Young, D. and Stephenson, J. (2007) 'The Use of an Interactive Learning Environment to Support Learning through Work', in D. Young and J. Garnett (eds), *Work-based Learning Futures* (Bolton: University Vocational Awards Council), 84–97.

Suggested further reading

Andrews, A. and Haythornthwaite, C (2007) *The SAGE Handbook of E-Learning Research* (London: Sage Publications).

Clarke, A. (2005) *IT Skills for Successful Study* (Basingstoke: Palgrave Macmillan).

Clarke, A. (2008) *E-Learning Skills*, 2nd edn (Basingstoke: Palgrave Macmillan).

Collis, B. and Moonen, J. (2001) *Flexible Learning in a Digital World: Experiences and Expectations* (London: Kogan Page).

Coombes, H. (2001) *Research Using IT* (Basingstoke: Palgrave Macmillan).

Dolowitz, D., Buckler, S. and Sweeney, F. (2008) *Researching Online* (Basingstoke: Palgrave Macmillan).

Ellis, R. and Goodyear, P. (2010) *Students' Experiences of E-learning in Higher Education: The Ecology of Sustainable Innovation* (London: Routledge).

McVay Lynch, M. (2004) *Learning Online: A Guide to Success in the Virtual Classroom* (London: RoutledgeFalmer).

Pulman, A. (2009) *Blogs, Wikis, Podcasts and More* (Basingstoke: Palgrave Macmillan).

Race, P. (2004) *500 Tips for Open and Online Learning*, 2nd edn (London: RoutledgeFalmer).

Santy, J. and Smith, L. (2007) *Being an E-learner in Health and Social Care: A Student's Guide* (London: Routledge).

Savin-Baden, M. (2007) *A Practical Guide to Problem-based Learning Online* (London: Routledge).

Simpson, O. (2003) *Student Retention in Online*, Open and Distance Learning (London: Kogan Page).

Talbot, C.J. (2007) *Studying at a Distance: A Guide for Students*, 2nd edn (Maidenhead: Open University Press).

8 Foundation Degrees: What They Can Do for You

Alix Pearson

In this chapter you will learn:

▶ what a Foundation degree is, how you can get on one and how it will be taught;
▶ what features you might expect to find on your programme once you enrol;
▶ what your qualification will lead to next – progression and post-graduate opportunities;
▶ how much it will cost;
▶ the kind of contribution and input your employer might make;
▶ the subjects/ sectors/professions covered.

● What is a Foundation degree?

> I couldn't see the point of doing an academic degree, not when I knew what I wanted to do. I thought I might as well learn something that I would end up using. (Student, Navigator, 2006: 20)

Foundation degrees are designed for people who work, for employers and for employability. They are equivalent to the first two years of an Honours degree, and are available in a range of different modes. They can be studied full time, but are most relevant to working students like yourself when they are available in part-time or work-based modes. They can allow you to use your work experience to achieve learning (also see Chapter 2). This in turn can allow you to enhance your skills and qualifications while in work, hence completing your award, sometimes, in no more time than is taken by a full-time undergraduate, even though you will have had less time to devote to study, but you have been allowed to use work-based learning which means that time at work, applying theories, testing ideas and researching and thinking count as study time.

Foundation degrees include a strong focus on work-based learning, and the effective use of work-based experiences to learn and gain academic credit. The work-based and vocational nature of Foundation degrees means that it is not always easy to categorize them into full-time or part time modes; but they do tend to fall into the categories intended for *employability and widening participation* (most often full-time) or designed for *workforce development* (might be part-time or work-based). Regardless of the mode of delivery the Foundation degree will have a strong vocational focus and address the key skills and knowledge required for real work in business sectors where a need has been identified. The Level Outcomes, defined by the QAA Foundation Degree Qualification Benchmarks (http://www. qaa.ac.uk/reviews/foundationdegree/benchmark/fdqb.asp) require academic challenge equivalent to that of Honours degree programmes at Levels 4 and 5 (see Appendix 1 and level descriptors in Chapters 1, 2 and 4).

The core features of a Foundation degree are:

- employer involvement;
- the development of skills and knowledge;
- application of skills in the workplace;
- credit accumulation and transfer (Chapter 2);
- progression – within work and/or to an honours degree.

There are currently nearly 3000 validated Foundation degrees in England. They are listed on a database compiled by Foundation Degree Forward which is checked against the data from education providers (http://www.fdf.ac.uk/courses/). Foundation degrees can be run by universities or colleges of further education who are able to offer higher education, but they must be validated by a university and the degree award you get is a university award. The Foundation degree is a qualification in its own right, designated by the letters FdA (Foundation degree Arts) or FdSc (Foundation degree Sciences), you will be a graduate and take part in the formal university graduation ceremonies, either at the university where you have enrolled or at the university which awards the HE level qualification for your college.

How long have Foundation degrees been around?

There has been a steady growth in students enrolled on Foundation degrees since the first 4320 students registered in 2001/02; enrolments for 2008/09 reached 87,339 (see Figure 8.1).

The Foundation Degree Task Force report to government ministers in 2003 suggested that the new award should aim to reach 100,000 Foundation degree places by 2010, a figure which became the unofficial success measure of Foundation degrees:

> Foundation Degrees continue to grow in popularity as both students and employers appreciate the innovative nature of these qualifications.

National growth in Foundation degree student numbers

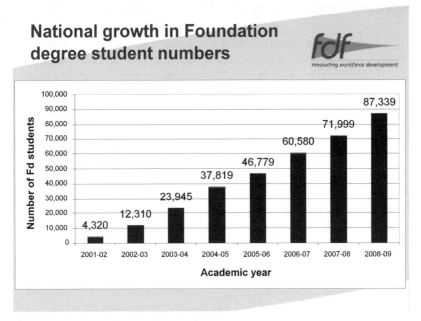

Figure 8.1   Increasing student numbers

Source: Foundation Degree Forward (fdf), based on HEFCE data published in the Foundation Degree Key statistics report. http://www.hefce.ac.uk/pubs/hefce/2008/08_16/

They are enabling individuals to develop their careers whilst helping business to remain strong in these challenging economic times.

I'm delighted with these latest enrolment figures, which confirm that we're well on the way to meeting our ambition for 100,000 Foundation degree students by 2010. (David Lammy MP, Minister of State for Higher Education, reported in fdf press release; http://www.fdf.ac.uk/page.aspx?id=4&newsid=7)

Much of the additional funding which has been made available to HE providers since 2004 has been for the provision of Foundation degrees. A recent policy, The Equivalent and Lower Qualification Policy (ELQ) withholds funding for students who already hold a degree qualification, unless they are studying for a Foundation degree. This illustrates the priority these degrees continue to have in government policy. The government's commitment to this style of award has ensured that both the number of Foundation degrees available and the number of students enrolling on them has increased dramatically (http://www.hefce.ac.uk/pubs/hefce/2008/08_13).

Foundation degrees for employability or widening participation

> This kind of thing is the best way forward. So you do a degree in geography ... you probably never use any of it, this kind of degree sounds good, sounds useful. Why would anyone want to do a basic boring academic degree, it makes me think twice about interviewing them? (Employer, micro business, Navigator, 2006: 20)

These programmes are full-time and can be run by universities or colleges. Entry is through the Universities and Colleges Admissions Service – UCAS (www.ucas.ac.uk/). The courses are often built on existing expertise within the university or college, through their Level 3 provision (immediately below HE level – see Appendix 1 for a table of Level 4 and above) They offer a mixed curriculum which blends taught elements with some work experience. Providing appropriate work experience is often a challenge as it is not easy to persuade employers to provide placement opportunities for students, especially if the college or university have not planned how the employer might benefit, as well as the student. The objectives of placements need to be integral to the programme and adequately prepared and designed.

Example: Paul – seamless progression from work placement to work

Paul gave his career in web design a great start when he chose a Foundation Degree. The course was all about employability and, in a field where all jobs attract a great number of applications, it gave Paul the edge he needed. Being ready to deliver value to an employer means more than having a collection of techniques. Paul says 'My personal development at College on the Foundation degree prepared me for presentations, group working and how to schedule and manage a project. Feedback was one-to-one and was very helpful in making improvements to my weaker areas. We had been given "live briefs" (design specifications from industry) in our college course and had the chance to listen to guidance from professional designers. We were well-prepared.'

The College staff say 'We want our Foundation degree students to feel comfortable as soon as they embark upon work experience of any sort. That means the systems and packages they use at college must be those chosen by the industry – and

> students need to be up to speed using the right techniques from
> the start.'
>   Paul's employer says, 'Paul quickly became very useful indeed.
> Soon I found I could trust him to deal face-to-face with
> customers and then to set up and manage delivery on our
> projects. He was too good to let go – so I didn't.'

If you are not employed, having a work placement is not the only way for you to gain experience of a workplace. For some sectors, colleges provide modern and specialized training facilities, which mirror real workplaces; these 'real work environments' allow you to practise skills safely, closely supervised by your tutors. Some examples of this are 'clean rooms' which are used for the manufacture of aseptic pharmaceuticals and Travel Agencies where college staff, other students, and members of the public come to book holidays and business travel through you. Modern and sophisticated college restaurants, for example, offer you the opportunity to undertake all levels of work, which mirror the job roles you would find in the commercial world. Some universities have created lifelike courtrooms and 'incident houses' to facilitate the training of crime and forensic investigation professionals.

In other sectors, such as art and design and media design, where the employment opportunities are often as sole traders, or as part of a small team, work experience can be arranged by the provision of 'live briefs' where tutors act as your client and assessment outline which requires you to, for example, develop a database, or a corporate image. The amount of time your Foundation degree programme spends on work experience reflects the complexity of the workplace and the job roles within it; your college or university will have consulted employers and/or employer organizations to get the content and balance of the programme just right.

Example: 'Apprentices' test skills without having to face 'Suralan'

> A student on a full-time Foundation degree in multimedia design
> needs to acquire a broad range of skills in order to become
> employable and successful in a very competitive industry. This
> FdA in multimedia design has modules covering web design,
> manipulation of sound, graphics and moving image using pack-
> ages which are commonplace in industry. Skills development

includes practice at presentations, and assessment tasks have students working in Sir Alan Sugar's 'Apprentice' style groups. Working with real design specifications from industry gives students the chance to practise project scheduling and management skills as well as their technical skills. By the end of the second year of the Foundation degree, students are working independently on a work-based project which will give them 30 per cent of the mark for the whole year. The college has strong contacts with local multimedia companies, inviting employers in to give guest lectures and master-classes and to cast their eyes over completed work. By the time they graduate, students really feel that they have the knowledge, skills and experience to work in the industry, either for themselves, or in a company.

Foundation degrees for workforce development

Basically that's the way the organisation is going, it's all getting a lot more technical and you've got to get your knowledge base up. (Student, Navigator, 2006: 21)

These are the second main category of Foundation degrees. The Foundation degrees described above 'for employment' tend to be full-time; those aimed at 'workforce development' are more likely to be part-time and developing you *while you also work*. Workforce development is about providing education and training for you while you are employed, the knowledge and skills involved are closely tailored to the needs of your company and sector. Because you have a job, much wider use can be made of work-based learning, so assessments can be directly related to making improvements in your workplace. You should expect to take an active part in your own learning; this often holds great appeal for students who have been disenchanted by more traditional approaches to education. An active approach is also required from your employer. This might be in the form of interest and input to what you are studying – it might also take the form of paying all or some of your fees. To justify this level of support you need to ensure that you demonstrate the workplace benefit and relevance of your academic activity.

What is work-based learning?

Within a Foundation degree the principles of WBL remain the same as those discussed in the other chapters of this book; WBL is the use of opportunities and experience available in the workplace to provide a nexus for the development of the higher-level cognitive skills which characterize higher education. A history graduate may develop higher-level critical and analytical skills by studying the fall of imperialism in Russia, whereas you too will develop these same critical and analytical skills – but perhaps by studying the increase in scrap and wastage rates on an automated production line. For you, as a work-based learner, your work is your 'subject'. However, WBL is not about attaching academic credit directly to functional skills; you are not given credit for your ability to operate a piece of machinery (a craft skill). What you *might* be given credit for is your ability to apply and reflect on different theories and models of production, quality and customer service in the manufacturing process.

There are three models of a Workforce Development Foundation Degree:

Programmes designed to train you to work for a particular company

> I applied to the Police and got in, and they used to send the new
> intake to regional training centres, but now you do a Foundation
> Degree. (Student, Navigator, 2006: 20)

The police force is one of several organizations that use Foundation degrees. Another example is the Network Rail partnership with Sheffield Hallam University, which has the following characteristics:

- Foundation degree in railway engineering;
- placements offered to students;
- interview with company is guaranteed for programme graduates;
- it is not available through UCAS.

This type of partnership is valuable to both employer and employee/potential employee. It helps the employer with succession planning and saves money on training costs as students enter employment already experienced in the processes of the company. This model is becoming more popular, but is not yet commonplace.

Example: BT Foundation degrees are a ringing success

> BT was one of the first companies to set up a Foundation degree
> when it launched a programme for Higher Apprentices in 2006.
> BT joined forces with a number of universities to create a series
> of Foundation degrees to attract 'A' level students who were

intending to go to university. Instead, students can earn while they learn, gain a recognized qualification and work experience and avoid student debts.

Students are based across the country and study subjects like network and communication technologies and telecoms and management using online learning, traditional classroom-based lectures and supported learning in the workplace. The course content has been designed not only to fit with the job placements students are assigned but also to give each student a broad knowledge which can open up wider career paths too.

The programme takes three years to complete and about 95 per cent of students complete the course and can have a successful career with BT.

Programmes designed to up-skill existing workers

These programmes are designed so that workers can carry out a broader range of tasks, or be promoted to greater responsibility. Companies involved include: Tesco, Rolls Royce and Thomson Travel.

> We've got people involved in Foundation Degrees and another about to be. We saw them as a recognisable qualification that fitted into our business, and they were flexible. (Employer, large company, Navigator, 2006: 21)

The features of the programme include:

- close partnership between universities and employers;
- content and assessment is related to the workplace;
- employer can share the delivery of the programme with master-classes and internal training programmes which are accredited.

Many of these programmes have leadership, management and wider business skills at their core, although some also contain some technical or professional updating as well. The employer would be expected to play a strong role in supporting students through such a programme, and not just by meeting all or some of the cost. Applications are made through the employer and normal undergraduate entry qualifications are generally waived if you have the right level of responsibility at work and have demonstrated your commitment and ability to undertake the course.

Example: Fd student saves company £150,000!

A company making a well-known brand of frozen seafood products helped design a Foundation degree in Food Manufacturing Management with a local college in Humberside. The content therefore, was very relevant to the company, but even they were surprised at the benefits they reaped. For example, one student improved the effectiveness of the packing area, negotiating with a customer for a change in size of the boxes used.

It sounds like a simple change, but the company hadn't considered it. The knowledge from the Foundation degree and the assessment project undertaken, allowed the area supervisor to look at things through a fresh pair of eyes, informed by the theory of operations management learned on the programme. Not only this, but another project, from another student improved the efficiency of the fish finger saws, resulting in savings on both rejects and planned maintenance costs of £150,000.

Programmes which meet the aspirations of students to develop themselves and enhance their career prospects

Such programmes might be paid for by employers and supported by them, but are not part of a company internal development or succession planning scheme. These programmes have the following characteristics:

- developed by colleges and universities;
- content of the programme guided by reference to employers;
- cater for a mixed group of students – you might work in different organizations, content often is generic;
- given context by you and your own workplace;
- use your own company data, policies and processes;
- applications are made directly to the university or college;
- can be completed in two years, sometimes three.

Example: Student writes company business plan

Lucy, a team leader in a customer contact centre, enrols on a Foundation degree in Customer Service Management offered at her local college. Her fellow students work in a variety of places, some in contact centres, some for the local authority, one runs an internet retailer, another works in a building society. What they have in common is that they are all responsible for managing systems and processes to provide excellent customer service. They all study six modules in the first year of the programme, five in the second year and they are trying to complete the Foundation degree in two years.

The first year modules cover the generic areas of:

- Managing Self and Others
- Marketing in a Customer Service Environment
- Managing Operations
- Managing and Learning from Customer Complaints.

They all do a personal development plan to improve some of their personal skills such as making presentations, or learning to say no. Each of the students undertakes the assignments based on their own organization, and with a confidentiality rule, they learn from each other as they make presentations about their projects and plans.

One of the projects Lucy completes reviews the customer complaints process in use at the contact centre, and she makes recommendations to improve this and presents it to her manager. She passes this assignment with a high mark, and is also noticed by her manager, which means she is kept in mind if any special project work needs to be done.

Where does a Foundation degree lead me? What can I do next?

They are challenging, and they're not an easy ride. (Employer, large company, Navigator, 2006: 20)

Foundation degrees are an innovative vocationally focused higher education qualification. They lead, via various routes, towards further HE awards, thus supporting lifelong learning. You may not want to study further at this time and you should not interpret that your Foundation degree is in any way deficient as a qualification in its own right, it is not. If you follow a traditional route through education, from GCSEs, to 'A' and 'AS' levels and then to a degree your qualifications might feel like they flowed smoothly and were achieved in a relatively short period of time. Progression to higher awards, through vocational routes is not usually this seamless. There are wide ranging and diverse vocational qualifications, such as NVQs, BTEC National qualifications or 14–19 diplomas. Vocational students tend to be older (and busier) and to be studying in part-time, work-based modes. There is a limited choice of relevant, accessible higher-level programmes to suit the needs of learners like yourself – who prefer to study in a work-based or work-related mode. A unique feature of Foundation degrees is the provision made for progression to an honours degree (known as articulation). This can involve mapping onto existing honours degrees.

This might be an added benefit – but you must ensure that what is being offered to you suits both your learning needs and your career profile as well as not in any way compromising the existing content and coherence of your completed Foundation degree:

> Validating institutions may experience difficulty in providing coherent progression routes for Foundation Degree students, and may, therefore, shape the qualification to 'fit' more traditional qualifications. (Longhurst, 2005: 50)

The design and provision of appropriate and accessible progression routes for Foundation degree graduates has been a subject of some debate. A Foundation degree is the *equivalent* of the first two years of a degree programme, it is not meant to be exactly *the same as*.

The full-time Foundation degrees, aimed at employability or widening participation and often based on more traditional, already existing awards, generally have suitable programmes available to provide progression routes. It is the part-time, work-based programmes which can present more of a challenge when an appropriate progression route is sought. If you complete your foundation degree by WBL then transferring to a traditional Honours route may not be what you want to do. Furthermore, these routes might not be appropriate for you in terms of the learning and teaching methods used and the practical requirements – for example, there may be extensive campus attendance. Your WBL experience will have (or soon will!) imparted a flavour of just how hybrid and relevant learning can be. Once you realize that your study route can be personalized and related to real life workplace activities why would you round that off with classroom study? Similarly, your employer, who may have paid your fees and allowed you time to study, will also favour the practical application of knowledge and skills in the workplace, which is the main principle of Foundation degrees, and of great benefit to both you and your employer. Generally, employers are disappointed if this stops because you have no choice but to top up with a more traditional route. You need to make enquiries about how you can progress your Foundation degree to an Honours degree (if that is what you think you might want to do). Ask about the availability of progression routes, which adopt the same principles of WBL as your Foundation degree has. Details of the processes and principles of such work-based routes are discussed in the other chapters of this text. For example, the accreditation of prior learning (APL) in Chapter 2; work-based projects in Chapter 5; work-based assessments in Chapter 4; WBL online in Chapter 7. The work-based studies programmes discussed earlier in this collection aim to address employer needs and demands in relation to work-force development, while also fulfilling your needs, as a student who is also accustomed to working and is ideally suited to a student-centred programme.

The nature of higher-level WBL and study changes as you progress through the HE levels. It is important that you continue to be stretched intellectually and, similarly, that what is on offer to you in the way of progression routes expects a greater level of responsibility or influence of you at work. In traditional programmes progression tends to be characterized by knowledge of a 'subject' and engaging in subject research. In programmes which are designed for the workplace, progression is characterized more by the role, responsibility and sphere of your influence in your workplace – as well as your intellectual and analytical capabilities.

For example, if you enrolled on a Foundation degree in Leadership and Management your progression might look like this:

- First year (Level 4) of programme – understanding the impact you can have on your team and your immediate area of production.
- Second year (Level 5) – learning about a broader sphere of influence, looking at the impact of your team, or task, on your department.
- Third/honours year (Level 6) – considering broader and higher level impact, looking at issues at organizational level, researching perhaps the impact your organization has on its operating environment, or the impact external issues might have on the company. This is about the 'bigger picture' – as your role matures.

The ability to address these more generic issues is typical of the higher-level skills which employers indicate they are looking for in graduates. The

Council for Industry and Higher Education's (CIHE) 2008 report on graduate employability cites 'commercial awareness' as the area where there is the largest gap between how important employers think this is, and how satisfied they are with the capabilities of graduates in this area (Archer and Davison, 2008: 10).

Example: Art and design students – practice running your own business, with support

Students gaining Foundation degrees in Art and Design at a college in the north-east of England can set themselves up as sole traders to get their BA in their progression year programme. Working in a disused industrial building, creating the atmosphere of an art studio collective, the students prepare business plans and aim to create commercially viable artwork.

Ceramicists work alongside fine artists, who work alongside photographers and graphic designers. Maximum creativity in enterprise is encouraged and supported and students have mounted exhibitions in car showrooms, taken large ceramic sculptures to major pottery festivals and taken selling space at popular craft fairs.

College staff help the students to reflect on their experiences, making sure that they learn from what are inevitable mistakes. The generic skills developed in this programme relate to business and financial planning, marketing and publicity, customer service, and project planning.

Some of the students go on to run successful businesses and the college has an adviser from Business Link on-site to provide support and information. Others use the experience to conclude that self-employment is not for them, but the experience they have had impresses potential employers.

The Framework for Higher Education Qualifications (www.qaa.ac.uk/academicinfrastructure/FHEQ/EWNI08/FHEQ08.pdf) published by the Quality Assurance Agency for Higher Education, defines the level of learning required of students at each stage of higher education programmes (see Chapters 1, 2 and 4). At Level 6, it is necessary for you to have some experience of research methods, so the generic progression routes require a work-based research project (Chapter 5), which is the equivalent of the more traditional dissertation that concludes most degree programmes and some programmes also include a taught Research Methods module. It is quite common for the research project to comprise half of the credit for this level (perhaps 40 credits for the project and 20 credits for the Research Methods module). The other half of the credit usually comes from negotiated elements, such as a critical review of learning with an action plan for career development, which includes a specialist area of personal skill such as 'project management' or 'creative thinking and action' (Chapter 3). You can be from any working context to pursue these generic framework programmes; you personalize the content by applying it to your own workplace and your own ambition.

Postgraduate opportunities

Because work-based Foundation degrees are post-experience programmes – that is, completed while you are in work – it may be appropriate for you to progress directly onto a post-experience Master's level award. A Master's programme such as a Master of Business Administration (MBA) or an MA in Management may be considered a suitable progression for you, especially if you have undertaken a Foundation degree because you have been away from learning for some time and lacked confidence academically, but hold a senior post with much responsibility at work.

Professional bodies

Similarly, it may be more appropriate for you to progress to professional qualifications and awards. It is important that the requirements of professional bodies are checked very carefully when embarking on any programme of education. If your chosen career progression demands professional qualifications or membership of professional bodies make sure that the Foundation degree is recognized by the professional body and check the progression arrangements. Some sectors, such as social work, will allow progression into year two of the Honours degree in order to become a qualified social worker.

There are a few Foundation degrees which have embraced professional qualifications as part of the Foundation degree curriculum, so that you can gain two awards on completion of your programme, or if you already hold the professional qualification you can add the necessary modules to it to gain a Foundation degree. For example, one college offers a Foundation degree in accounting, which is built around the curriculum of the Association of Accounting Technicians. This means that the Foundation degree curriculum includes studying which accountants would have had to do anyway. Another college offers a Foundation degree in Counselling which also gives students the professional qualification of the British Association of Counselling Practice (BACP).

● What subjects are Foundation degrees available in?

As Foundation degrees are designed for the workplace, reflecting the skills and knowledge requirements of real jobs, they are not categorized on an academic subject basis, but by employment sector. Early Foundation degree development was concentrated in areas where there was no history of qualification in order to support new technical and professional job roles, so it is perhaps not surprising that early growth, and subsequent high numbers of programmes are in areas of public sector workforce development, through education and health.

Figure 8.2, compiled by Foundation Degree Forward, shows the range and number of Foundation degrees across employment sectors.

There are high numbers of full-time students on programmes in health and social care, medical science and pharmacy, nursing, sports science, technology, tourism, transport and travel and all creative arts and design. Although there is no reliable data to indicate whether the full-time students on these programmes are work-based or full-time institutionally based students, my professional experience and knowledge suggests that subjects allied to medicine will have some work-based students in the full-time number. The other areas are likely to be programmes designed to enhance employability.

At the opposite end to the popular sectoral areas (for example, education, business and computing), the sectors where there has been no strong tradition of training in higher-levels skills appear, such as retailing, or where the existing professional route to qualification is well-established and does not

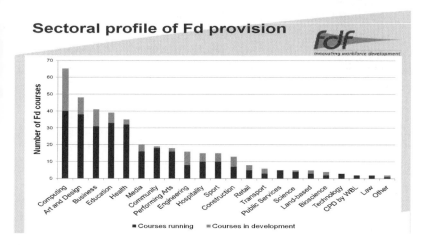

Figure 8.2 How Foundation degrees span sectors
Source: Foundation Degree Forward.

embrace Foundation degrees, such as law. Foundation degrees are well suited to all sectors who recognize the importance and need for higher-level skills among the workforce, and where new emerging job roles require a robust qualification to establish standards of professional competence. This is particularly vital as the speed of the twenty-first century global market-place accelerates and we are increasingly reminded that the workforce of the future will need to adapt to rapid change, including changing jobs and job roles more frequently than in the past, and working in industries which may not even exist yet. To quote a recent government policy document, 'We require a skills system that not only responds to demand but is also able to anticipate future growth in the economy' (BERR, 2009: 15).

Example: Foundation degree creates a new appetite for learning

A care home offering high quality residential nursing care for elderly people, some with dementia, recognizes that demo-graphic changes will have a big impact on their work. The popu-lation is ageing, creating greater demand for care, and this applies to their workforce too, with many staff approaching retirement age themselves.

The care home wishes to improve the skills of the existing workforce, in order to achieve continuity of high quality care and a lower staff turnover. The workforce already has qualifications in social care and dementia, but in order to encourage profes-sional development, more is required. Clinical skills need to be firmly embedded in an HE approach.

By working in partnership with HE the care home has created a new role of 'Lead Carer', and existing healthcare assistants can prepare for this role by undertaking a Foundatioin degree in health and social care practice.

The entire curriculum of the Foundation degree has been developed in consultation with the care home. Studying is done both at university and in the workplace and staff are taking on more senior duties as they progress through the programme as well as exploring other HE opportunities.

Teaching assistants, paralegal advisers, police officers, assistant practi-tioners in podiatry and radiography, aircraft engineers and nuclear de-commissioners are all professions which have a work-based Foundation degree as a signal of competence. Fingerprint experts and Crime Scene Investigators working in police forces are qualified by a Foundation degree, which is awarded by a university, although all the teaching, work-based learning and assessment is done by the employer.

Some employers who invest their resources in providing in-house training for their staff have had their training analysed to see if it is worthy of academic credit. A number of companies, small ones as well as household names, have partnered with universities and as a result their training now carries HE level credits. This means that as you undertake in-house training with your employer you not only get the skills, knowledge and information you need but you might also be adding up credits which can be used towards an HE award; or if the in-house programme is a substantial one, it might even represent an award in its own right. Robust quality assurance measures ensure that standards are kept high, and some programmes, such as those named in the paragraph above, are considered creditable as an entire foundation degree. In other cases, the university identifies a programme which students can progress to, or designs a special route for further staff development.

Example: Foundation degree helps to reduce operating costs

A medium-sized logistics company working with tight profit margins wanted to introduce a flatter company structure, devolving decision-making down to the lowest practical level and removing a tier of high-level management. They create and deliver a management development programme for their middle management staff, covering team and performance management, change management, effective leadership and cost control. Although the company only has 500 staff, the management development programme is targeted at 80 staff and over a period of three years, all 80 staff became part of the programme.

fdf advice encourages the company to consider academic accreditation for the programme.

Initial analysis shows that, with the addition of work-based assignments, the programme is equivalent to the first year of a Foundation degree.

An articulation arrangement is agreed with a university, allowing members of staff who have completed the programme to enter the second year of the Foundation degree in management.

The company could have chosen to have an award for their own programme, but decided against the cost and time commitments as there were a small number of students in total. The articulation agreement rewards those who are keen to continue their own development by signing up for further study.

'If the Fd uses my work, do I still have to go to lectures and do exams?' – How will your Fd be taught?

The aim of a work-based Foundation degree is to provide you with a structured opportunity to reflect upon your current workplace activity and to more fully understand your own competence as it fits with the operational requirements of your current and future job roles. Although you may not have much experience as a 'student', you do have experience of your job and your workplace, and a good Foundation degree curriculum will work with this, offering you modules which have a blend of teaching and learning approaches. There should be a balance of things you have to do yourself, such as work-based projects (Chapter 5) or personal development plans (Chapter 3), and areas which have a more theoretical base. You should not have to spend a lot of time in formal lectures – there are lots of other ways for you to learn – and being on a Foundation degree may feel quite different from your expectations. When we think of learning, we quite often think of memorizing, as this was the way many of us were taught at school; we were taught to memorize times tables or spellings or vocabulary from a foreign language, or formulae in mathematics.

Skills development requires a different kind of learning, which is not based on memory but is based on understanding and application. The focus for teaching and learning on a Foundation degree programme should be work-based action learning. This means that you should be able to apply theories and models you have learned about to solve real practical problems in your workplace. For example, you may plan a work-based project which looks at reducing scrap waste in a particular area of manufacturing production; you will need to have knowledge of methods of data collection and analysis as well as production efficiency and effectiveness. In order to present a proposal for change, you may need to have knowledge of financial systems and procedures, as well as the financial systems in place at your work; a rudimentary knowledge of marketing and business planning may also be appropriate to this project. In addition to this, personal skills will be required to bring the project to an effective conclusion. As well as learning and study skills, you will require presentation skills, IT skills, influencing skills and organizational skills. You will gather the knowledge you need from a variety of sources, for example:

- attending part-time lectures;
- e-learning using appropriate material;
- attending work-place training events;
- reading books and articles;

- attending master-classes or guest lectures;
- mentoring by an appropriate work colleague;
- attending conferences or professional updating events.

It wouldn't really work trying to assess complex learning and development such as this in an examination. Your project could be assessed using a blend of methods (Chapter 4). The written business plan with all its research and analysis would be supported by a video or observation of the presentation; testimonials from managers and colleagues; and a reflective report of the learning process from you.

What do I need to get onto a Foundation degree?

All programme providers will have their own rules about this. Generally, as you will be doing a work-based programme, you are likely to be over 21, an age when most institutions apply different rules for entry. You may not need any Level 3 (for example, 'A' level or BTEC) qualifications, as the education provider will instead be looking for evidence that you can benefit from the programme and have the ability to succeed. You may be asked to have an interview so that they can find out what you have been doing since you left school. What is most important is that you have the right kind of responsibility in your job to be able to do work-based assessment tasks at the right level. Some institutions may ask for a letter of support from your manager to demonstrate this. In some cases, if you want to study a subject area which has a firm foundation in academic principles, for example mathematics and engineering, and you do not have the necessary entry qualifications at Level 3, you may be offered the opportunity to demonstrate that you have the required knowledge by submitting a portfolio of evidence of your relevant experience. There may also be opportunities for you to undertake a taster module, or submit a piece of written work to demonstrate that you have the ability to complete the course.

If my employer has to support my study what will they be expected to do?

It is very useful to have someone at work who is on your side when it comes to undertaking work-based assignments and projects. They will be helpful in negotiating access for you, to areas of work, or people whom you may not normally come across. For example, if you work in production, you may rarely speak to someone from marketing. However, it would be quite likely that a work-based project would require you to show some knowledge of how marketing was approached in your organization. Having someone supporting you at work, especially if they are more senior, can often help smooth the way to negotiate spending some time in the marketing department, or with the marketing manager. This can be similarly helpful if you require access to plans or documents which are not in the public domain – someone to speak to senior managers on your behalf can be helpful. This person can sometimes be referred to as a 'work-based mentor' but that need not be taken literally. Smoothing the way for you in your learning at work is only one part of what a work-based mentor might do to facilitate your Foundation degree study.

A mentor might offer you:

- advice and support on good practice;
- underpinning knowledge and understanding relating to your occupational knowledge and practices;
- underpinning knowledge and understanding relating to their fulfilment and management of day-to-day work practices and the management of change;
- support in arranging for activities to take place to enable you to attain your objectives;
- advice on portfolio building and evidence collection (especially if your mentor has a training background);
- support in identifying and carrying out research to develop practices in your specialist occupational field;
- support in identifying and developing personal, generic and key skills.

Achievement in work-based programmes relies not just on you and your tutors at the college or university, but on your operating in a supportive working environment. If you are fortunate enough to have a formalized or very supportive mentoring arrangement use it well. Try to remain self-sufficient, it is your programme after all, not theirs, but use the help and expertise they can offer you. If you cannot find anyone to support you in this way at work do not worry as this is not unusual. You will need to rely more on your tutors at the university or college (Chapter 6).

● How much will a Foundation degree cost?

Education providers are autonomous bodies who have the liberty to set their own fees, so it is not possible to give accurate information about this. Some may charge the standard full-time fee of over £3000 per year; others may charge a part-time fee of around £1200 per year, for three years; some institutions charge by the module (around £400 for a 20 credit module). You may find further education colleges charge lower fees than universities for their Foundation degrees, but this is not prescribed. Some institutions will allow you access to students union and sports facilities, others do not; it is always wise to check if this is very important to you. As a work-based student who is registered part-time (even if you are studying full-time hours) you are not able to apply for any student loans.

● What features should I look for in a Foundation degree?

Education is a very important purchase. It can often cost more than your first car and will take up a significant amount of your time. It is easy to find information and guidance on buying a car, and a trusted friend to take along with you. Often, a purchase of education is based upon an unspoken understanding that moral and ethical principles will apply, followed by a quick search through the prospectus of a delivery institution which has accessible car parking. When thinking about a Foundation degree, try and find the answers to the following issues – it won't always be easy to get this information:

- *Is it really work-based?* Will you be able to use real work projects to meet some of the learning outcomes of the programmes?
- *How many modules are there and how are they scheduled?* A work-based programme should not consist of lots of small subject-oriented modules all running together – ideally there should be a progression of modules gradually developing your capabilities.
- *How much assessment is there? What kind of assessment is it?* This type of programme should have plenty of *formative* assessments (giving you feedback) and a key *summative* assessment related to each module. Chapter 4 gives an idea of what is possible – so don't settle for essays and exams!
- *How much contact time is there?* Beware of programmes which offer one day, or even half a day, per week contact time. The curriculum is unlikely to be work-based and likely to be subject-based.
- *Ask yourself searching questions about your own motivation to undertake a work-based programme requiring a lot of self-sufficiency.* Do you have the discipline to set aside time for study and doing assessments when you are not driven along in a class-room environment?

- *How much support will there be for you?* Ask about the assignment of tutors, the support for any on-line elements (for example, is there a 7 × 24 hour hot line?) will you get access to a mentor at work?
- *How is the involvement of your employer arranged?* For example, will your tutor come and visit you and your manager at work? Can your manager come to the induction of the programme? Can you get credit for things you can already do or are scheduled to do in your current job role? Will it be possible to create special tasks at work to help your learning and provide for interesting summative assessments?

The relationship between yourself and the university is not exactly that of a customer talking to a retail company – it is more complex than that. Think of seeing a fitness coach or visiting a doctor; you have every right to ask detailed questions and be sure that the opportunity is right for you.

Summary

Foundation degrees are:

1   Designed with employers.

2   A combination of academic study and relevant workplace learning.

3   Ideal to equip people with the knowledge and skills to improve performance and productivity.

4   The first new higher education qualification for 25 years.

5   Part of the work-based learning revolution, which places students and their employment at the centre of curriculum.

6   On target to reach their 100,000 student numbers objective. (Stop press! Figure achieved – April 2010.)

7   A route to higher-level learning outcomes being achieved via thoughtful, reflective, professional practice in the workplace.

References

Archer, W. and Davison, J. (2008) *Graduate Employability: What Do Employers Think and Want* (London: CIHE).

BERR (2009) *New Industry, New Jobs – Building Britain's Future* (online). Available at http://www.berr.gov.uk/files/file51023.pdf (accessed 3 December 2009).

Foundation Degree Forward, Course Search (online). Available at http://www.fdf.ac.uk/single.aspx?id=5 (accessed 3 December 2009).

Higher Education Funding Council for England (2008) *Foundation Degrees: Key Statistics 2001–02 to 2006–07* (Bristol: HEFCE).

Longhurst, D. (2005) 'Are Foundation Degrees Designed for Widening Participation?', in C. Duke and G. Layer (eds), *Widening Participation: Which Way Forward for English Higher Education?* (Leicester: NIACE), Chapter 5, pp. 45–59.

Navigator (2006) *Foundation Degrees: Message Testing,* Report prepared for COI on behalf of DfES (London: COI, DfES).

Quality Assurance Agency for Higher Education (2004) *Foundation Degree Qualification Benchmark* (Gloucester: QAA).

Quality Assurance Agency for Higher Education (2008) *The Framework for Higher Education Qualifications in England, Wales and Northern Ireland* (Gloucester: QAA).

Suggested further reading

Blunkett, D. (2000) *Speech at University of Greenwich,* 15 February, Press Notice 2000/0064 (London: DfES).

Boud, D., Cressey, P. and Docherty, P. (eds) (2006) *Productive Reflection at Work* (Oxford: Routledge).

Boud, D. and Solomon, N. (eds) (2001) *Work Based Learning: A New Higher Education?* (Buckingham: SRHE and Open University Press).

Brotherton, G. and Parker, S. (eds) (2008) *Your Foundation in Health and Social Care: A Guide for Foundation Degree Students* (London: Sage).

Department for Education and Skills (2003) *The Future of Higher Education* (London: HMSO).

Department for Education and Skills (2004) *Foundation Degree Task Force Report to Ministers* (London: HMSO).

Department for Education and Skills (2005) *White Paper, Skills: Getting on in Business, Getting on at Work* (London: HSMO).

Dransfield, R., Needham, D., Guy, P., Fox, E. and Wilde, J. (2004) *Business for Foundation Degrees and Higher Awards* (London: Heinemann).

Fanthome, C. (2004) *Work Placements: A Survival Guide for Students* (Basingstoke: Palgrave Macmillan).

Hammersley-Fletcher, L., Lowe, M. and Pugh, J. (2006) *The Teaching Assistant's Guide: An Essential Textbook for Foundation Degree Students* (London: Routledge).

Higher Education Funding Council for England (2000) *Foundation Degree Prospectus* (Bristol: HEFCE).

Jenner, S. (2000) *The Graduate Career Handbook: Making the Right Start for a Bright Future* (Harlow: Financial Times Prentice Hall).

Leitch, S. (2006) *Leitch Review of Skills: Final Report, Prosperity for all in the Global Economy: World Class Skills* (London: HMSO).

Moon, J. (2004a) *Reflection and Employability* (York: LTSN).

Moon, J. (2004b) *Learning Journals* (London: RoutledgeFarmer).

Neugebauer, J. and Evans-Brain, J. (2009) *Making the Most of your Placement* (London: Sage).

Zachary, L.J. and Fischler, L.A. (2009) *The Mentee's Guide: Making Mentoring Work for You* (San Francisco: Jossey-Bass).

Appendix 1
Credit Values Typically Associated with Programmes Leading to Main HE Qualifications in England

HE qualifications as set out in the Framework for Higher Education Qualifications	Level	Minimum credits for award	Minimum credits at the level of the qualification
PhD/DPhil	8	Not typically credit-rated	
Professional doctorates (only if credit based) (EdD, DBA, DClinPsy)		540	360
Research master's degrees (MPhil, MLitt)	7	Not typically credit-rated	
Taught MPhil		360	240
Taught master's degrees (MA, MSc, MRes)		180	150
Integrated master's degrees (MEng, MChem, MPhys, MPharm)		480	120
Postgraduate diplomas		120	90
Postgraduate Certificate in Education (PGCE)		60	40
Postgraduate certificates		60	40
Bachelor's degrees with honours (BA/BSc Hons)	6	360	90
Bachelor's degrees		300	60
Professional Graduate Certificate in Education (PGCE)		60	40
Graduate diplomas		80	80
Graduate certificates		40	40

HE qualifications as set out in the Framework for Higher Education Qualifications	Level	Minimum credits for award	Minimum credits at the level of the qualification
Foundation Degrees (FdA, FdSc)	5	240	90
Diplomas of Higher Education (DipHE)		240	90
Higher National Diplomas (HND)		240	90
Higher National Certificates (HNC)	4	150	120
Certificates of Higher Education (Cert HE)		120	90

Appendix 2
Example of Questions asked in Training Needs Analysis

Company Training Needs Analysis

1 What are the key components of the work being performed in your company/department?
2 What skills and knowledge are required to perform the work?
3 What are the measures of successful performance of the work?
4 Are people performing at the levels required?
5 Which roles require specific technical/professional training and what is it?

Suitability Training Needs Analysis

1 In what areas do staff under-perform in your department?
2 Is there under-performance among specific groups of employees?
3 What are the causes of under-performance?
4 What training will help bridge the gap between the standards of performance needed and the actual performance?
5 How does the training the business currently provides meet these requirements (please see attached list)?
   a Technical training
   b Business skills training
   c Other company funded training (state which).
6 What else could be provided?
7 Is anything provided internally which could be improved or deleted?
8 Is under-performance due to any other reason other than a lack of knowledge and skills? If so what?
9 What solutions can be used to remedy under-performance caused by factors other than a lack of knowledge and skills?

Appendix 3
Example of a Personal Statement

If I were asked to describe myself in a professional capacity, then I would label myself as being hard working, conscientious, flexible, open-minded and patient. Some of these qualities are natural attributes; others have developed over time with experience.

My intention now is to build on these strengths and become a successful primary school teacher. No one is more surprised at that statement than me, as I never thought that I would want a career that involved working with children.

I have always been in occupations that involved working with people and have relished the variety and challenges that this has brought. Six years ago, I made the move into adult training and decided that adult teaching was the direction that I wanted to go in. At this stage, I thought that teaching adults would be more fulfilling, as the subject matter would be at a higher level. I changed my opinion two years ago when I started working at the Media Centre. As a media tutor at the Centre, I teach all age groups including school children and have been surprised by how much more challenging and rewarding I have found this.

Children, particularly at primary school age, are not as conditioned to giving the responses that they think they should. Primary children instantly let you know when they are bored or do not understand something, then it is up to you to turn the teaching session around. Primary children also express their appreciation more readily when they have enjoyed a teaching session and have learnt something. It is a constant challenge to make their lessons interesting and think of new ways to add value to their learning. Each new step taken in this direction is extremely satisfying.

In my spare time, I am also a Brownie leader and have seen firsthand the ways in which a child can develop when they are given the right opportunities. For a child to develop into a well-rounded adult they need more than just academic skills; they also need life and social skills. I am now aiming to become a qualified primary practitioner, but more than that, I want to be able to enrich the lives of the students I teach by ensuring they have a positive and valuable learning experience.

Appendix 4
Extract from a Learning CV

Post-secondary Education

Qualification	Date Achieved
BTEC National Diploma in Business and Finance with Travel and Tourism	1997
Certificate in Education	2008
Studying Media Studies	Due to complete 20-credit university module in April 2010

Employment

Media Company 2 – November 2007 to date – Media ICT Tutor

Achievements to date:

- Developed and delivered training courses to company employees including Company Induction, Stress Management and Customer Care
- Liaised with all departments to ensure the company maintained Investors in People status
- Developed and delivered training courses to external businesses including Presentation Skills and Train the Trainer

Media Company 1 – February 2006 – November 2007 Design and Development Officer

- Designed a range of training courses for UKLG's National Retail Training Team

Travel Agency – November 2003 – January 2006 Systems Trainer

- Delivered training in a new computer system as part of the National Training Team

Voluntary work

Assistant Brownie Guide Leader for the past 5 years. Training for holiday licence.

Appendix 5
Extract from a Job Description

Job Title: **Media/ICT trainer**
Department   **Media Centre**

Main purpose of job:

- To raise the profile of the company to develop long-term readership for children, young people and adults.
- To support the company's lifelong learning initiative through teaching in the Media Centre and in local education establishments.
- Providing innovative teaching materials relating to the newspaper and the internet.

Personal Qualities

- Self-motivator, flexible, enthusiastic, team player, calm and friendly disposition.
- Fully qualified primary or secondary teacher
- English/ICT specialist preferred.

Reporting to:

Newspapers in Education manager

- To teach children and adults to use the ICT equipment in the company's Media Centre and encourage them to prepare front page news sheets, school newspapers and meet end of session deadlines.
- To develop teaching programmes, with appropriate lesson plans, to meet the demands of the National Curriculum and other Educational criteria, relating to the use of newspapers and the internet.

Appendix 6
Example of a Project
Proposal

a. Working title of project
Improving the literacy and attainment in Secondary School Business Studies

b. Introduction
This project is set in a secondary school where I am a teacher of business studies. In my role I deliver a programme to encourage less able pupils to pursue vocational courses to equip them for future work. Researchers have tried to link literacy and achievement in all Key Stages in secondary education, but many pupils and some teachers do not recognize the importance of enhancing literacy beyond Key Stage 3.

As a teacher I propose to focus on developing strategies to improve literacy to improve attainment in business studies. I have observed how literacy and comprehension impact negatively on attainment and surmise that this may be the case for other subjects as well. My project would result in the creation of a handbook with detailed strategies to disseminate across the department (and possibly the school), to raise attainment by improving literacy ...

c. Main aims of the project and its significance
A case study approach will be used to determine appropriate strategies as it facilitates both qualitative and quantitative data collection approaches. Bell (2000) states that although case studies are generally qualitative approaches, quantitative data can also be used. It is best suited to this project due to the limited time available but allows for some in-depth study of the research question ...

The aim of this project is to raise the attainment of pupils on the vocational business course. It will identify factors that contribute to literacy ability among pupils and determine strategies that enhance levels of literacy. It will test these strategies for effect on attainment and achievement. Lewis and Wray (1999) argue that current evidence from national testing of pupils suggests that 30–40 per cent fail to achieve reading standards expected for their age group, thus suggesting that underperformance may be a consequence of poor literacy. ...

The project will inform other teachers as to literacy strategies that are available to aid pupil understanding. It will raise the participants' understanding of the need for strengthening their literacy abilities in order to improve their attainment across all subjects.

d. The worker/researcher role, and relevant expertise

As a business studies teacher the pupils are already familiar with me and I relate well to them and their parents/carers. I know the school wants to improve performance and this will contribute to that objective.

I have sought and gained permission from the senior leadership team in the school. I will be sending all the parents of the pupils involved letters asking for their permission to participate in this. I have access to the necessary information and I have spoken to the gatekeepers of the relevant data who are prepared to share it with me.

As their teacher I will be able to observe the participants' responses to the new strategies firsthand. If there are any signs that things are not going according to plan I can intervene and implement changes quickly ...

I have permission to use the school resources such as the literacy co-ordinator and the lesson times in which to do this. I am planning the interventions into my lesson plans in a way that ensures that there will not be any learning lost for the pupils, and it should make a difference to learning achieved overall.

e. Your main research questions and objectives

My research questions are:

1. What factors contribute to lower levels of literacy among pupils studying business studies?
2. What learning activities may improve literacy levels among these pupils?
3. What learning interventions can be used effectively to influence attainment?
4. Are pupils aware how literacy levels may impact on their performance?

Consequently the project objectives are to:

1. Undertake a literature review on literacy and attainment
2. Interview participants to gauge their perceptions of literacy level and ability
3. Review pupil achievement records and data regarding attainment before and after the introduction of new strategies
4. Undertake observations of levels of participant engagement with new literacy learning activities in the classroom
5. Analyse documentary data and interviews
6. Write a handbook of suitable literacy activities that support learning in business studies for the department.

During the introduction of new topics in class, additional literacy strategies will be used alongside the usual learning materials. The effect of these activities will be evaluated to determine if there are any improvements in comprehension and appreciation of learning materials. Any impact on attainment levels over the period may indicate a positive contribution to learning achievement long term ...

f. Identify a rationale for research approach, considering and excluding alternative approaches

I will use a case study approach as it will allow me to investigate using a variety of data. Case study is concerned principally with the interaction of factors and events and Bell (2000) considers that it is particularly appropriate for individual researchers as it allows exploration of a problem in some depth within a limited time frame. I shall focus on a small group of individuals.

g. State rationale for data collection, analysis of data and how will this address your research questions

Data will be collected through interviews, questionnaires, documents, structured observations and records. Most of the data will be qualitative and will look for themes from the interviews and documents. The quantitative data will be from pupil records and will be in Excel so will be analysed in percentages. These methods will give the most complete piece of research (Bell, 2000) as Cohen and Manion (1994: 240) state that 'multiple methods are suitable when a controversial aspect of education needs to be evaluated more fully'.

The participants are currently a class of eighteen 15-year-olds and are a typical group in that they are considered to be low achievers who need to raise their achievement levels. They are similar to other vocational business groups we teach.

By using both quantitative and qualitative data the data will be reliable as it can be checked by other types of data. If the questionnaire gives me the answers to the research questions, it will confirm the validity of my approach. Triangulation of data will occur through using different data such as participant interviews, my observations and pupil result records.

I will need to learn how to analyse qualitative data into themes. I will ask colleagues and my tutor to help. I understand the pupil records but will have to collect individual pupil profiles and will need assistance from the head of department to do this.

h. Project feasibility, time scale, resources, and ethical issues

This project has to be undertaken between February and May. I will be preparing data collection tools while waiting for permission from the university to proceed and from the senior management team.

The time frame is in the Gantt chart:

Activity	Wk 1	2	3 Term starts	4	5	6	7	8	9
Plan and design data collection instruments	■	■							
Obtain ethics approval	■	■							
Literature search and review	■	■	■						
First and second class observations			■ (1)				■(2)		
Interviews				■	■				
Questionnaires				■					
Results recorded			■				■		
Data analysis					■	■	■		
Write up							■	■	■
Submission date									19th

Because the pupils are under the age of sixteen I need to gain permission from their parents and the school, but also the participants need to give me informed consent and show they understand what I am trying to do. I have devised a consent form for this purpose. Confidentiality and anonymity of participants will be ensured although I will know which individuals are involved. I will protect the participants' identities and not allow access to data to anyone not directly involved in the research.

i. Project report and target audience
The results will be a valuable resource within the department to enhance pupil attainment. My colleagues in the department will be informed of the progress and results of the project, which will be shared at an inset session. The results will also be used to inform pupils and parents on literacy and how it is affecting their current educational attainment.

j. Strengths and weaknesses of research proposal
This will benefit the school and the pupils and will provide evidence for increased literacy activities. Basing the research with a real group of pupils will strengthen the application of the findings. However, the participants may not be open about their literacy difficulties because of social taboos. Absenteeism may result in incomplete data collection.

This project is relevant to the school objectives of raising attainment in this particular group of low achievers. I can do it as part of my teaching so even if the results are inconclusive I will be developing diversity in my teaching activities to improve pupil literacy.

References

Bell, J. (2000) *Doing your Research Project: A Guide for the First Time Researcher in Education and Social Science,* 3rd edn (Buckingham: Open University).

Cohen, L. and Manion, L. (1994) *Research Methods in Education,* 4th edn (London: Routledge).

Lewis, M. and Wray D. (1999) *Literacy in the Secondary School* (London: Fulton Books).

Index